INTERPROFESSIONAL COLLABORATION AND SERVICE USER PARTICIPATION
Analysing Meetings in Social Welfare

Edited by
Kirsi Juhila, Tanja Dall, Christopher Hall and
Juliet Koprowska

First published in Great Britain in 2022 by

Policy Press, an imprint of
Bristol University Press
University of Bristol
1–9 Old Park Hill
Bristol
BS2 8BB
UK
t: +44 (0)117 374 6645
e: bup-info@bristol.ac.uk

Details of international sales and distribution partners are available at
policy.bristoluniversitypress.co.uk

© Bristol University Press 2022

British Library Cataloguing in Publication Data
A catalogue record for this book is available from the British Library

ISBN 978-1-4473-5663-9 hardcover
ISBN 978-1-4473-5664-6 paperback
ISBN 978-1-4473-5666-0 ePub
ISBN 978-1-4473-5665-3 ePdf

The right of Kirsi Juhila, Tanja Dall, Christopher Hall and Jukiet Koprowska to be identified as editors of this work has been asserted by them in accordance with the Copyright, Designs and Patents Act 1988.

All rights reserved: no part of this publication may be reproduced, stored in a retrieval system, or transmitted in any form or by any means, electronic, mechanical, photocopying, recording, or otherwise without the prior permission of Bristol University Press.

Every reasonable effort has been made to obtain permission to reproduce copyrighted material. If, however, anyone knows of an oversight, please contact the publisher.

The statements and opinions contained within this publication are solely those of the editors and contributors and not of the University of Bristol or Bristol University Press. The University of Bristol and Bristol University Press disclaim responsibility for any injury to persons or property resulting from any material published in this publication.

Bristol University Press and Policy Press work to counter discrimination on grounds of gender, race, disability, age and sexuality.

Cover design: Dave Worth
Front cover image: istock-488364348

Research in Social Work series

Series Editors: **Anna Gupta**, Royal Holloway, University of London, UK and **John Gal**, Hebrew University of Jerusalem, Israel

Published together with The European Social Work Research Association (ESWRA), this series examines current, progressive and innovative research applications of familiar ideas and models in international social work research.

Also available in the series:

The Settlement House Movement Revisited: A Transnational History

Edited by **John Gal**, **Stefan Köngeter**, and **Sarah Vicary**

Social Work and the Making of Social Policy

Edited by **Ute Klammer**, **Simone Leiber**, and **Sigrid Leitner**

Research and the Social Work Picture

By **Ian Shaw**

Find out more at:

policy.bristoluniversitypress.co.uk/research-in-social-work

Research in Social Work series

Series Editors: **Anna Gupta**, Royal Holloway, University of London, UK and **John Gal**, Hebrew University of Jerusalem, Israel

---

Forthcoming in the series:

*Adoption from Care:
International Perspectives on Children's Rights, Family Preservation and State Intervention*

Edited by **TarjaPösö**, **Marit Skivenes** and **June Thoburn**

*Involving Service Users in Social Work Education, Research and Policy:
A Comparative European Analysis*

Edited by **Kristel Driessens** and **Vicky Lyssens-Danneboom**

Social Work Research Using Arts-Based Methods

Edited by **Ephrat Huss** and**Eltje Bos**

Critical Gerontology for Social Workers

Edited by **Sandra Torres** and**Sarah Donnelly**

*Power and Control in Social Work:
An Ethnographic Account of Mental Health Practice*

By **Hannah Jobling**

Find out more at:

policy.bristoluniversitypress.co.uk/
research-in-social-work

Research in Social Work series

Series Editors: **Anna Gupta**, Royal Holloway, University of London, UK and **John Gal**, Hebrew University of Jerusalem, Israel

---

Forthcoming in the series:

*Migration and Social Work:
Approaches, Visions and Challenges*

Edited by **Emilio J. Gómez-Ciriano, Elena Cabiati** and **Sofia Dedotsi**

*The Origins of Social Work:
Western Roots, International Futures*

By **Mark Henrickson**

Find out more at:

policy.bristoluniversitypress.co.uk/
research-in-social-work

Research in Social Work series

Series Editors: **Anna Gupta**, Royal Holloway, University of London, UK and **John Gal**, Hebrew University of Jerusalem, Israel

International Editorial Board:

Andrés Arias Astray, Complutense University of Madrid, Spain
Isobel Bainton, Policy Press, UK
Inge Bryderup, Aalborg University, Denmark
Tony Evans, Royal Holloway, University of London, UK
Hannele Forsberg, University of Tampere, Finland
John Gal, Hebrew University of Jerusalem, Israel
Anna Gupta, Royal Holloway, University of London, UK
Todd I. Herrenkohl, University of Michigan, US
Ephrat Huss, Ben-Gurion University of the Negev, Israel
Stefan Köngeter, Eastern Switzerland University of Applied Science (OST), Switzerland
Judith Metz, Saxion University of Applied Sciences, The Netherlands
Manohar Pawar, Charles Sturt University, Australia
Ian Shaw, National University of Singapore and University of York, UK
Darja Zaviršek, University of Ljubljana, Slovenia

Find out more at:

policy.bristoluniversitypress.co.uk/research-in-social-work

Contents

List of figures and tables — viii
Notes on contributors — ix
Acknowledgements — xi

Introduction — 1
Kirsi Juhila, Tanja Dall, Christopher Hall and Juliet Koprowska

1   From a collaborative and integrated welfare policy to frontline practices — 9
Kirsi Juhila, Suvi Raitakari, Dorte Caswell, Tanja Dall and Monika Wilińska

2   Examining talk and interaction in meetings of professionals and service users — 33
Christopher Hall and Tanja Dall

3   How chairs use the pronoun 'we' to guide participation in rehabilitation team meetings — 63
Tanja Dall and Dorte Caswell

4   Working within frames and across boundaries in core group meetings in child protection — 83
Christopher Hall and Stef Slembrouck

5   Alignment and service user participation in low-threshold meetings with people using drugs — 115
Suvi Raitakari, Johanna Ranta and Sirpa Saario

6   Sympathy and micropolitics in return-to-work meetings — 141
Pia H. Bülow and Monika Wilińska

7   Negotiating epistemic rights to knowledge concerning service users' recent histories in mental health meetings — 171
Kirsi Juhila, Lisa Morriss and Suvi Raitakari

8   Relational agency and epistemic justice in initial child protection conferences — 197
Juliet Koprowska

Conclusion — 225
Kirsi Juhila, Tanja Dall, Christopher Hall and Juliet Koprowska

Postscript — 241
Index — 247

List of figures and tables

Figures

6.1	The seating arrangement in meeting no. 5	151
6.2	Extract 3: Interaction in the background (meeting no. 5, time 11:15–11:40)	156
6.3	Subordinate and dominant communication	157
6.4	Sympathy gift	157
6.5	The seating arrangement in meeting no. 2	159

Tables

3.1	Inclusive and exclusive 'we' in rehabilitation team meetings	69
6.1	Participants in the studied meetings	148
8.1	Characteristics of the ICPCs in the two LAs	202

Notes on contributors

The contributors of this book are members of an international research group, Discourse and Narrative Approaches to Social Work and Counselling (DANASWAC). First established in 1997, the group has worked together on a number of research projects and a wide range of publications on the subject.

Pia H. Bülow, Professor of Social Work, Department of Social Work, School of Health and Welfare, Jönköping University, Sweden and Department of Social Work, University of the Free State, South Africa.

Dorte Caswell, Professor, Department of Sociology and Social Work, Faculty of Social Sciences, University of Aalborg, Denmark.

Tanja Dall, Postdoctoral Researcher, Department of Sociology and Social Work, Faculty of Social Sciences, University of Aalborg, Denmark.

Christopher Hall, Associate Senior Research Fellow, Department of Social Work and Social Care, University of Sussex, UK.

Kirsi Juhila, Professor of Social Work, Faculty of Social Sciences, Tampere University, Finland.

Juliet Koprowska, Honorary Fellow in Social Work, Department of Social Policy and Social Work, University of York, UK.

Lisa Morriss, Lecturer in Social Work, Faculty of Arts and Social Sciences, Lancaster University, UK.

Suvi Raitakari, Senior Lecturer in Social Work, Faculty of Social Sciences, Tampere University, Finland.

Johanna Ranta, Postdoctoral Researcher in Social Work, Faculty of Social Sciences, Tampere University, Finland.

Sirpa Saario, Senior Lecturer in Social Work, Faculty of Social Sciences, Tampere University, Finland.

Stef Slembrouck, Professor of English Linguistics, Department of Linguistics, Ghent University, Belgium.

Monika Wilińska, Associate Professor in Welfare and Social Science, Department of Social Work, School of Health and Welfare Jönköping University, Sweden.

Acknowledgements

First of all we wish to thank the service users and the professionals in our field sites. Without their active participation and engagement, we would not have been able to study the reality of multi-agency meetings as they unfold. This book is dedicated to them.

We would also like to thank the many colleagues who have supported, encouraged and challenged our studies of meeting interactions in social welfare over the past four years. The original idea for this book surfaced at the 13th meeting of the Discourse and Narrative Approaches to Social Work and Counselling (DANASWAC) network in Tampere, Finland in August 2016, where one of the sessions focused on multi-party meeting talk. Since then, the chapters have been discussed and developed yearly at DANASWAC meetings. Early versions of the chapters were also presented at the seventh International and Interdisciplinary Conference on Applied Linguistics and Professional Practice (ALAPP) in Ghent, Belgium in November 2017, where we held a panel on multi-party meetings in interprofessional work.

Research presented in Chapters 1, 5 and 7 was partially funded by the Academy of Finland (decision number 307661).

Research presented in Chapter 3 was funded by the Department of Sociology and Social Work, Aalborg University, Denmark and the Department of Social Work, University College Copenhagen, Denmark.

Research presented in Chapter 8 was partially funded by the UK Economic and Social Research Council's Impact Acceleration Account through the University of York, UK.

Introduction

Kirsi Juhila, Tanja Dall, Christopher Hall and Juliet Koprowska

> I walked into the room, and I was nervous as it was, because obviously you're going into something that is like judge and jury on you. And you walk in and you look at the people and I thought to myself, I've got to sit here in front of all these people being judged and ... Well, everyone introduced themselves, like they do, they all go round the table. You don't take it all in, because there's so many people, all going, 'Hello my name is so and so'. You have to acknowledge them, but you don't take it in ... (Packman and Hall, 1998, p 222)

These words, from a parent talking about participating in an initial child protection conference, encapsulate the tension at play when service users participate in multi-agency meetings in social welfare. The number of participants alone can make the meetings hard to 'take in', and differences in status confer predetermined roles of judging and being judged before the meetings even begin. At the same time, however, multi-agency meetings constitute an opportunity for shared discussions that may increase both cooperation and understanding between different professionals and service users. It is this opportunity that has made meetings where professionals from different disciplines and service users are co-present become commonplace in health and social welfare in Western welfare states. This has happened as part of a larger development, where collaborative and integrated welfare is promoted as a solution to the perceived ineffectiveness of health and social services that are professional-led and dispersed (Kitto et al, 2011). Two themes in particular are presented as essential for the success of collaborative and integrated welfare: interprofessional collaboration and service user participation. This book is about how such aims are realised in multi-agency meetings. The words of the parent that open this chapter represent a service user's reflections on a meeting after the event. By contrast, this book analyses audio- and video-recordings of the naturally occurring interactions that 'talk the meetings into being'.

Multi-agency meetings are understood as boundary spaces where professionals from different disciplines and welfare agencies, service users and their lay representatives are brought together to work on a common task. Such an understanding brings forward the negotiated and interactional character of social welfare, casting interprofessional collaboration and service user participation as complex practices, involving work across professional and organisational boundaries, the integration of aims and perspectives, comprehensiveness in assessment and efforts, and shared goals and synergy (see Chapter 1).

The core idea of this book is to examine empirically how professional participants in the meetings collaborate with each other (or do not), and the kinds of alliances they create, as well as how service users position themselves and are positioned as participants in the information gathering, reasoning, assessing and decision making about their personal and institutional circumstances. By analysing the specific setting of multi-agency meetings across a range of social welfare fields, the book contributes to the ongoing discussion about collaborative and integrated welfare through the thematic lenses of interprofessional collaboration and service user participation. The ambition is to facilitate a deeper understanding of how collaborative and integrated welfare is brought about in meetings between professionals from different disciplines and service users, and to develop a conceptual and analytical framework that can support further examination of the doing of interprofessional collaboration and service user participation.

Doing interprofessional collaboration and service user participation in multi-agency meetings

Increasingly, multi-agency meetings are the locus for implementing the policies and procedures of interprofessional working (Blom, 2004; Julkunen and Willumsen, 2017). The meetings explored in this book have certain characteristics that differentiate them from other professional and workplace practices:

- They are multi-agency in that they include practitioners from a number of agencies – for example, social work, education, health, the police, housing, social security, employment services and third sector organisations.
- The terms and conditions of some meetings are prescribed by statute or institutional policy and procedures.

- The meetings focus on individual families or service users.
- The meetings are the place where professionals organise their work with the service user in terms of the goals set at one meeting and reviewed at the subsequent one.
- The meetings often have decision-making or reviewing functions, meaning that they result in the provision (or denial) of a service or establishment of an institutional category for an individual or family, for example child concern or adult risk.
- The service user, their family and perhaps an advocate are encouraged or required to attend.

In these – and other – ways, the practical accomplishments of multi-agency meetings in social welfare become the realisation of collaborative and integrated welfare policy. Henneman et al (1995, p 108) make the observation that collaboration is 'a process which occurs between individuals, not institutions, and only the persons involved ultimately determine whether or not collaboration occurs'. Arguably, the same can be said of service user participation. Several studies have demonstrated that having users present at meetings does not ensure their inclusion in decision making or care planning (for example, Hall and Slembrouck, 2001; Hitzler and Messmer, 2010). When seeking to understand how policies come about in practice, then, looking at what actually happens as professionals and service users meet around a common task brings us closer to the details of 'doing' interprofessional collaboration and service user participation. Research in health care and business organisations has illustrated that meetings require participants to pay attention to certain conventions and constraints on what can be brought up, how and by whom (for example, Asmuß and Svennevig, 2009; Svennevig, 2012; Halvorsen and Sarangi, 2015). The opening quote in this Introduction illustrates one small aspect of this, as participants 'go round the table' following a certain format in introducing themselves while the service user sits back trying to take it all in. By examining the details of how participants orient to and act out such interactional conventions and devices, this book demonstrates how the realisation of policy becomes contingent on the interactional practices of professionals and service users, situated in particular meetings.

The organisation of the book

The book revolves around two themes, alluded to earlier: (a) how professionals negotiate professional boundaries, responsibilities and hierarchies; and (b) how service users participate and are formulated as participants in their own personal matters at multi-agency meetings. These themes are closely interrelated, and especially so in multi-agency meetings where both the service user and several professionals are present. Thus, while some chapters of the book may focus on one theme more than the other, both interprofessional collaboration and service user participation are present in all chapters.

Chapters 1 and 2 make up the introductory section of the book, with the first conceptualising interprofessional collaboration and service user participation and the second, multi-agency meetings as communicative events. Chapter 1 (Juhila, Raitakari, Caswell, Dall and Wilińska) discusses collaborative and integrated welfare as a current policy trend and defines the concepts of interprofessional collaboration and service user participation. The two themes are introduced as relational and interactional activities that require and constitute relational expertise. The chapter goes on to address the potential and challenges of interprofessional collaboration and service user participation – themes that are most often presented in uncritical and idealised ways. Finally, the chapter introduces multi-agency meetings and teamwork as frontline arenas and boundary spaces to 'do' collaboration based on shared aims and common knowledge. Chapter 2 (Hall and Dall) moves closer into the interactional makeup of multi-agency meetings, reviewing the literature on meeting talk. The chapter outlines literature that has approached meetings as ceremony and ritual and discusses a number of key analytical concepts related to meeting talk: the structure of meetings, the role of the chair, turn-taking, topic progression and decision making. The conceptualisations and analytical concepts introduced in Chapters 1 and 2 are taken up in the empirical chapters (Chapters 3 to 8), which analyse concrete instances of interprofessional collaboration and service user participation in multi-agency meetings.

Chapters 3 to 8 draw on research in different sectors of social welfare in different countries, formulated through different legal jurisdictions. The chapters are all empirically based in multi-agency talk and preoccupied with the details of accomplishing interprofessional collaboration and service user participation, along with the interactional practices and dilemmas that follow. Depending on the practice field, literature and author preference, a variety of descriptions are used in discussing the two themes (for example, client/patient/parent and inclusion/involvement/ownership). To ensure coherence of terminology, all the chapters refer to 'interprofessional collaboration' and 'service user participation', except when referencing literature that uses other terms, for example professional–client talk.

Chapter 3 (Dall and Caswell) examines rehabilitation team meetings in Danish employment services. Meetings are led by a chairperson who represents one of the attending agencies, and the chapter analyses how chairs use the pronoun 'we', to include or exclude other team members and the service user in decision making. The authors find that chairs' use of 'we' contributes to a practice that places 'the team' as a unit in a position of authority and dissuades disagreement from service user and team members. Chapter 4 (Hall and Slembrouck) examines chairs' practices in child protection core group meetings in England. The authors draw on the concepts of 'framing' and 'boundary work' to explore how different professionals contribute to the multi-agency meeting and how the meetings emerge as arenas for competing interprofessional claims. The chapter concludes that constructing and managing professional contributions involves complex boundary work by all participants.

Chapter 5 (Raitakari, Ranta and Saario) examines multi-agency meetings in low-threshold services for people using drugs in Finland. The concept of 'alignment' is applied as a linguistic device that supports a cooperative flow of interaction, making visible how collaborative participation is only ever partially achieved and at risk of failing. The authors find, for example, that question–answer sequences and positioning both service users and professionals in alternating ways as 'tellers' and 'recipients' are essential alignment techniques to advance collaborative participation. Chapter 6 (Bülow and Wilińska) examines return-to-work meetings within the Swedish social insurance system and, uniquely in this book, studies video recordings, enabling the analysis of posture and gesture. The concepts of 'sympathy' and 'sympathizing' are used to explore emotions and micropolitics in multi-agency meetings concerning work ability. The authors demonstrate how sympathizing becomes an integral part of the institutional frame, with the institutional actors stepping outside their specific meeting roles to sympathize with the service user.

Chapter 7 (Juhila, Morriss and Raitakari) examines mental health meetings undertaken as part of the Care Programme Approach context in England. In this chapter the concepts of 'epistemic status' and 'epistemic rights' are used to analyse the ownership of knowledge concerning service users' recent histories. The authors demonstrate how not only service users but professionals, too, display access to and ownership of such knowledge. They go on to find that meetings contain both collaborative practices that strengthen service user participation and practices that produce epistemic injustice for service users. Chapter 8 (Koprowska) examines interactions between chairs and service users in initial child protection conferences in two local authorities in England. The author finds that frontline practices differ between the two authorities, influencing the way the chair takes up the role. The concepts of 'relational agency', 'epistemic rights' and 'epistemic justice' are utilised to show that the chair's interactional approach advances or constrains service user participation.

The book then concludes by synthesising the main findings of Chapters 3 to 8 in a discussion of how to understand multi-agency meetings in social welfare settings as interactional accomplishments. Four themes are highlighted: the role of the chair and turn-taking; information-giving and decision-making roles; different uses of 'we' and alignments; and owning, prioritising and producing knowledge. The Conclusion argues that multi-agency meetings have the potential to be both integration ceremonies, which make possible the creation of common knowledge, and degradation ceremonies, which devalue the knowledge and status of both service users and professionals. It ends by outlining some of the specific areas of attention that may facilitate more constructive meetings for both professionals and service users.

References

Asmuβ, B. and Svennevig, J. (2009) 'Meeting talk', *Journal of Business Communication*, 46(1): 3–22.

Blom, B. (2004) 'Specialization in social work practice: Effects on interventions in the personal social services', *Journal of Social Work*, 4(1): 25–46.

Hall, C. and Slembrouck, S. (2001) 'Parent participation in social work meetings – the case of child protection conferences', *European Journal of Social Work*, 4(2): 143–60.

Halvorsen, K. and Sarangi, S. (2015) 'Team decision-making in workplace meetings: The interplay of activity roles and discourse roles', *Journal of Pragmatics*, 76: 1–14.

Henneman, E.A., Lee, J.L. and Cohen, J.I. (1995) 'Collaboration: A concept analysis', *Journal of Advanced Nursing*, 21(1): 103–9.

Hitzler, S. and Messmer, H. (2010) 'Group decision-making in child welfare and the pursuit of participation', *Qualitative Social Work*, 9(2): 205–26.

Julkunen, I. and Willumsen, E. (2017) 'Professional boundary crossing and interprofessional knowledge development', in B. Blom, L. Evertsson and M. Perlinski (eds) *Social and Caring Professions in European Welfare States: Policies, Services and Professional Practices*, Bristol: Policy Press, pp 115–30.

Kitto, S., Reeves, S., Chesters, J. and Thistlethwaite, J. (2011) 'Re-imagining interprofessionalism: where to from here?', in S. Kitto, J. Chesters, J. Thistlethwaite and S. Reeves (eds) *Sociology of Interprofessional Health Care Practice: Critical Reflections and Concrete Solutions*, New York: Nova Science Publishers, pp 207–11.

Packman, J. and Hall, C. (1998) *From Care to Accommodation: Support, Protection and Control in Child Care Services (Studies in Evaluating the Children Act 1989)*, London: The Stationery Office.

Svennevig, J. (2012) 'Interaction in meetings', *Discourse Studies*, 14(1): 3–10.

1

From a collaborative and integrated welfare policy to frontline practices

Kirsi Juhila, Suvi Raitakari, Dorte Caswell, Tanja Dall and Monika Wilińska

Introduction

During recent decades, Western welfare states have gone through a number of substantial transformations. One such transformation was the turn to active welfare states, based on the neoliberalist ideas of limiting the role of the state in welfare provision and emphasising citizens' responsibilities instead of rights. Along with this, there has been a transition to a managerialist mode of governance, calling for more effective and efficient welfare services, and an increasing demand to understand service-using citizens as active participants in service provision. Common to these kinds of transformations is that they travel across countries and are often defined as indispensable steps to maintaining welfare states and to securing effective, fair and flexible responses to citizens' wishes and needs. In other words, these are globally promoted and shared policies of welfare states, which are then realised in national legislation and guidelines.

New managerialist modes of governing have, among a range of other features, facilitated an increasingly specialised organisation of work in health and social care services. The idea is that specialised units of professionals will be able to develop more effective and productive service delivery due to both a specialisation of professional skills and an optimisation of procedures guiding work. However, this specialisation has produced fragmented services, which lack coherence and coordination in individual cases and between services more broadly. This has led to a call for collaborative and integrated welfare services across service sectors and national contexts. The resulting collaborative and integrated welfare policy and its accomplishments and implications in frontline social welfare service practices are at the core of this book. This policy stems from the aforementioned welfare state transformations, but it also has specific roots and justifications. It is promoted as a solution to overcoming the challenges of ineffective, dispersed and professional-led health and social care services. 'Collaboration' in this book refers to both collaboration between different professionals and organisations, and collaboration between professionals and citizens as service users. 'Integration', for its part, refers to the view that health and social care services should be seen as a whole, responding comprehensively to people's complex problems and service needs, in contrast to segmented sections concentrating solely on strictly targeted issues (Cameron et al, 2014; Fenwick, 2016, p 112).

Collaborative and integrated welfare is approached in this book from two aspects that are presented in the existing literature as essential for the renewal of welfare services, namely interprofessional collaboration and service user participation. These are both seen as premises for achieving collaborative and integrated welfare, and also as markers of the successful implementation of such a policy. These two aspects are examined in the book as they are achieved in frontline everyday practices and encounters between professionals and service users through which the realisation of collaboration and integration is sought. Thus, the focus is not on policy and collaboration at the organisational level, but on communicative and interactional processes, which are often mentioned as critical for the successful implementation of collaborative and integrated welfare services (Bokhour, 2006; Cameron et al, 2014; Goodwin, 2015). Furthermore, the book focuses on a specific organisational form of work: multi-agency meetings. Alongside the policy-level call for collaborative and integrated welfare services, an increase in the number of multi-agency meetings has been observed (Blom, 2004; Julkunen and Willumsen, 2017). These meetings are regarded as boundary spaces that bring together professionals from different professions and welfare agencies, service users and (sometimes) their next of kin or lay representatives.

The following section specifies what lies behind a transnational idea of a collaborative and integrated welfare policy. The subsequent sections review the literature on interprofessional collaboration and service user participation. These sections do not just promote but also challenge the two aspects of collaborative and integrated welfare.

A globally promoted idea to solve complex problems

The idea of collaborative and integrated welfare has been promoted by the World Health Organization (Cameron et al, 2014; Fenwick, 2016, p 114), and has been adopted as one of the core emphases in government programmes for future welfare services in many Western countries (Kitto et al, 2011, p 208). As Cameron et al (2014, p 225) stated in relation to the UK context: 'A consistent theme of policy over the past 40 years has been a concern that welfare services could be improved if agencies worked together more efficiently. In the field of adult health and social services, a variety of strategies have been introduced to encourage this agenda.' Similar movements are seen in the Scandinavian countries, such as in Finland where the government's large health and social service reforms seek more efficient and effective practices, and more integrated and well-functioning health and social care packages for individual citizens and families. Furthermore, the reforms aim to make countries responsible for giving people the opportunity to participate in developing health and social services.

The policy interest in and turn to collaborative and integrated welfare have been justified with a wide range of arguments. First, certain social problems and health problems are seen as interconnected (complex problems), demanding that they be dealt with together, not separately. Second, it is believed that by combining the professional expertise of various frontline workers with the experiential expertise of citizens and service users, it is possible to reach a more profound understanding of complex problems and to solve them more effectively and efficiently (Goodwin, 2015). Third, it is argued that collaborative and integrated welfare creates relational and joined-up talking and thinking that produces new and shared knowledge, instead of a mixed selection of professionals' and service users' views. Fourth, collaborative and integrated welfare is claimed to be a user-centred practice, since it treats citizens and service users as collaborators and participants, and approaches their problems and needs holistically, thereby constructing integrated care pathways (Huby and Rees, 2005; Vanhaecht et al, 2010). Fifth, the advantages of shared responsibility in providing and receiving welfare services is emphasised; solving complex problems should be everyone's duty (for example, the idea of a 'Big Society').

Despite justifying arguments, collaborative and integrated work faces several challenges. Leathard (2003) cites issues at five different levels:

- structural, such as fragmentation and gaps between different services;
- procedural, such as different budgetary and planning cycles;
- financial, such as different funding mechanisms and flows of financial resources;
- organisational, such as the division and organisation of work and professional groups;

- professional, such as issues of status and legitimacy, and different values and views.

Following the literature on frontline organisations, important decisions are made at each of these levels that are not just procedural or organisational, but which also translate and transform policy aims in ways that impact the frontline 'doing' of collaborative and integrated work in practice. Thus, collaborative and integrated work may take place at system and organisational levels as well as at the service user level in an effort to organise professionals' work and clients' service packages into seamless entities (Van der Klauw et al, 2014; Valentijn et al, 2015). This means that policy is not implemented through the formulation of policy aims or a reorganisation of work alone, but must also be adopted and acted out by professionals and service users in their encounters. In the words of Henneman et al (1995, p 108): 'Although organisations can be instrumental in supporting collaboration, they cannot ensure its success. Collaboration is, in fact, a process which occurs between individuals, not institutions, and only the persons involved ultimately determine whether or not collaboration occurs.'

Interprofessional collaboration

Cooperation between different professionals representing different organisations, services or professions has been defined with various concepts, such as 'multidisciplinary', 'cross-disciplinary', 'interagency', 'interorganisational' and 'interprofessional' work or practice. Although these concepts have different nuances (Kvarnström, 2011, pp 22–4), the authors of this book use the concept 'interprofessional' with an affix of 'collaboration' (interprofessional collaboration), which is commonly used in the health and social care literature. Fenwick (2016, p 113) defines interprofessional practice as 'integrated forms of practice involving workers in two or more different organisations or services', whereas Hammick et al (2009, p 205, cited in Morrison and Glenny, 2012, p 369) see it as occurring 'when multiple workers from different backgrounds provide comprehensive services by working together synergistically'. Collaboration, in turn, is described, for example, by Chesters et al (2011, p 4) as 'a key attribute of working together rather than working alongside, with the setting of shared goals (including, where possible, those of patients and their relatives)'.

Interprofessional collaboration is thus characterised by such attributes as working together across professional and organisational boundaries, integration, comprehensiveness, shared goals and synergy.

It is argued that this kind of orientation is especially needed when encountering complex, wicked (Rittel and Webber, 1973) and multidimensional problems that cannot be solved by applying the narrow or specialised knowledge of a single profession, service or agency (Goodwin, 2015). Interprofessional collaboration is argued to increase the holistic wellbeing of service users with complex service needs, rather than just concentrating on certain domains or problems in their lives.

From a critical perspective, interprofessional collaboration is perceived as an inherently good and skilled practice, with limited reflection on both its advantages and its disadvantages (Chesters et al, 2011; Morrison and Glenny, 2012; Fenwick, 2016). Fenwick (2016, p 113) writes that '"collaboration" tends to be over-simplified in practice as a romanticised ideal of communication, and in policy as a universal governing imperative for professional work in public service'. Chesters et al (2011, p 1) describe interprofessional health care as an uncritically accepted 'common sense' that is close to being a dominant discourse. Accordingly, Morrison and Glenny (2012, p 368) claim that 'for the protagonists, being inter-professional is, above all, the essence of being or becoming professional, previous forms seen as increasingly irrelevant or reprehensible'. Hence, education that strengthens interprofessional skills has been promoted and developed intensively in recent decades (for example, see the *Journal of Research in Interprofessional Practice and Education*).

Collaboration is an appealing term (Morrison and Glenny, 2012, p 367). It is hard to resist the idea that collaboration, rather than individual and singular specialised efforts, produces innovative solutions to complex problems in health and social care and increases service users' positive service experiences and wellbeing. Total resistance to collaboration would not even be reasonable, since interprofessional collaboration has been shown to be an effective, responsive and user-centred practice in many service occasions and for many different service user groups. However, the evidence is not always sufficiently robust and solid (Cameron et al, 2014; Goodwin, 2015). In fact, the appealing connotations of the term should not obscure the fact that the evidence of the functionality of interprofessional collaboration is mixed; it can produce both negative and positive practices and impacts (McNeil et al, 2013). It is therefore dangerous to regard interprofessional collaboration as a superior practice that works in all 'complex cases' without taking into account the specific requirements of the working environment, resources and the personal needs and wishes of service users.

Gaining knowledge of collaboration in practice — whether it is a suitable approach in a given context or not and what outcomes it produces — demands looking closely at naturally occurring frontline service practices, where interprofessional collaboration is applied and displayed in service user–professional encounters processing individual cases.

Relational agency, boundaries and common knowledge

Interprofessional collaboration has been studied and developed as a field of research based on various theories and philosophies of knowledge, agency and interaction. For the purposes of this book, Anne Edwards' work on collaboration is interesting, since she emphasises the everyday relational processes of interprofessional practices (Edwards, 2005, 2010, 2017, Edwards et al, 2009). Her work draws on cultural-historical activity theory, whose origins can be found in the writings of Vygotsky (1978) and Leontyev (1981), and which has been elaborated further from the point of view of learning in working life and developmental work research by Yrjö Engeström and his colleagues (Engeström, 1987, 1999, 2001).

Edwards (2011, p 33) uses the term 'relational turn' to describe necessary and ongoing changes in expertise demanding interprofessional and interagency activities in working life. The foundation of the turn is in the idea of relational agency. By relational agency, she is referring to:

> a capacity for working with others to strengthen purposeful responses to complex problems. It arises in a two stage process within a constant dynamic which consists of:
>
> (i) working with others to expand the 'object of activity' or task being worked on by recognising the motives and the resources that others bring to bear as they, too interpret it; and
> (ii) aligning one's own responses to the newly enhanced interpretations with the responses being made by the other professionals while acting on the expanded object. (Edwards, 2011, p 34)

Relational agency is thus based on constant responsive interactions with other professionals, with the aim of producing solutions to complex problems (objects of activity) that are more than just a combination of individual professionals' expertise and interpretations of problems. Interactions occur at intersecting practices that create boundary spaces where it is possible to build beneficial new common knowledge and relational expertise (Edwards, 2011, pp 33–5).

Building common knowledge and relational expertise is not an easy, straightforward process. Conflict between areas of specialised expertise is an inevitable part of the process, since the familiar boundaries of professions and organisations are broken down (Frost et al, 2005). Relying on Engeström's (1999) theory, Frost et al describe the processes, discussing conflict in the following way:

> At this point, implicit knowledge must often be made explicit. Professionals have to find a common language to make knowledge accessible to their colleagues from other disciplines. ... To understand these processes, we drew on Engeström's (1999) activity theory model in the field of knowledge creation and exchange. An important premise in Engeström's model is that conflict is inevitable as tasks are redefined, and distributed within changing organizations and teams. His premise is that such conflicts must be debated openly, as communities/teams come together with different knowledge, expertise and histories to pursue a common goal, if progress is to be made towards creating new forms of knowledge and practice. (Frost et al, 2005, p 189)

Ideas about relational agency, interaction and common knowledge are linked to constructionist and discursive theories of knowledge (Berger and Luckmann, 1966; Potter, 1996; Edwards, 1997; Burr, 2015). According to these theories, knowledge is not something that is simply possessed by individuals, based for example on their education or experiences, and occasionally delivered to other people. Instead, knowledge is seen as continually produced, negotiated and challenged in textually mediated conversations, such as scientific literature concerning knowledge about interprofessional collaboration, or in face-to-face encounters, such as interprofessional team meetings grappling with complex problems. There are differences between the theory of relational agency based on the activity theory model and constructionist theories. The former sees intersecting boundaries as a promising space for joined-up thinking and talking, producing innovative and useful new knowledge, although usually only after conflicts have been debated. By contrast, the latter is more open to the possibility that interactions in boundary spaces can also result in competitive struggles between different types of knowledge and the repression of certain stakeholders or 'voices'. In the end, it is a matter for empirical research to find out how knowledge is created, contested and shared in the boundary spaces of frontline services, and with what consequences. As Edwards (2011, p 34) notes, 'we know all too little about how common knowledge is built at the boundaries of systems or practices'. Hence, one aim of this book is to demonstrate both how common knowledge is constructed in boundary spaces such as multi-agency meetings, and how different domains of knowledge may come into conflict with one another or be given hierarchical value.

Blurring boundaries, power relations and the risks of shared responsibility

Edwards' conceptualisation of collaboration as relational processes that are continually produced and negotiated in responsive interactions calls attention to the actual doing of collaboration in frontline practices in health and social services. The potential of interprofessional collaboration is contingent on the practical accomplishment of such work; however, interprofessional collaboration may also produce negative results. The often taken-for-granted potential of interprofessional collaboration is challenged by literature that identifies risks in this approach. Here three lines of concern are addressed.

The first line of concern is that interprofessional collaboration threatens professional identities, creates intolerant attitudes towards differences in professional knowledge and requires professionals to 'assimilate' into a generic care culture with generic roles (McNeil et al, 2013). Certainly the opposite view exists, that interprofessional collaboration depends on strong professional identities and domains of expertise, with the sharing of a wide range of professional knowledge without it being merged into a single entity. Nevertheless, professionalism is often mentioned as one of the main obstacles or even threats to the strengthening of integrated care, since 'professionalism would seem to progress individualistic rather than cooperative tendencies as professionals seek to protect specific tasks and craft knowledge which may determine the type of team practice' (Coyle et al, 2011, p 45). Professionalism can easily result in boundary work, where different professions and service agencies draw rigid demarcation lines by claiming that their skills and jurisdictions cover one particular domain of work but not another (Gieryn, 1983; Abbott, 1995; Allen, 2000; Hall et al, 2010, 349).

Frost et al argue that:

> [J]oined-up thinking has profound implications for the concept of professionalism and how we think about professional knowledge

and practice. It can be argued that traditional claims to professional expertise are based on developing expertise in specific professional fields, the antithesis of joined-up thinking (Frost, 2001). In multi-agency teamwork, professional knowledge boundaries can become blurred and professional identity can be challenged as roles and responsibilities change. (Frost et al, 2005, p 188)

On the one hand, more permeable boundaries between professions can be seen as a precondition for interprofessional collaboration and innovative joined-up thinking. On the other hand, there is a danger that distinctive professional knowledge and approaches to solving complex problems are lost in the process of blurring boundaries and reaching for a shared understanding. Sometimes 'orientations of different professions to the same problem can be diametrically opposed' (Fenwick, 2016, p 115). Accordingly, Morrison and Glenny write that:

[S]ervices enjoined to 'collaborate' may be on different projects and, indeed, varied epistemological and action-oriented 'pathways', sometimes towards divergent 'destinations'. For example, educators intervene to include children and young people in education, social workers to protect those children most vulnerable, and health services to heal; in each case, these endeavours are driven with internal contradiction. (Morrison and Glenny, 2012, p 371)

All these endeavours by educators, social workers and health professionals are valuable in their own right and require specialist knowledge and expertise. Therefore, bypassing these domains of specialised expertise and the tasks of different welfare organisations to concentrate primarily on common knowledge creation and shared aims can, at worst, produce negative impacts for people with complex problems by missing the opportunity to reach genuinely interprofessional, multifaceted conclusions.

The second line of concern brings up power relations between different professionals. The sociology of the professions has a long history of discussing such issues as interprofessional competition, monopolies of practices and hierarchies between professions (Reeves, 2011). In the pursuit of interprofessional collaboration it is essential to understand and challenge culturally embedded power relations (Fenwick, 2016, p 116). The professions do not enter arenas for interprofessional collaboration as equal partners free from stereotypical categorisations and expectations. For instance, the dominance of the medical model in health and social care settings and the authoritative roles of health professionals, especially doctors, have frequently been discussed and demonstrated in the literature (Abramson and Mizrahi, 2003; Long et al, 2006, pp 509, 516; Nugus et al, 2010). However, medical dominance does not necessarily mean that the expertise of other domains is not respected; rather, it is regarded as complementary to the primary medical expertise.

The third line of concern discusses the responsibilities of different professional parties in interprofessional collaboration. Joined-up thinking and talking includes the idea of members of interprofessional teams having shared responsibility for solving complex problems in individual cases (Hewitt et al, 2014). According to Morrison and Glenny (2012, p 380), this diffuses responsibility, and there is a risk that a 'reduction in personal responsibility is not complemented by a comparable assumption of responsibility by service coordinating teams'. Sharing and blurring responsibility might obscure who has the final decision-making power, and who ultimately takes responsibility for what in complex cases (Fenwick, 2016, p 113; Dall, 2018). This sometimes leads to situations where, from the point of view of service users, no one seems to have decisive responsibility.

The concerns that have been raised in relation to the idea of interprofessional collaboration should be taken seriously and studied carefully in a variety of settings. Doubts and contradictions about interprofessional collaboration may materialise in some health and social care settings but not necessarily all, nor in every individual case, nor at all times in the same way. Empirical research that concentrates on everyday interprofessional collaboration is the means for finding out how interprofessional collaboration in shifting contexts is realised in practice, and whether the abovementioned concerns are justified. Such research lies at the heart of this book.

Service user participation

In recent decades, the topic of service user participation has been widely discussed and studied in health and social care across Western societies (for example, Beresford, 2002; Kvarnström, 2011; Kvarnström et al, 2012, 2013; Matthies and Uggerhoej, 2014; Raitakari et al, 2015; Juhila et al, 2017, pp 36–7). In the literature, participation is related to concepts such as 'self-determination', 'human rights', 'full citizenship', 'user involvement', 'consumer choice' and 'empowerment'. The basic argument is that citizens should occupy a position of authority and, along with that, have the opportunity to influence and make decisions on matters of importance to them.

The expectation that service users should have a more active and powerful role regarding their own wellbeing and the health and social care services they receive has emanated from a variety of sources (Pilgrim and Waldron, 1998; Drake et al, 2010). National policy documents and legislation globally have articulated the importance of service user involvement. Similarly, service users, as well as health and social care professionals in various settings, have promoted the principle of participation (Cahill, 1996; Collins et al, 2007; Browne and Hemsley, 2008; Kvarnström, 2011, p 8; Kvarnström et al, 2012). Service user participation is also a core principle in the ethics codes of health and social care professions, and the service user movement has played a significant role in highlighting user participation as a human rights issue (see for example Bassman, 1997; Cook and Jonikas, 2002). Professionals, for their part, are seen as responsible for encouraging, enabling and supporting users to use this right.

The ideal of service user participation challenges interprofessional collaboration that occurs solely between different professionals and agencies. As Kvarnström (2011, p 24) writes, the use of the term 'interprofessional collaboration' seems to exclude service users and people close to them. Thus, her suggestion is that it is better to replace that concept simply with 'collaborative practices', where service users are understood as partners with their own expertise. Nowadays, it is a widely held view that collaborative practices should not be exclusively interprofessional, but should include service users and their significant others, such as their parents and carers (Morrison and Glenny, 2012, p 369).

Service user participation is commonly understood in terms of both individual and collective participation. At the individual level, it is considered important that service users are provided with information and that they are active in setting goals, defining support measures and making choices regarding the services they receive. At the collective level, it is emphasised that service users, as an important stakeholder group, should be involved in the planning, providing, assessing and researching of services (Beresford, 2002; Lammers and Happell, 2003; Kvarnström, 2011; Raitakari et al, 2015). In this book, the focus is on individual participation in that it examines how service users participate and are treated as participants in their own personal matters in integrated, collaborative and multi-agency health and social care meeting practices. We thus use the term 'participation' in the broad sense of service users being present and participating in discussions regarding their individual case and situation. Whether or not this amounts to having an active influence on decision making and care planning is an empirical question to be examined in the individual encounters.

Service users as participants in creating knowledge in collaborative practices

Applying Edwards' (2010, 2011) ideas about interprofessional work and relational expertise to collaborative practices, including both professionals and service users, means that service users are understood as important participants with relational agency, producing solutions to complex problems. This corresponds with the general shift described earlier – from services provided *by* professionals *for* clients, to the increasingly common view that practices (should) unfold *with* service users as active participants (Hopwood and Edwards, 2017, p 108). Service users' expertise and interpretations of problems concerning themselves are regarded as important resources in creating common knowledge and relational expertise in boundary spaces. What is also in focus here is the communicative construction of common knowledge in mutually responsive ways. This relational foundation of professional–service user collaboration places specific demands on professionals, who have to balance the use of their specialist expertise against the risk of compromising the idea of collaboration and partnership with clients. Hopwood and Edwards (2017, p 109) suggest that the establishment of common knowledge can be an important mediating factor in achieving such a balance, but they also emphasise that the concept of 'common knowledge' 'does not imply that ... "what matters" must be(come) the same. Indeed the different insights associated with different motives are seen as strengths in partnership approaches'. Professionals (and service users) should thus attempt to facilitate encounters in which it becomes possible to work with differences and explore what they mean for the unfolding collaboration.

Such a conceptualisation highlights service user participation as 'a complex, emergent phenomenon located in practices and specific settings, rather than something that can be reduced to procedural prescription' (Hopwood and Edwards, 2017, p 117). It also means that the question of whether participation is best understood as service users relaying information, offering interpretations, collaborating in defining and solving problems or autonomously making decisions in their own case becomes an empirical question to be examined in naturally occurring encounters between service users and professionals.

Power relations, responsibilities and the risks of social engineering and stigmatisation

Following the conceptualisation of service user participation as contingent on communicative and negotiated practices, it is perhaps no surprise that the ideals of participation are met with certain concerns regarding its realisation and fulfilment in health and social care. Here, three concerns are addressed.

The first concern is similar to the second concern regarding interprofessional collaboration, namely power relations in interactions. Just as different professions do not enter collaborations as equally valued and trusted participants, free from pre-existing stereotypes, nor do service users. Service users might be treated more like objects than subjects in interactions, whose situation and troubles are 'diagnosed' and conceptualised by various professionals using their specialised expertise and knowledge. Furthermore, service users can be categorised in advance into certain 'client types', such as someone with a substance-abuse addiction or a long-term unemployed person with predetermined attributes, which does not give them much space to present their identities in different and personal ways. It can also be the case that instead of equal and shared collaborations between all parties, particular alliances or subgroups emerge. For example, professionals may ally with each other 'against' the service user's interpretation of their own situation, or one professional may ally with the service user to advocate their right to their own voice in interactions. Boundary spaces then become 'battle fields' for different viewpoints and blocs.

The second concern relates to the balance between service users' right to be involved versus their responsibility to participate. Kvarnström (2011, p 18) writes that 'the concept of service user participation is associated with the dimension of active social citizenship as well as rights to be active in contacts with health and social care services'. The rights perspective includes, for instance, such privileges as being entitled to: getting information and support from professionals in increasing one's self-determination; having a strong voice in interpreting one's own situation and needs; making choices concerning services; and having permission to challenge professionals' judgements and discretionary power. In addition to the rights perspective, the service user's active citizenship and participation are increasingly understood as the service user's responsibility. However, it can be argued that individuals should also have the right *not* to become involved or participate (Juhila et al, 2017, p 37). Since service users have different interests and capacities to participate, the option to be non-active must be available (Hickey and Kipping, 1998; Lammers and Happell, 2003, p 387; Fischer and Neale, 2008; Raitakari et al, 2015). When emphasising the service user's responsibility to participate, it is not understood as an individual's choice and right, but as a duty of citizenship and as a governmental tool to overcome exclusion and welfare dependency (Jayasuriya, 2002; Paddison et al, 2008).

The third concern raises the question of whether collaboration is always in the best interests of the service user. Is it what the service user wants and hopes for? For service users, collaborative and integrated practice means that instead of different professionals working with them separately in different organisations, several professionals from various organisations deal with their situation and problems simultaneously, towards shared aims. The principle of integrated care is based on the holistic idea that health problems and social problems are somehow connected and should be met and tackled together with all relevant parties. This can mean, for instance, endeavours to create one, shared assessment process (see Dickinson, 2006) and one care plan in collaborative practices for each service user. Certainly, collaborative and integrated practice can have many advantages for service users. For example, it may reduce visits to different services and the so-called 'revolving door' phenomenon. And it can create comprehensive interpretations of service users' life situation that service users find useful in their life planning. However, from a critical point of view, collaborative and integrated practice can be seen as a form of social engineering, purporting to reach into all domains of life (Morrison and Glenny, 2012, p 371). Service users might sometimes prefer not to participate in interprofessional collaboration, if given the option to make that choice. For example, service users may regard their mental health problems and unemployment issues as unrelated issues that should not be dealt with simultaneously with every professional involved. They may prefer discussions with one trusted professional at a time, if they feel uncomfortable discussing their lives in multi-agency meetings with several people present. They may also feel that being a service user in integrated services is stigmatising, since they are defined as a person with complex problems and needs. According to Morrison and Glenny (2012, p 371), 'service users may have to present themselves as dysfunctional, helpless, or disabled in some way before integrated service is made available to them'. In terms of the possible negative sides of collaborative and integrated practice, a relevant question is whether the principle of service user participation allows the user the choice of refusing or challenging such participation.

Collaboration and integration in action: teamwork and multi-agency meetings

Collaborative and integrated practice that includes both different professionals and service users cannot exist without interactional arenas where it can be accomplished. Multi-agency meetings constitute one such arena and one that has been increasingly utilised, as welfare policies have emphasised the need for collaborative and integrated services (Blom, 2004; Julkunen and Willumsen, 2017). The literature in health and social care often covers such meetings in terms of 'teamwork', and the ability to conduct teamwork is seen as a fundamental element of health and social care systems (Coyle et al, 2011, p 39; Morrison and Glenny, 2012, p 376).

Multi-agency meetings in health and social care may take the shape of case conferences, case planning meetings, network meetings, team meetings and so on. Each type of meeting has specific aims for assessing, planning for or resolving the service user's complex case, and may also be structured around specific interactional norms and procedures. Multi-agency meetings are a common way to structure and implement collaborative and integrated welfare; however, we still know very little about communication and interaction in such meetings (Bokhour, 2006).

The established way to understand teamwork in health and social care is as communication and work done together by professionals representing different professions and agencies. In a literature review, Xyrichis and Lowton (2008) found that enhanced communication achieved through team meetings is a means to ensure effective teamwork, and conversely that a lack of communication is the source of misconceptions, conflicts and the breakdown of teamwork. When teamwork is successful, it may fulfil the following primary aims: '(1) to provide the best patient care possible, (2) to make joint interdisciplinary decisions, (3) to coordinate care amongst professionals, and (4) to complete the written treatment plan' (Bokhour, 2006, p 353). However, in practice, service users are not necessarily seen as having an active role in achieving these goals in teams and their multi-agency meetings.

At one extreme, service users may not even be present at meetings, leaving the discussion of their situation and problems to the professionals. However, the growing policy-level emphasis on the importance of service user participation means that nowadays service users are often invited as participants to multi-agency meetings regarding their personal matters, and their presence can even be considered indispensable for successful meetings. Nonetheless, even where service users are present in meetings, their position may still vary a great deal. For example, some studies have shown that service users are treated mainly as informants about their current situation, troubles and wishes, with professionals retaining the power to process this information and make plans and decisions concerning the service user's future (Hitzler and Messmer, 2010; Juhila et al, 2015). Furthermore, multi-agency meetings can place high demands on vulnerable service users in terms of the communicative abilities needed to make their voice heard, even when professionals are attuned to the service user as an active participant.

Despite these challenges in the very structure of meetings, multi-agency meetings that include service users can, and should ideally, function as arenas in which 'the "best" possible knowledge about the client's situation is present and where the participants share and negotiate the responsibilities for working toward common goals' (Berger and Eskelinen, 2016, p 100). Indeed, if the idea of collaborative and integrated practice is taken seriously, service users must be viewed as full team members, whose knowledge is understood and valued equally with that of other participants (Chesters et al, 2011, p 3). This resonates with Edwards' (2010, 2011) concept of 'relational agency' and the building of common knowledge in responsive interactions. However, it is important to ask whether and what kind of roles, rights and responsibilities service users and individual professionals have in relational agency and in the creation of knowledge.

While the policy movements towards more collaborative and integrated welfare are present and almost universally supported across health and social care settings, as well as across national welfare states, the realisation of such ideals in practice is less clear cut. In particular, this is related to the various challenges of implementing policy in practice. As the literature on street-level bureaucracy and organisations (Lipsky, 1980; Brodkin, 2011) has effectively demonstrated, frontline organisations can be understood as *de facto* policy makers in the sense that they informally (re)construct policy in the course of everyday organisational life (Brodkin, 2011, p i253), although they do not determine the explicit policy content. How collaborative and integrated welfare policy is brought about in practice is thus highly contingent on the organisation and management of work as well as the conduct of professionals and clients in everyday encounters. This book focuses on analysing encounters in multi-agency meetings, which although crucial for accomplishing collaborative and integrated welfare, can also reveal the dilemmas, complexities and failures in implementing this policy-level ideal. This raises several questions for further examination, some of which include:

- How are relational agency, (new) boundary spaces and common knowledge constructed (or not constructed) in the meetings?
- Can blurred professional boundaries be dysfunctional, for instance by obscuring responsibilities between the parties, and if so, how can this be identified in meeting interactions?
- What patterns of participation among professionals and service users appear in the meetings?
- Do service users have a choice regarding whether and how to participate in the meetings (responsibility versus right to participate)?
- Who collaborates with whom in meetings – professionals with each other, some professionals with service users or all participants together?
- What kinds of positions are given to and taken by service users in multi-agency meetings (outsiders, informants, decision makers and so on)?
- How are hierarchies of different knowledge and expertise, including service users' knowledge and expertise, produced and negotiated (or not) in the meetings?
- How is service user knowledge based on personal experiences valued (in relation to professional knowledge) in the meetings?
- Are there signs of the stigmatisation or downgrading of service users in the course of meeting conversations?

This list encapsulates our preliminary interests in examining multi-agency meetings as arenas where it is expected that collaborative and integrated welfare will be realised. The next chapter provides more precise methodological premises and analytic tools for doing such analyses.

References

Abbott, A. (1995) 'Boundaries of social work or social work of boundaries?', *Social Service Review*, 69(4): 545–62.

Abramson, J.S. and Mizrahi, T. (2003) 'Understanding collaboration between social workers and physicians', *Social Work in Health Care*, 37(2): 71–100.

Allen, D. (2000) 'Doing occupational demarcation: The "boundary work" of nurse managers in a district general hospital', *Journal of Contemporary Ethnography*, 29(3): 326–56.

Bassman, R. (1997) 'The mental health system: Experiences from both sides of the locked doors', *Professional Psychology: Research and Practice*, 28(3): 238–42.

Beresford, P. (2002) 'User involvement in research and evaluation: Liberation or regulation?', *Social Policy and Society*, 1(2): 95–105.

Berger, N.P. and Eskelinen, L. (2016) 'Negotiation of user identity and responsibility at a prerelease conference', *Qualitative Social Work*, 15(1): 86–102.

Berger, P.L. and Luckmann, T. (1966) *The Social Construction of Reality: A Treatise in The Sociology of Knowledge*, New York, NY: Penguin Books.

Blom, B. (2004) 'Specialization in social work practice: Effects on interventions in the personal social services', *Journal of Social Work*, 4(1): 25–46.

Bokhour, B.G. (2006) 'Communication in interdisciplinary team meetings: What are we talking about?', *Journal of Interprofessional Care*, 20(4): 349–63.

Brodkin, E. (2011) 'Policy work: Street-level organizations under new managerialism', *Journal of Public Administration Research and Theory*, 21(2): i253–i277.

Browne, G. and Hemsley, M. (2008) 'Consumer participation in mental health in Australia: What progress is being made?', *Australasian Psychiatry*, 16(6): 446–9.

Burr, V. (2015) *Social Constructionism* (3rd edn), London: Routledge.

Cahill, J. (1996) 'Patient participation: A concept analysis', *Journal of Advanced Nursing*, 24(3): 561–71.

Cameron, A., Lart, R., Bostock, L. and Coomber, C. (2014) 'Factors that promote and hinder joint and integrated working between health and social care services: a review of literature', *Health and Social Care in the Community*, 22(3): 225–33.

Chesters, J., Thistlethwaite, J., Reeves, S. and Kitto, S. (2011) 'Introduction: A sociology of interprofessional healthcare', in S. Kitto, J. Chesters, J. Thistlethwaite and S. Reeves (eds) *Sociology of Interprofessional Health Care Practice: Critical Reflections and Concrete Solutions*, New York, NY: Nova Science Publishers, pp 1–8.

Collins, S., Britten, N., Ruusuvuori, J. and Thompson. A. (2007) 'Understanding the process of patient participation', in S. Collins, N. Britten, J. Ruusuvuori and A. Thompson (eds) *Patient Participation in Health Care Consultations: Qualitative Perspectives*, Maidenhead: McGraw-Hill, Open University Press, pp 3–21.

Cook, J.A. and Jonikas, J.A. (2002) 'Self-determination among mental health consumer/survivors: Using lessons from the past to guide the future', *Journal of Disability Policy Studies*, 13(2): 87–95.

Coyle, J., Higgs, J., McAllister, L. and Whiteford, G. (2011) 'What is an interprofessional health care team anyway?', in S. Kitto, J. Chesters, J. Thistlethwaite and S. Reeves (eds) *Sociology of Interpersonal Health Care Practice: Critical Reflections and Concrete Solutions*, New York, NY: Nova Science Publishers, pp 39–53.

Dall, T. (2018) 'Distribution of responsibility in inter-professional teams in welfare-to-work', *Nordic Social Work Research*, 10(1): 80–93.

Dickinson, A. (2006) 'Implementing the single assessment process: Opportunities and challenges', *Journal of Interprofessional Care*, 20(4): 365–79.

Drake, R.E., Deegan, P.E. and Rapp, C. (2010) 'The promise of shared decision making in mental health', *Psychiatric Rehabilitation Journal*, 34(1): 7–13.

Edwards, A. (2005) 'Relational agency: Learning to be a resourceful practitioner', *International Journal of Educational Research*, 43(3): 168–82.

Edwards, A. (2010) *Being an Expert Professional Practitioner: The Relational Turn in Expertise*, Dordrecht: Springer.

Edwards, A. (2011) 'Building common knowledge at the boundaries between professional practices: Relational agency and relational expertise in systems of distributed expertise', *International Journal of Educational Research*, 50(1): 33–9.

Edwards, A. (ed) (2017) *Working Relationally In and Across Practices: Cultural-Historical Approaches to Collaboration*, New York, NY: Cambridge University Press.

Edwards, A., Daniels, H., Gallagher, P., Leadbetter, J. and Warmington, P. (2009) *Improving Inter-Professional Collaborations: Multi-Agency Working for Children's Wellbeing*, London: Routledge.

Edwards, D. (1997) *Discourse and Cognition*, London: Sage Publications.

Engeström, Y. (1987) *Learning by Expanding: An Activity-Theoretical Approach to Developmental Research*, Helsinki: Orienta-Konsultit Oy.

Engeström, Y. (ed) (1999) *Perspectives on Activity Theory*, Cambridge: Cambridge University Press.

Engeström, Y. (2001) 'Expansive learning at work: Toward an activity theoretical reconceptualisation', *Journal of Education and Work*, 14(1): 133–56.

Fenwick, T. (2016) *Professional Responsibility and Professionalism: A Sociomaterial Examination*, London: Routledge.

Fischer, J. and Neale, J. (2008) 'Involving drug users in treatment decisions: An exploration of potential problems', *Drugs, Education, Prevention, and Policy*, 15(2): 161–75.

Frost, N. (2001) 'Professionalism, change and the politics of lifelong learning', *Studies in Continuing Education*, 23(1): 5–17.

Frost, N., Robinson, M. and Anning, A. (2005) 'Social workers in multidisciplinary teams: Issues and dilemmas for professional practice', *Child and Family Social Work*, 10(3): 187–96.

Gieryn, T. (1983) 'Boundary work and the demarcation of science from non-science: Strains and interests in professional ideologies of scientists', *American Sociological Review*, 48(6): 781–95.

Goodwin, N. (2015) 'How should integrated care address the challenge of people with complex health and social care needs? Emerging lessons from international case studies', *International Journal of Integrated Care*, 15: e037.

Hall, C., Slembrouck, S., Haigh, E. and Lee, A. (2010) 'The management of professional roles during boundary work in child welfare', *International Journal of Social Welfare*, 19(3): 348–57.

Hammick, M., Freeth, D., Copperman, J. and Goodsmith, D. (2009) *Being Interprofessional*, Cambridge: Polity Press.

Henneman, E.A., Lee, J.L. and Cohen, J.I. (1995) 'Collaboration: A concept analysis', *Journal of Advanced Nursing*, 21(1): 103–9.

Hewitt, G., Sims, S. and Harris, R. (2014) 'Using realist synthesis to understand the mechanism of interprofessional teamwork in health and social care', *Journal of Interprofessional Care*, 28(6): 501–6.

Hickey, G. and Kipping, C. (1998) 'Exploring the concept of user involvement in mental health through a participation continuum', *Journal of Clinical Nursing*, 7(1): 83–8.

Hitzler, S. and Messmer, H. (2010) 'Group decision-making in child welfare and the pursuit of participation', *Qualitative Social Work*, 9(2): 205–26.

Hopwood, N. and Edwards, A. (2017) 'How common knowledge is constructed and why it matters in collaboration between professionals and clients', *International Journal of Educational Research*, 83: 107–19.

Huby, G. and Rees, G. (2005) 'The effectiveness of quality improvement tools: Joint working in integrated community teams, *International Journal for Quality in Health Care*, 17(1): 53–8.

Jayasuriya, K. (2002) 'The new contractualism: neo-liberal or democratic?', *Political Quarterly*, 73(3): 309–20.

Juhila, K., Hall, C., Günther, K., Raitakari, S. and Saario, S. (2015) 'Accepting and negotiating service users' choices in mental health transition meetings', *Social Policy & Administration*, 49(5): 612–30.

Juhila, K., Raitakari, S. and Hansen Löfstrand, C. (2017) 'Responsibilities and welfare discourses', in K. Juhila, S. Raitakari and C. Hall (eds) *Responsibilisation at the Margins of Welfare Services*, London: Routledge, pp 35–56.

Julkunen, I. and Willumsen, E. (2017) 'Professional boundary crossing and interprofessional knowledge development', in B. Blom, L. Evertsson and M. Perlinski (eds) *Social and Caring Professions in European Welfare States: Policies, Services and Professional Practices*, Bristol: Policy Press, pp 115–30.

Kitto, S., Reeves, S., Chesters, J. and Thistlethwaite, J. (2011) 'Re-imagining interprofessionalism: where to from here?', in S. Kitto, J. Chesters, J. Thistlethwaite and S. Reeves (eds) *Sociology of Interprofessional Health Care Practice: Critical Reflections and Concrete Solutions*, New York, NY: Nova Science Publishers, pp 207–11.

Kvarnström, S. (2011) *Collaboration in Health and Social Care: Service User Participation and Teamwork in Interprofessional Clinical Microsystems*, Jönköping, Sweden: School of Health Sciences, Jönköping University, Dissertation Series No. 15.

Kvarnström, S., Hedberg, B and Cedersund, E. (2013) 'The dual faces of service user participation: Implications for empowerment processes in interprofessional practice', *Journal of Social Work*, 13(3): 287–307.

Kvarnström, S., Willumsen, E., Andersson-Gäre, B. and Hedberg, B. (2012) 'How service users perceive the concept of participation, specifically in interprofessional practice', *British Journal of Social Work*, 42(1): 129–46.

Lammers J. and Happell, P. (2003) 'Consumer participation in mental health services: Looking from a consumer perspective', *Journal of Psychiatric and Mental Health Nursing*, 10(4): 385–92.

Leathard, A. (2003) 'Introduction', in A. Leathard, *Interprofessional Collaboration: From Policy to Practice in Health and Social Care*, Hove: Brunner-Routledge, pp 2–10.

Leontyev, A.N. (1981) *Problems of the Development of the Mind*, Moscow: Progress Publishers.

Lipsky, M. (1980) *Street-Level Bureaucracy: Dilemmas of the Individual in Public Services*, New York, NY: Russell Sage Foundation.

Long, D., Forsyth, R., Iedema, R. and Carroll, K. (2006) 'The (im)possibilities of clinical democracy', *Health Sociology Review*, 15(5): 506–19.

Matthies, A.-L. and Uggerhoej, L. (eds) (2014) *Participation, Marginalisation and Welfare Services: Concepts, Politics and Practices Across European Countries*, Farnham: Ashgate.

McNeil, K., Mitchell, R. and Parker, V. (2013) 'Interprofessional practice and professional identity threat', *Health Sociology Review*, 22(3): 291–307.

Morrison, M. and Glenny, G. (2012) 'Collaborative inter-professional policy and practice: In search for evidence', *Journal of Education Policy*, 27(3): 367–86.

Nugus, P., Greenfield, D., Travaglia, J., Westbrook, J. and Braithwaite, J. (2010) 'How and where clinicians exercise power: Interprofessional relations in health care', *Social Science & Medicine*, 71(5): 898–909.

Paddison, R., Docherty, I. and Goodlad, R. (2008) 'Responsible participation and housing: Restoring democratic theory to the scene', *Housing Studies*, 23(1): 129–47.

Pilgrim, D. and Waldron, L. (1998) 'User involvement in mental health service development: How far can it go?', *Journal of Mental Health*, 7(1): 95–104.

Potter, J. (1996) *Representing Reality: Discourse, Rhetoric and Social Construction*, London: Sage Publications.

Raitakari, S., Saario, S., Juhila, K. and Günther, K. (2015) 'Client participation in mental health: Shifting positions in decision-making', *Nordic Social Work Research*, 5(1): 35–49.

Reeves, S. (2011) 'Using the sociological imagination to explore the nature of interprofessional interactions and relations', in S. Kitto, J. Chesters, J. Thistlethwaite and S. Reeves (eds) *Sociology of Interprofessional Health Care Practice: Critical Reflections and Concrete Solutions*, New York, NY: Nova Science Publishers, pp 9–22.

Rittel, H. and Webber, M. (1973) 'Dilemmas in a general theory of planning', *Policy Sciences*, 4(2): 155–69.

Valentijn, P., Boesveld, I., Van der Klauw, D., Ruwaard, D., Struijs, J., Molema, J., Bruijnzeels, M. and Vrijhoef, H. (2015) 'Towards a taxonomy for integrated care: A mixed-methods study', *International Journal of Integrated Care*, 15: e003.

Van der Klauw, D., Molema, H., Grooten, L. and Vrijhoef, H. (2014) 'Identification of mechanisms enabling integrated care for patients with chronic diseases: A literature review', *International Journal of Integrated Care*, 14(21): e024.

Vanhaecht, K., Panella, M., van Zelm, R. and Sermeus, W. (2010) 'An overview on the history and concept of care pathways as complex interventions', *International Journal of Care Pathways*, 14(3): 117–23.

Vygotsky, L.S. (1978) *Mind in Society: The Development of Higher Psychological Processes*, Cambridge, MA: Harvard University Press.

Xyrichis, A. and Lowton, K. (2008) 'What fosters or prevents interprofessional teamworking in primary and community care? A literature review', *International Journal of Nursing Studies*, 45(1): 140–53.

2

Examining talk and interaction in meetings of professionals and service users

Christopher Hall and Tanja Dall

Introduction

In institutional settings such as health and social care services, multi-agency meetings are the forum for implementing policies and procedures of interagency operations and service user participation. In Chapter 1, multi-agency meetings are conceptualised as boundary spaces that bring together professionals from different professions and welfare agencies, service users and (sometimes) their next of kin or lay representatives. This makes the communicative and interactional processes important, as it is through face-to-face meetings that the everyday practices of professionals and service users are examined, directed and reviewed in a formal setting.

The multi-agency meetings examined in this book are from a number of countries, contrasting welfare regimes and different sectors of health and social care, and they are formulated through different legal jurisdictions. However, as will become clear, there are a number of important similarities. The book does not propose to provide a comparative analysis, but together the analyses suggest that there is something particular about the frame, structure and function of multi-agency meetings that promotes certain interactional practices and addresses interactional dilemmas. This reflects the function of the multi-agency meeting as an organisational procedure for processing people and entities, as occurs in a team meeting or home visit, which requires participants to conform to certain conventions and constraints of turn allocation, topic progression, role performance, politeness, delicacy and so on.

This chapter first questions the notion that meetings should be treated as formal events for making plans and decisions. Instead, it argues that they should be approached as complex social and interactional encounters that draw on everyday notions of what constitutes appropriate organisational interaction. Second, the chapter examines the literature that depicts meetings as rituals and ceremonies in which the values and expectations of organisational practice are enacted. It presents the concept of 'degradation and integration ceremonies' as particularly relevant to social welfare meetings where the identity of service users is exposed to the scrutiny of professionals. Third, the literature on talk and interaction in meetings is discussed, with key analytical concepts examined, such as the organisation and structure of meetings, the role and action of the chair, turn-taking and selection, topic management and progression, and decision making.

Meetings as social and interactional occasions

Meetings in organisations have been the subject of extensive research, although there is little research that examines meetings that include professionals from different agencies and service users and their supporters. Even so, some of the concepts that are applied to other types of organisational meetings are relevant here. Swartzman provides a definition of a meeting:

> [A] meeting is defined as a communicative event involving three or more people who agree to assemble for a purpose ostensibly related to the functioning of an organization or group, for example, to exchange ideas or opinions, to solve a problem, to make a decision or negotiate an agreement, to develop policy and procedures, to formulate recommendations, and so forth. A meeting is characterized by multiparty talk that is episodic in nature, and participants either develop or use specific conventions ... for regulating this talk. (Swartzman, 1989, p 9)

A number of writers have argued against an analysis of meetings in complex organisations that concentrates on formal structures and roles and evaluates action in terms of rational decision making. Harris (1999, p 247) criticises approaches that characterise professional activity as 'technical-rationality', while Måseide (2011, p 526) describes medical team meetings as 'social and discursive events ... [with] an emergent rather than a determined character'. More generally, there is a view that organisational work is investigated less in terms of structural and formal relations and more in terms of social and cultural factors such as values, norms, meanings, interaction and talk. Meyer and Rowan (1977, p

341) argue that 'the formal structures of many organisations in post-industrial society dramatically reflect the myths of their institutional environments instead of their work activities'.

Gephart (1978, p 557) notes that participants require 'a background stock of knowledge' to manage organisational structures: 'the organization is constituted by linguistic devices and interpretational schemes which members use to make sensible certain conduct, events, and states of affairs and to methodically locate them as falling within the purview of "the organization".'

Quoting Bittner (1974), Gephart (1978) notes three verbal forms that participants use to construct the organisation: compliance (invoking rules of the organisation), stylistic unity (highlighting versions of proper organisational behaviour) and functional integrity (attending to activities that affect the functioning of the organisation). Similarly, Peck et al (2004, pp 100–1) contrast the work of organisational meetings as 'instrumental, palpable and explicit' with approaches that see meetings as 'social, symbolic and implicit: they are held to maintain organisational cohesion above all'. What constitutes appropriate organisational work is therefore under constant review, suggesting less of an orientation towards making decisions or formulating plans and goals and more of a concern with constructing the organisation (such as its rules, values, formulations of appropriate professional practice and ways of working). Hughes et al emphasise the routine, orderly nature of meetings:

> [M]eetings must, at least in part, be seen as symbolic affairs, not only because they are ritualized and patterned but because they function as routine yet vital face-to-face encounters in a bureaucratic and technocratic society that has long since surpassed the practical need to gather people into close proximity. (Hughes et al, 2011, p 136)

Social welfare meetings in particular involve the construction of social problems and the formulation of candidate solutions. As shown in Chapter 1, developing agreements, establishing ways of working together and displaying values of inclusion or participation are often stated aims of meetings. However, we suggest that multi-agency meetings draw on, construct, negotiate and manage a wide variety of interactional and local features and do not merely implement symbolic features, such as the inclusion of service users or the participation of different professionals.

Meetings as organisational rituals and ceremonies

There is extensive literature on organisational rituals and ceremonies (Meyer and Rowan, 1977; Islam and Zyphur, 2009; Smith and Stewart, 2011; Koschmann and McDonald, 2015). Islam and Zyphur (2009, p 116) define ritual action as 'a form of social action in which a group's values and identity are publically demonstrated or enacted in a stylized manner, within the context of a specific occasion or event'.

Koschmann and McDonald (2015, p 230) point out that 'when organizational practices take on a level of sacredness, formality, and aesthetic value, they go beyond mere routine and can achieve the status of ritual'. Islam and Zyphur (2009) identify a number of elements in rituals:

- repetition in content, form or occasion;
- practices being 'acted out' in planned ceremony rather than being spontaneous;
- behaviour that is out of the ordinary or overtly draws attention away from the mundane;
- a high level of organisation where even chaotic elements are given prescribed places;
- the use of evocative presentation;
- an orientation towards collective rather than individual consumption.

Islam and Zyphur (2009) reviewed the research using Trice and Beyer's (1985) taxonomy of organisational rituals, although they note there are few empirical studies. Much of this research explores rituals and ceremonies within an organisation that engage, reward and integrate workers with regard to adopting the values and goals of the organisation. Islam and Zyphur note rites of passage, such as graduation ceremonies, and rites of enhancement, such as awards ceremonies. In terms of multi-agency meetings in social welfare, Chapter 1 examined how policy in social welfare has explicitly attempted to bring professionals from different organisations together to share perspectives and values and promote joint decision making, as might be characteristic of integration and conflict resolution ceremonies. In terms of the inclusion of the service user, degradation and integration functions have been examined.

Degradation and integration ceremonies

The study of degradation ceremonies has been the focus of empirical study since an early paper by Harold Garfinkel. These ceremonies are characterised as follows:

> Any communicative work between persons, whereby the public identity of an actor is transformed into something looked on as lower in the local scheme of social types, will be called a 'status degradation ceremony' ... The degradation ceremonies here discussed are those that are concerned with the alteration of total identities. (Garfinkel, 1956, p 420)

In such ceremonies, 'a person loses eligibility (relationships that confer status or behaviour potential) in a particular community' (Schwartz, 1979, p 139). There is an event and a perpetrator who is under examination. The ceremony is in public with a denouncer and witnesses 'who adhere to a set of values required for membership in good standing' (Schwartz, 1979, p 139). Garfinkel (1956, p 424) sees the court as having 'a fair monopoly over such ceremonies', and the concept can be seen as an ideal type (Murray, 2000, p 40). Bergner (1987, p 25) illustrates a military demotion ceremony as an extreme example of a degradation ceremony: an officer appears in front of his assembled company, the breach of his military duties is announced, and he is described as having been a questionable individual all along and stripped of his rank. This illustration omits the process of the degradation – laying out the charges and dismissing the perpetrator's rebuttal – before the decision is made; however, it captures the public nature of the degradation and the shaming of the perpetrator.

There does not appear to be research that evaluates the function of meetings to criticise or shame professionals. Research on child protection meetings reports little overt conflict between professionals when parents are present (Hall and Slembrouck, 2001, p 143). Asmusβ and Svennevig (2009, p 17) describe how the chair aims to manage disagreements but they also note the potential for alliances to form to support counterproposals while avoiding overt conflict, which suggests that participants find more subtle ways to manage potential criticism.

A number of studies have developed the concept of 'degradation ceremonies' to examine meetings or processes in various health, criminal and welfare settings. Murray (2000) examines 'deniable degradation' – bureaucratic procedures that are seen as instrumental but still contain symbolic messages of degradation. Gustafson (2013) describes various procedures as degradation ceremonies that target lower-class women in receipt of welfare and transform their identity. Small transgressions associated with living in poverty are changed via shaming processes into criminal and bureaucratic transgressions – for example, the use of drug tests for welfare recipients, reactions to giving fake addresses for school registration or penalties for buying stolen baby food. Psychotherapist Bergner considers such degradation as a frequent experience for his service users:

> Our psychotherapy service users, more often than not, have been degraded. That is, they have in the course of their lives been subjected to treatment by others which has given them reason to conclude that they were not fully entitled, coequal members of their communities. (Bergner, 1987, p 25)

From a different perspective, Kahan (2006) suggests 'shaming rituals' as a legitimate and cheaper alternative to imprisonment.

At the same time, service users might experience meetings as supportive or enhancing, integrating them into the welfare network and their community. Approaches in juvenile justice and child welfare promote a notion of 'successful reintegration ceremonies' (Braithwaite and Mugford, 1994). Researchers and policy makers have developed the significance of ceremonies to encourage strategies of restorative justice and supportive displays of service users by friends and families. In particular, such approaches attempt to separate the act from the actor. While the act may have been unacceptable, the character of the service user is not condemned: 'the event and the perpetrator must be uncoupled' (Braithwaite and Mugford, 1994, p 143). Epstein (2013, p 9) notes the possibility of the 'mirror image' of the degradation ceremony as 'elevation, praise, and inclusion'.

Degradation and integration ceremonies are therefore seen in practices across health and social welfare settings as ongoing features of shaming or integrating practices rather than one-off public events. The concept draws attention not only to the extent to which the service user is disempowered or denigrated by the ceremony but also to how the professionals, the 'denouncer' and the 'witnesses' display that they are 'invested with the right to speak in the name of ultimate values' (Garfinkel, 1956, p 423).

There are a few studies that consider the ceremonial characteristics of meetings in health and social welfare by examining the details of talk and interaction: Garfinkel (1956) on the courts, Strong (1979) on medical consultations, Harris (1999) on child protection conferences, Peck et al (2004) on health boards and Helsel (2014) on case conferences. Perhaps the most pertinent research materials for studying meetings in social welfare are the publications of Miller (1983) and Miller and Holstein (1995) on meetings between professionals and service users on a work incentive programme (WIN). These are 'conciliation sessions' arranged when it is decided that a service user has stopped cooperating with the programme, and 'WIN hearings' conducted when the service user is asked to leave the project. Miller (1983, p 142) notes the moral character of the meetings, as workers seek to make the service users 'responsible for their behaviour and accountable to the government for the welfare they receive'. The meetings are organised around a complaint–excuse process whereby the worker makes a complaint about the service user's lack of cooperation, the service user accounts for their behaviour by making excuses and the professionals accept (or reject) the service user's appeal to extenuating circumstances (Miller, 1983).

Miller and Holstein (1995) note how, as the disagreements move from everyday practice to meetings, they take on more formal features. There are invitation letters and an agenda, records are kept and a history is created: 'The rhetorical resources that made for locally persuasive arguments were more available to staff members' (Miller and Holstein, 1995, p 44). The WIN hearings become quasi-legal:

> Movement of WIN disputes into this quasi-legal domain brought a new procedural environment and focus to the disputing process. In contrast to other dispute domains, talk in WIN hearings was formally limited to direct and cross-examination of witnesses. Speakership rights were procedurally allocated; each person had specifically designed opportunities to speak and their speech was strictly oriented to specific questions. (Miller and Holstein, 1995, pp 51–2)

Organisational rituals and ceremonies display more formal features compared with other face-to-face encounters such as home visits or office interviews, drawing on moral formulations relevant to the organisation.

Promoting a discursive and interactional approach

Examination of multi-agency meetings in social welfare as ceremonies and rituals engages with cultural approaches to the study of organisations. There are, however, problems with approaches that consider only the function of organisational ceremonies, particularly if they concentrate on instrumental functions and the efficacy of the ritual – 'whether or not rituals work' (Koschmann and McDonald, 2015 p 232. For example, Epstein (2013, p 7) uses the concept of 'ceremony' to argue that empowerment practices in health and social welfare 'are without material content, they are "make-believe," constructed only of symbols whose meaning lies in what they signify rather than in what they contain'. He provides an example of psychotherapy:

> Psychotherapy as a production function is intended to achieve its goals of assuaging a variety of mental problems ... as a ceremony, psychotherapy only expresses a series of values – idealized self-reliance and extreme individualism – that may have little relationship to its own clinical goals. (Epstein, 2013, p 7)

Epstein quotes Trice and Beyer (1984, p 655), who state that the ritual is 'a standardized, detailed set of techniques and behaviours that manage anxieties, but seldom produce intended, technical consequence of practical importance'. Rituals are standardised but ultimately have little instrumental consequence in terms of achieving the goals of the organisation. In contrast, Koschmann and McDonald (2015) see organisational rituals less as outcomes of the intentions of organisational actors and more as occasions to display and promote the organisation, often with unintended consequences. They are occasions to apply the values, norms and ideals of the organisation in order to manage everyday practical dilemmas.

There appears, however, to be a paradox in the literature. As noted earlier, Koschmann and McDonald (2015) discuss rituals as sacred and formal, and Islam and Zyphur (2009, pp 120–1) characterise them as 'out of the ordinary', whereas Hughes et al (2011, p 136) emphasise that they are 'orderly' and 'ritualized and patterned but function as routine encounter'. Boden (1994, p 106) states that meetings are both 'routine' and 'ritualized'. Does the depiction of meetings as rituals suggest that they are routine or out of the ordinary? All investigators observe the ways in which organisational meetings take on a patterned character with consistent and formulaic practices, for example the actions of the chair, who is invited to speak, and so on (concepts that will be examined later in this chapter). The difference appears to be the orientation of the investigation. For Koschmann and McDonald (2015, p 242), a meeting can move beyond 'an empty routine'. For example, they describe a practice in team meetings in a non-governmental organisation in which all team members signed birthday cards for donors and volunteers:

> Rather than an administrative detail to hurry through, the card signing was a time for reflection and bonding. We came to see the card signing as a ritualistic practice because of its patterned

behaviours and its symbolic significance beyond its immediate instrumental purposes. (Koschmann and McDonald, 2015, p 242)

This practice had taken on the status of a sacred ritual because it symbolised and 'made present' the norms, values and history of the agency concerned. For the agency, these norms included the 'inclusion' of service users, which formed 'the abstract ideal to coordinate their work' (Koschmann and McDonald, 2015, p 246). In this way, the performance of the ritual 'reminded' and 'disciplined' team members and served to 'actualize their agency': 'Rituals are powerful precisely because they cannot be reduced to the actions of individuals, but make present the full force of the organisation – its values, norms and relations of power' (Koschmann and McDonald, 2015, p 247).

In Chapter 1, we noted the importance of themes such as the participation and inclusion of service users in multi-agency meetings and policy discussions. Now we can begin to see how such professional and practical justifications for policy and practice also draw on sacred and moral connotations that are present in everyday organisational rituals and ceremonies such as meetings.

However, this orientation to concepts outside and above individuals hints at meetings having an abstraction independent of organisational members and their practices. Koschmann and McDonald's (2015, p 235) identification of inclusion as the 'authoritative text' that constitutes 'an official conception of the organisation' is, in fact, a researchers' notion: 'We combed through our field notes and key [agency] documents to discover key ideas and concepts that seemed to have traction and influence at [the agency]' (2015, p 246). While such texts are created by organisational members, especially in organisational rituals, it is the researchers who are identifying and summarising the sacred notion of inclusion as 'lurking' throughout the rituals, which is 'not explicitly recognized in the moment' (2015, p 247).

Writers from an ethnomethodological perspective are reluctant to seek explanations that go beyond the constructions and categories of members. Hughes et al (2011, p 133) criticise approaches which contend that behind social interaction 'lies a "real" explanatory, objective reality of social and cultural forces and processes of which, in the main, social actors are unaware'. Participants in organisational rituals are aware that they are part of a large organisation 'working in a system which transcends their here-and-now' (Hughes et al, 2011, p 142). However, Hughes et al suggest that such larger formulations are brought into interactions by members to manage local issues: 'Such "macro" phenomena as the "wider organisation" are not so much instantiated within local interactions ... but rather "called forth" and so, reflexively, make an interaction an instance of a particular kind of social activity' (Hughes et al, 2011, p 143).

When a service user is invited to talk at a meeting, or when professionals comment on policy implementation, different versions of what constitutes 'inclusion' are brought into the discussion strategically to manage dilemmas and create agreements. How service users are included or to what extent their contributions are valued on such occasions is a matter of investigation. Similarly, Boden (1994, p 35) considers that 'meaning is constituted in the interplay of people and objects under the concrete conditions of a particular setting ... no social act is "objective" or "exterior" to action'. Furthermore, 'far from simply reproducing institutionalised rituals and routines, social actors know how to produce a specific next action that, seen from afar, will look plausible' (Boden, 1994, p 36).

So, organisational rituals such as meetings are constructed, negotiated and accomplished by participants through a series of displays of agreement and alignment about what is rational and typical. As we will see in the rest of this chapter, such interactional work is complex and fraught with dilemmas, but participants can draw on a wide range of discourses and interactional resources to manage the meeting.

> As they shift through locally relevant possibilities, however, social actors use their own agendas and understandings to produce "answers" that are fitted to "questions." The result is oddly reasonable and is, in any case, imbued with rationality and purposiveness through the accounts provided by both the immediate agents and those who must, later, make sense of the actions. Rationality is thus, through and through, an enacted affair. (Boden, 1994, p 41)

Boden (1994, pp 59–63) examined a meeting of hospital managers who are trying to reduce costs. She notes the quick and immediate exchanges as speakers monitor and respond to one another's contributions. Although such meetings are 'routine', she notes that 'it would be hard to characterize the talk as "routinized" or "ritual"' (1994, p 61). By this, she is suggesting that although such meetings are frequent, the complexity of exchanges does not follow a strict format, even if they are carefully negotiated: it is 'not some woolly social construction but a finely ordered and consequential alignment of differing perspectives, goals and agendas' (Boden, 1994, p 63). They are not rituals in the sense of set procedures that merely act out organisational values; instead, participants carefully make their contributions to accord with others and negotiate the essence of the formulations of the everyday organisational work of determining what constitutes a saving or policy change.

In summary, organisational rituals and ceremonies are important ways of characterising multi-agency meetings in social welfare. However, it is advisable to avoid approaches that concentrate on examining the instrumental features of rituals or merely display some underlying interprofessional value. Rather, it is better to examine how concepts such as 'effectiveness' and 'inclusion' are constructed and negotiated to manage complex interactions and accomplish affiliation and agreement. Furthermore, in contrast to the small meeting of managers described by Boden, multi-agency meetings in social welfare are likely to display more formal features that can be characterised as ritualistic, for example the activities of the chair, the management of participants' turns, the role performance of different professionals and the participation of the service user.

Meeting talk and interaction

A number of core analytical concepts from studies of talk and interaction in various types of organisational meetings are relevant for the study of how collaborative and participatory policies are acted out in multi-agency meetings. While multi-agency meetings in social welfare display particular characteristics and dilemmas because of the presence of the service user and multi-agency participation, we have already seen the value of examining ideas developed through research into other kinds of organisational meeting. Meetings are central to the functioning of all organisations. Boden (1994, p 81) says that 'meetings are where organizations come together ... [they] remain the essential mechanism through which organizations create and maintain the practical activity of organizing'. Meetings are 'occasioned' by the organisation and at the same time 'accomplish' the organisation (Boden, 1994, p 82). Halvorsen (2010, p 274) notes that 'professions are thus faced with new modes of collaboration requiring communicative skills as well as multiprofessional competencies'.

Participants are constrained in their talk and interaction by obligations of being part of a meeting (Halvorsen and Sarangi, 2015, p 4). Asmuß and Svennevig (2009) and Svennevig (2012a) note a number of formal features that distinguish meetings from other institutional interactions: they are planned in advance for a pre-specified organisational purpose; participants are invited (by letter, email and so on); the time is scheduled; and they often take place in designated meeting rooms. Meetings are managed by a chair and there is a range of documents – such as agendas and reports – and name tags. They become a matter of institutional record with minutes and action plans. Holmes and Stubbe (2015) emphasise that meetings are task oriented and concerned with workplace business. Boden (1994) makes a distinction between formal and informal meetings. The formal meeting displays the features described earlier, whereas the informal meeting has a more conversational character and less control by the chair, perhaps more characteristic of a team meeting. In social welfare meetings, however, such a distinction is not straightforward. There is a wide diversity of teams with members from different professions and organisations, some of whom are co-located and work together on a daily basis, while others only meet one another at the meeting.

Asmuβ and Svennevig (2009) identify the key topics in the analysis of meeting talk, including the role of the chair, openings and closings, the allocation of turns, and topic progression and leadership. To that list can be added decision making and the performance role of participants. In this book, the presence of the service user calls attention to considerations of affiliation, emotional displays and differing rights to knowledge.

Organisation and structure of a meeting

Meetings are structured around agendas, goals and a clear participation structure (Halvorsen and Sarangi, 2015, p 3). The chair directs the participants to address the topics on the agenda. Halvorsen and Sarangi (2015, p 12) suggest the following phases for a business meeting: introduction, status, discussion, decision making and closure. Hall and Slembrouck (2001, p 149) suggest introduction, information gathering and assessment, discussion and decision making, and planning. In their study, Gunther et al (2015, p 69) pinpoint five phases in care planning meetings in mental health at which the service user was present:

- orientation towards planning the service user's care and starting the plan's recording;
- creating a service user portrait;
- interpreting the service user's problems;
- defining the help and support methods;
- making a care agreement.

They note in particular how attention to writing the care plan document provided a structure to the meeting. In these meetings, the service user was addressed first and contributed in dialogue with the professionals throughout the meeting. In contrast, Hall and Slembrouck (2001) report how the social worker in a child protection meeting was invited to provide the current status of the case during the meeting and how each professional was allocated a turn, with the service user restricted to particular slots for comment. During the professional contribution, the service user was often referred to in the third person (Hall et al, 2006, p 58). Arminen and Perälä (2002, p 19) similarly note that multiprofessional meetings concerning substance abuse are organised around extended professional contributions, which constitute institutional versions of the service user.

However, there remain opportunities for digression and negotiation. The structure of the meeting has to be managed by participants. Svennevig (2012b) notes the emergent character of meetings:

> [T]he scheduling of a topic does not determine its deployment in the meeting in itself. The agenda has to be invoked and attended to by the participants in local turns at talk, and thus, topic progression is also a matter of local and contingent emergence. (Svennevig, 2012b, p 54)

Holmes and Stubbe (2015) make a distinction between linear and 'spiral' patterns in meetings. In the former, each topic is introduced and completed before moving on to the next, whereas spiral meetings are more exploratory, with earlier discussions informing later ones. Holmes and Stubbe (2015) note in particular that meetings where participants regularly work together tend to be more informal and democratic. In multi-agency meetings in social welfare, it is likely that some participants work together regularly and others only occasionally. Similarly, service users have varying experience with meetings. Occasional participants might be 'outsiders' to the conventions of such formal meetings.

Multi-agency meetings in social welfare can be organised around various artefacts, for example the completion of a form or checklist. They can be organised around a decision that is to be reached, for example to provide services. They can also be seen in terms of reviewing the service user's progress. However, achieving decisions, conducting reviews or managing checklists and agendas requires local management.

Role and action of the chair

Sacks (1992) describes an omnipresent identity as one where an activity is tied to an identity in the interaction. A chair is both an identity and an activity with rights and obligations that can be attended to at any moment. Following from this, it is usually the chair who manages the meeting by inviting participants to contribute and by controlling the agenda. Boden (1994, p 86) says that 'speaker selection depends on the chairperson, who has both rights and obligations' in relation to assembled members and the purpose of the meeting'. Asmuβ and Svennevig (2009, p 11) note that the chair is 'given institutional authority to moderate the talk', but this may be in a facilitating or authoritative role, encouraging participation or directing and controlling the participants' contributions. Holmes et al illustrate the distinction in the following:

> Kenneth's meetings tend to be characterized by a strictly linear discussion of a fixed agenda. Moreover, he is not only in control of the topics to be discussed, he is also the sole selector of speakers. Tricia's meetings, in contrast, contain many spiral discussions in which everyone participates and to which they freely contribute. (Holmes et al, 2007, p 442)

On occasion the chair addresses the meeting as whole, for example stating: 'With your permission, I'll move on.' Asmuβ and Svennevig (2009, pp 12–13) note in particular how the chair summarises the findings of the meeting, seeking agreement for a decision or conclusion: 'the group is treated as a single addressee'. They further report research that highlights the uncertainty of consensus when such concluding statements are not explicitly acknowledged. Ford (2008, p 50) reports that the aim of a chair is to direct the pace of the meeting: 'When I chair a meeting I'm pretty hard core about what's going to get accomplished, because time is precious.' Markaki and Mondada describe the chair's role:

> the central structuring and monitoring action of the chair (Boden, 1994; Pomerantz and Denvir, 2007; Svennevig, 2008) who organises the allocation of turns in a way that considers the distribution of rights to speak among the co-participants and the respect of the topical agenda of the meeting as well as the time schedule. In this context, meetings frequently appear as organized in two *parties* (Schegloff, 1995) with either the 'chair'/'facilitator'

or the selected 'speaker' on the one side and the remaining 'audience' on the other side. (Markaki and Mondada, 2012, p 33)

The chair allocates turns to a speaker whose response is likely to be directed back to the chair but who is aware of the overhearing audience. Following the completed turn, the chair selects the next speaker. Hall and Slembrouck (2001, p 149) note how in child protection meetings the selection of the next speaker appeared to follow a hierarchy of appropriate institutional representatives in child protection meetings – social work, family centre, education, health, the police – often invited in the name of the institution (Hall et al, 2006, p 64).

In multi-agency meetings in social welfare, the presence of the service user provides important decisions for the chair as to how they are invited to make a contribution – in particular, whether are they 'talked about' or 'talked to', as Campbell (1997, p 4) says, 'to present their own "case" or hear the "case" being constructed by others'. Two extreme participation structures might be suggested. At one extreme, the service user is addressed directly by the chair. In such meetings, the chair–service user dialogue is the main exchange of the meeting, with other professionals invited to contribute, but the evaluation of that contribution is examined by the chair–service user dyad. Gunther et al observe a case planning meeting:

> The professional starts the meeting by addressing the service user by name. The professional uses an inclusive expression, 'we will make' … to invite the service user to join in the making of the care plan. The use of the passive/inclusive form emphasizes the collaboration between the key worker and the service user. (Gunther et al, 2015, p 70)

At the other extreme, the chair invites the professionals to make their contributions, with the service user restricted to particular slots after the professionals have selected the key topics for consideration. Hall et al (2006, p 60) note how the service user's interruption in a child protection conference is quickly rebuffed by the chair: 'I'll come back to you, go on (social worker).' In between these extremes, there are a variety of alliances and joint recalls by service users and professionals.

Turn-taking and selection

As previously discussed, the chair is expected to manage the turns of the participants. In formal meetings, turns are more tightly monitored by the chair, 'functioning as a kind of central switching station for the meeting' (Boden, 1994, p 99). However, even in formal meetings there are opportunities to interrupt the pre-allocated structure (Boden, 1994, p 89). Boden contends that it is the management of turns that makes meetings formal, not the context of the meeting. In informal meetings, turn-taking is more likely to resemble everyday conversational turn-taking but with a tolerance of long turns without interruption. Even so, given the constraints of time, speakers are likely to monitor, and be monitored, in terms of the relevance and appropriateness of their contributions. The chair might invite speakers with instructions of what is expected, for example to be brief (Koprowska, 2016, p 112), and interrupt if topics are not addressed (Boden, 1994, p 101).

Participants might select themselves as the next appropriate speaker. Ford (2008, p 66) notes participants making a bid by raising their hand during a speaker's contribution and selecting themselves as the next speaker without referring to the chair. Others self-select if the topic is seen as theirs, for example if it is about their institution's practices: 'the person identified in this way has not only the right, but also the obligation to speak ... participants recognize and attribute identities in a locally situated way' (Markaki and Mondada, 2012, p 48). Markaki et al (2010, p 1531) examine how members in an international business meeting draw on membership categories to organise the selection and self-selection of participants, glancing at the next appropriate speaker, in this case, mentioning a particular country ('I will speak for ...'). Mondada (2007) notes the use of pointing to allocate the next turn but also to limit speakership.

In terms of the content of the turn, Boden (1994, p 99) notes: 'As in courtroom or plea-bargaining settings, speakers accomplish and are heard to accomplish legitimately long organisational stories, using these accounts to construct positions and realize agendas.'

Boden (1994, p 102) talks of 'discourse identities' being created in meetings to indicate the ways in which participants speak in terms of professional roles, but this is achieved in the turn-by-turn development of the talk (Clifton, 2009, p 63). A speaker might be invited to contribute in terms of being the teacher or doctor, but they must also perform as a teacher or doctor. Housley observes meetings in which the role of participants is identified for supporting families after a flood:

> In the case of multidisciplinarity and team organisation, role is viewed as a primary mechanism through which different knowledge bases (disciplines) inform the decision-making practices and communication acts within the team framework

> ... (however) role identities and distinctions in practice (e.g., the multidisciplinary meetings examined) are occasioned, situated, interactionally achieved resources for getting the day's work done. (Housley, 1999, p 2)

Identities are created and negotiated in meetings. Housley provides examples of how team members draw on, for example, what tasks a social worker or volunteer should or should not take on, in order to establish the role identities of team members and allocate responsibilities. Koprowska (2016, p 112) observes how social workers warrant their contribution to child protection meetings: 'They explained how the concerns justified the meeting and demonstrated their professional accountability by showing they had followed proper procedures.'

In their presentation, speakers may take on different participation roles. Some participants will attempt to display expertise and be treated as an expert on their topic (Holmes and Stubbe, 2015, p 79). Others do not necessarily provide a report but display a professional analysis and version of the matter at hand to a designated hearer. Goffman (1981, p 144) investigated participation status as 'the relation between a single participant and his or her utterance when viewed from the point of reference of the larger social gathering' (Goodwin and Goodwin, 2004, p 223). He makes the distinction between: the Animator, 'an individual active in the utterance production'; the Author, 'someone who has selected the sentiments that are expressed and the words in which they are encoded'; and the Principal, 'someone whose position is established by the words that are spoken, someone whose beliefs have been told, someone who is committed to what the words said'. Virkkula (2010) reports how a manager who is translating in a multilingual business meeting moves between the animator and author roles, between a literal and nuanced translation of the talk. In social welfare meetings, a professional might report the views of their colleagues or quote institutional protocol or hearsay, often using reported speech. Similarly, there is a distinction between the addressee and the audience. Whereas the chair is often the addressee, the service user or another professional is the person to whom the comments might be aimed – the 'ratified participant in the encounter'. Other participants may be 'ratified' or 'unratified' recipients.

The service user's turn in a social welfare meeting, as already mentioned, varies from being in the form of a dialogue with the chair to being restricted to limited turns when invited by the chair. It is often acknowledged that the service user has authority to speak about their own personal and family circumstances. Ekberg and LeCouteur state:

> Although they carry the authority of professional perspective, therapists only ever have secondary access to knowledge about a service user's life and situation, based on what the client has shared within the therapy session. Clients will always have the ultimate epistemic access to how situations have played out in their lives, and how their behaviour may affect their situation in the future. (Ekberg and LeCouteur, 2015, p 13)

However, the relative importance attached to the service user's assessment of the state of affairs is often less likely to direct the discussion. In a child protection meeting, Hall and Slembrouck (2001, p 151) note the distinction between relating the facts and identifying patterns: 'In general (the service user) continues to deal with instances, whereas the social worker and the chair are concerned with establishing patterns that allow generalizations.' The chair is concerned with establishing categories of child risk that enable the meeting attendees to process the case.

Topic management and progression

As already mentioned, the agenda is the central artefact for formulating and monitoring the topic progression of meetings. Svennevig (2012a, p 7) notes that topics are specified in advance, a fundamental difference from everyday conversation. Boden (1994, p 112) sees a 'statement plus question' as a method for establishing a topic or changing it, asking, for example: 'Anything else on this matter?' This might invite a response in the question–answer sequence, or, as Barnes (2007) notes, silence can be a key pointer to topic change. The chair is usually responsible for opening and closing topics, particularly summarising and moving on, which, as Svennevig (2012a, p 7) observes, provides the chair with a 'privileged opportunity to influence the collective sense-making process'.

There are, however, opportunities for digression from the agenda (Asmusβ and Svennevig, 2009, p 15) or resisting the closing down of a topic, for example by asking: 'Can I ask a question before we move on?' (Boden, 1994, p 112). Boden explains the link between an agenda and topics:

> To define an organisational agenda is to define not so much a specific conversational procedure in talk as to describe a talk-based activity through which organisational members pursue local issues, maintain and advance departmental positions and occasionally follow a stated agenda. Their management is akin to topic management in that they are achieved through shifts of emphasis and rekeyings that are placed with precision in the ongoing flow of talk. Often participants move 'stepwise' toward or away from a particular topic, while simultaneously 'holding' their own agenda intact across these interactional shifts and across interactions. (Boden, 1994, p 156)

Svennevig (2012a, p 8) notes that, unlike in everyday conversation, speakers can orient their contribution to the agenda or an earlier speaker rather than the previous speaker: 'the result may be longer and more "monological" turns'. Housley (2000, p 432) examines 'the use of stories as a means of holding the floor, [which] can be heard as a method of responding to difficult questions'. Furthermore, stories display 'a moral character ... that seek to account for events, service users and experiences' (Housley, 2000, p 440).

Of particular importance is how topics are introduced and managed, especially those that are delicate or unwelcome. Politeness strategies in meetings, concerning the ways in which participants are careful to avoid threatening or undermining one another, have been the focus of previous research. Holmes and Stubbe (2015) identify a variety of relational features: thanking participants, humour, compliments, attention to collegiality and rapport, and consideration of participants' 'face'. Friess (2013, p 310) provides an example of both high and low concern for face:

Sloane: Sorry, well, I don't know if this is the right time, it's maybe a little off-topic, and I know that you've dealt with this a lot more than me, but could we discuss the hardware issue a little more?
Derek: No. Not now.

The turn by Sloane includes apologies, hedging and indirectness, whereas in response Derek shows little concern for Sloane's face, with an immediate rejection ('no'), although it is mitigated a little with 'not now'. Mullany (2004) examines the ways in which managers use humour in meetings to disguise directives to staff to take on unwelcome tasks.

In multi-agency meetings, participants are cautious about managing professional boundaries. Arber (2008) investigated how questions are asked in palliative care team meetings in ways that do not challenge the expertise of other professionals but still make a bid for action. For example, a nurse asks a consultant: 'I mean is it worth me trying to get an appointment at B hospital?' This is a question that is both cautious and polite:

> Therefore, the [nurse] is proceeding cautiously by using hedges to mark areas of uncertainty and potential alignments; she is also using questions in a way that is masking a command related to the referral procedure. This masking is a way of avoiding upsetting interprofessional relations. (Arber, 2008, p 1329)

Politeness is also evident when addressing service users, especially when addressing potentially embarrassing topics. Koprowska (2016, p 114) describes in child protection conferences the delicacy of social workers' descriptions of service users' circumstances, using 'downgraded and soft terms for descriptions of family life'. Direct accusations are avoided, and 'narratives of redemption' acknowledge the difficulties families have faced.

Decision making

A particular aspect of meeting talk is the realisation of decision making as a shared task for participants. In much of the organisational and practice literature, it is assumed that meetings are essentially concerned with making decisions and plans. Meetings are often notionally organised around models of rational decision making that involve identifying a problem, gathering information, analysing the situation, evaluating options and selecting an option. Furthermore, professional decision making in social welfare institutions is increasingly organised around standardised procedures and guidelines (Rexvid et al, 2012; Evertsson et al, 2017) that are seen to support evidence-based and non-biased decision making (van de Luitgarden, 2009).

However, studies of what actually happens in meetings show that decisions are not cognitively processed following set procedures but are negotiated in talk and interaction (Clifton, 2009, p 64). This is in line with theories that approach decision making as sense making rather than as a rational process (Weick, 1995). According to this view, problems and decisions are talked into being in interactive processes of interpretation and meaning construction. What constitutes a meaningful understanding is predicated on both the knowledge and inference of the participants, and on organisational categories and procedures that stabilise the practice of ongoing interpretation (Weick et al, 2005). One aspect of this concerns the categories and identities available for service users as well as professionals. The identity construction of service users has been demonstrated to be part of the decision-making process. For instance, once the character of the service user or type of case has been established, the decision inevitably follows, whether to offer or refuse help, establish an action plan, make a referral and so on (for example, Nikander, 2003; Hall et al, 2006; Messmer and Hitzler, 2011).

In multi-agency meetings, attempts are made at reaching consensus on agreements, which necessitates participants outlining at least some part of their reasoning and argumentation to others. This provides the opportunity to study the meaning making that goes into decision making, yet several researchers have pointed out that the decisions themselves are hard to pin down. Huisman (2001, p 70) defines a decision as a 'commitment to future action', while Hitzler and Messmer (2010, p 206) suggest that decisions can be described as 'the choice between two or more alternatives, when no one option is preferable from the outset'. What is crucial when studying meetings is that the 'commitment' or 'choice' is constructed and constituted through interactional and linguistic features. Huisman (2001, p 72) suggests that 'we can locate the emergence of decisions at the turn-by-turn level of the interaction in which participants exchange information and opinions'.

Boden makes the distinction between decisions and decision making:

> As real-time phenomena, *decisions* are, in fact, largely invisible and thus empirically unavailable, whereas *decision-making* can be located in the fine laminations of actions and reactions. As outcomes, decisions are real enough, of course, but only as long as a static, snapshot observation is made. But in the flux of organisational life neither decisions nor their "reasons" stand still. (Boden, 1994, p 22, emphasis in original)

Boden states that meetings might merely rubberstamp a decision already made, or decisions may be deferred to later meetings. Halvorsen (2010, p 276) says that 'decision-making processes are often incremental activities consisting of many minor steps, and decisions can rarely be connected to one singular utterance'. For similar reasons, Clifton (2009, p 60) suggests developing 'an understanding of decision-making in flight'. Måseide (2011, p 526) talks of 'medical problem solving' rather than 'decision making': 'decisions are rarely made. When a solution to a problem was found, it usually came [as] an inevitable result of the presentations, discussions or negotiations characteristic of the collaborative problem-solving process.'

When examining decision making in relation to questions of service user participation and/or interprofessional collaboration, the distinction between decisions and decision making is particularly important. As Hitzler and Messmer (2010, p 221) have demonstrated regarding meetings in child welfare, 'participation (in the interaction) ... does not safe-guard a partaking (in the decision)'. On the other hand, having the service users present and active in the interaction is a first step in including them in the sense making that goes into reaching a decision.

At the interactional and analytical level, the distinction between decisions and decision making directs attention to the sometimes 'invisible' character of decisions. Decisions become real when they are invoked as decisions, for example when they are summarised by the chair or recorded in the minutes. Clifton (2009) describes 'decision announcing' as the point when the chair states the decision, although this is only made possible after considerable negotiation during which the chair takes ownership of the decision, drawing on the agreement of the other participants. Decisions may also be clearly marked as such when meeting participants ask for confirmation ('Do we agree that ... ?') or declare an agreement to be reached ('We will do X, then.'). In either situation, the announcement or declaration is made retrospectively, marking that a decision *has been* made, rather than signalling the singular moment of making a decision.

In other instances, a decision may be more implicit yet still recognisable by the consequences of that decision in talk. This is the case, for instance, when a discussion emerges of who should take responsibility for a certain intervention when the decision to institute that intervention has not been made explicit. Hitzler and Messmer (2010, p 208) suggest that a decision is recognisable if it is treated as a decision in the given interaction, and that this can be done in a more or less explicit manner. However, as Huisman (2001) argues, a decision can appear to be clear and unambiguous to some participants while simultaneously appearing vague and fluid to others in the same meeting. Hitzler and Messmer (2010) themselves illustrate this phenomenon with an extract from a care planning meeting where 13-year-old Janine has asked permission to continue participating in a girls' group. This is followed by a lengthy discussion by the professional participants in which only positive evaluations of the option are presented. While this can be seen as an example of 'performances of affirmation' through which the professionals make their agreement clear to each other (Hitzler and Messmer, 2010, p 212), this is not clear to Janine, who returns to the question:

[Janine]: Well and now what about the girls' group? (2.0)
[Carer]: Oh but we said that, that'll be all right.

Hitzler and Messmer (2010, p 212) point out that the response from the carer indicates that he considers the decision has been made, that it has been explicitly stated, even though there was no such comment in the transcription. Huisman (2001) argues that what can be recognised as a decision by meeting participants fundamentally depends on the orientation of the participants and the procedural norms of the specific context. In social welfare settings, familiarity with such norms about what constitutes a legitimate and reasonable decision may vary considerably between professionals and service users and even between professionals from different agencies. In these cases, the explicitness of both the decision-making process and the decisions themselves may be an important aspect of making both service user participation and interprofessional collaboration possible.

Conclusion

This review of the literature on organisational meetings has examined a range of analytical concepts and theoretical approaches. The notion of organisational ritual and ceremony is particularly appealing. It has been developed in studies across a range of organisations. It alludes to the character of formal meetings, which is in sharp contrast to the more intimate and relational everyday encounters between service users and professionals in social welfare, such as in home visits, office meetings, placement visits, activities supporting service user access to other agencies and services, and so on. It also resonates with comments in consumer studies regarding the embarrassment reported by service users (for example, Campbell, 1997; Lawson et al, 1999; Buckley et al, 2011).

The importance of meetings to the operation of modern organisations has been emphasised. However, it has been suggested that research should avoid treating organisational meetings as separate from and determining the everyday actions of professionals and service users in meetings. While features of the meeting act as constraints on the behaviour of participants, nonetheless the meeting has to be brought into existence by professionals and service users at a particular time and in a specific location. The meeting is an accomplishment and is occasioned by the talk and interaction of those present, albeit within a bricolage of procedures and expected ways of working.

Of particular interest is the way in which the elements of organisational meetings emerge as typical across a range of business, voluntary organisations and public service groups. The role of the chair, the management of turns and topics, the formality of the interactions, the display of the professional roles of participants and the delicacy of the exchanges have been identified as key elements of meetings talk and interaction. The decision-making function of organisational meetings is also questioned in the literature. Clearly, participants are oriented to making decisions and plans; however, the existing literature is clear that it is impossible to identify 'decisions' or 'plans' as entities outside the interactional practices.

In sum, there is considerable research concerning team meetings within a single organisation. There is also research on meetings between different professionals, for example: Måseide (2011) in health, Markaki and Mondada (2012) in business and Arminen and Perälä (2002) in a multiprofessional team. Additionally, research exists on meetings between professionals and service users, for example: Miller (1983) in work incentive programmes Hitzler and Messmer (2010) in child care. However, little research examines meetings where professionals from different agencies and also service users and their supporters are included.

The studies in this book offer a contribution to fill this gap. The meetings involve professionals from various agencies, all of whom have some relation with the service user. While some may be new to such meetings, for others attendance is a regular feature of their working week. Similarly, service users and their supporters have varying degrees of knowledge about and investment in the outcome of the meetings. It is likely that the topic of such meetings will be highly consequential for both service users and key professionals. The meeting may involve confirming or denying whether someone is entitled to a disability pension; categorising a service user as at risk or vulnerable; or providing, removing or insisting on interventions. It is probable, therefore, that the chair and all participants are active in addressing (or avoiding) the dilemmas in constructing the service user's problems, managing the different participants' involvement, seeking agreements and alignments, and attending to the emotional tone of the meeting. These are complex encounters in which participants attempt to attend to a wide range of interactional dilemmas, and this book aims to understand more about the way such encounters unfold.

References

Arber, A. (2008) 'Team meetings in specialist palliative care: Asking questions as a strategy within interprofessional interaction', *Qualitative Health Research*, 18(10): 1323–35.

Arminen, I. and Perälä, R. (2002) 'Multiprofessional team work in 12 step treatment: Constructing substance abusers and alcoholics', *Nordic Studies of Alcohol and Drugs*, 19: 18–32.

Asmusβ, B. and Svennevig, J. (2009) 'Meeting talk', *Journal of Business Communication*, 46(1): 3–22.

Barnes, R. (2007) 'Formulations and the facilitation of common agreement in meetings talk', *Text and Talk*, 27(3): 273–96.

Bergner, R. (1987) 'Undoing degradation', *Psychotherapy*, 24(1): 25–30.

Bittner, E. (1974) 'The concept of organization', in R. Turner (ed) *Ethnomethodology,* London: Penguin, pp 69–81.

Boden, D. (1994) *The Business of Talk: Organizations in Action*, Cambridge: Polity Press.

Braithwaite, J. and Mugford, S. (1994) 'Conditions of successful reintegration ceremonies', *British Journal of Criminology*, 34(2): 139–71.

Buckley, H., Carr, N. and Whelan, S. (2011) 'Like walking on eggshells: Service users' views and expectations of the child protection system', *Child and Family Social Work*, 16(1): 101–10.

Campbell, L. (1997) 'Family involvement in decision making in child protection and care: Four types of case conference', *Child and Family Social Work*, 2(1): 1–11.

Clifton, J. (2009) 'Beyond taxonomies of influence: "doing" influence and making decisions in management team meetings', *Journal of Business Communication*, 46(1): 57–79.

Ekberg, K. and LeCouteur, A. (2015) 'Service users' resistance to therapists' proposals: Managing epistemic and deontic status', *Journal of Pragmatics*, 90: 12–25.

Epstein, W. (2013) *Empowerment as Ceremony*, New Brunswick: Transaction Publishers.

Evertsson, L., Blom, B., Perlinski, M. and Rexvid, D. (2017) 'Can complexity in welfare professionals' work be handled with standardised professional knowledge?', in B. Blom, L. Evertsson and M. Perlinski (eds) *Social and Caring Professions in European Welfare States: Policies, Services and Professional Practices*, Bristol: Policy Press, pp 208–21.

Ford, C. (2008) *Women Speaking Up: Getting and Using Turns in Workplace Meetings*, London: Palgrave Macmillan.

Friess, E. (2013) '"Bring the newbie into the fold": politeness strategies of newcomers and existing group members within workplace meetings', *Technical Communication Quarterly*, 22: 304–22.

Garfinkel, H. (1956) 'Conditions of successful degradation ceremonies', *American Journal of Sociology*, 61: 420–4.

Gephart, R. (1978) 'Status degradation and organizational succession: An ethnomethodological approach', *Administrative Science Quarterly*, 23(4): 553–81.

Goffman, E. (1981) *Forms of Talk*, Philadelphia, PA: University of Pennsylvania Press.

Goodwin, C. and Goodwin, M. (2004) 'Participation', in A. Duranti (ed) *A Companion to Linguistic Anthropology*, London: Wiley Blackwell, pp 222–44.

Gunther, K., Raitakari, S. and Juhila, K. (2015) 'From plan meetings to care plans: Genre chains and the intertextual relations of text and talk', *Discourse and Communication*, 9(1): 65–79.

Gustafson, K. (2013) 'Degradation ceremonies and the criminalization of low-income women', *UC Irvine Law Review*, 3(2): 297–358.

Hall, C. and Slembrouck, S. (2001) 'Parent participation in social work meetings – the case of child protection conferences', *European Journal of Social Work*, 4(2): 143–60.

Hall, C., Slembrouck, S. and Sarangi, S. (2006) *Language Practices in Social Work: Categorisation and Accountability in Child Welfare*, London: Routledge.

Halvorsen, K. (2010) 'Team decision making in the workplace: A systematic review of discourse analytic studies', *Journal of Applied Linguistics and Professional Practice*, 7(3): 273–96.

Halvorsen, K. and Sarangi, S. (2015) 'Team decision-making in workplace meetings: the interplay of activity roles and discourse roles', *Journal of Pragmatics*, 76: 1–14.

Harris, J. (1999) 'Multi-professional decision-making: The myth of the rational', *Educational Psychology in Practice*, 14(4): 246–52.

Helsel, P. (2014) 'Definitional ceremonies as counter-rituals to case conferences in pastoral care', *Practical Matters*, 7: 63–75.

Hitzler, S. and Messmer, H. (2010) 'Group decision-making in child welfare and the pursuit of participation', *Qualitative Social Work*, 9(2): 205–26.

Holmes, J., Schnurr, S. and Marra, M. (2007) 'Leadership and communication: Discursive evidence of a workplace culture change', *Discourse and Communication*, 1(4): 433–51.

Holmes, J. and Stubbe, M. (2015) *Power and Politeness in the Workplace: A Sociolinguist Analysis of Talk at Work*, Abingdon: Routledge.

Housley, W. (1999) 'Role as an interactional device and resource in multidisciplinary team meetings', *Sociological Research Online*, 4(3), www.socresonline.org.uk/4/3/housley.html

Housley, W. (2000) 'Story, narrative and team work', *The Sociological Review*, 48(3): 425–43.

Hughes, J., Randall, D., Rouncefield, M. and Tolmie, P. (2011) 'Meetings and the accomplishment of order', in M. Rouncefield and P. Tolmie (eds) *Ethnomethodology at Work*, Basingstoke: Ashgate, pp 131–50.

Huisman, M. (2001) 'Decision-making in meetings as talk and interaction', *International Studies of Management and Organisations*, 31(3): 69–90.

Islam, G. and Zyphur, M. (2009) 'Rituals in organisations: a review and expansion of current theory', *Group and Organisation Management*, 34(1): 114–39.

Kahan, D. (2006) 'What's really wrong with shaming sanctions', *Yale Law School Faculty Scholarship Series*, Paper 102.

Koprowska, J. (2016) 'The problem of participation in child protection conferences', *International Journal of Child and Family Welfare*, 17(1/2): 105–22.

Koschmann, M. and McDonald, J. (2015) 'Organisational rituals, communication and the question of agency', *Management Communication Quarterly*, 29(2): 229–56.

Lawson, M., Strickland, C. and Wolfson, P. (1999) 'User involvement in care planning: The care programme approach (CPA) from the user's perspective', *Psychiatric Bulletin*, 23: 539–41.

Markaki, V., Merlino, S., Mondada, L. and Oloff, F. (2010) 'Laughter in professional meetings: The organisation of an emergent joke', *Journal of Pragmatics*, 42: 1526–42.

Markaki, V. and Mondada, L. (2012) 'Embodied orientations towards co-participants in multinational meetings', *Discourse Studies*, 14(1): 31–52.

Måseide, P. (2011) 'Morality and expert systems: Problem solving in medical team meetings', *Behaviour and Information Technology*, 30(4): 525–32.

Messmer, H. and Hitzler, S. (2011) 'Declientification: Undoing client identities in care planning conferences on the termination of residential care', *British Journal of Social Work*, 41: 778–98.

Meyer, J. and Rowan, B. (1977) 'Institutionalized organisations: Formal structure as myth and ceremony', *American Journal of Sociology*, 83(2): 340–63.

Miller, G. (1983) 'Holding service users accountable: The micropolitics of trouble in a work incentive program', *Social Problems*, 31(2): 139–51.

Miller, G. and Holstein (1995) 'Dispute domains: organisational contexts and dispute processing', *Sociological Quarterly*, 36(1): 37–59.

Mondada, L. (2007) 'Multimodal resources for turn-taking: Pointing and the emergence of possible next speakers', *Discourse Studies*, 9: 194–225.

Mullany, L. (2004) 'Gender, politeness and institutional power roles: Humour as a tactic to gain compliance in workplace business meetings', *Multilingua*, 23: 13–37.

Murray, H. (2000) 'Deniable degradation: The finger-imaging of welfare recipients', *Sociological Forum*, 15(1): 39–63.

Nikander, P. (2003) 'The absent client: case description and decision-making in interprofessional meetings', in C. Hall, K. Juhila, N. Parton and T. Pösö (eds) *Constructing Clienthood in Social Work and Human Services: Interaction, Identities and Practices*, London: Jessica Kingsley Publishers, pp 123–40.

Peck, E., Six, P., Gulliver, P. and Towell, D. (2004) 'Why do we keep on meeting like this? The board as ritual in health and social care', *Health Services Management Research*, 17: 100–9.

Rexvid, D., Blom, B., Evertsson, L. and Forssen, A. (2012) 'Risk reduction technologies in general practice and social work', *Professions and Professionalism*, 2(2): 1–18.

Sacks, H. (1992) *Lectures on Conversation*, Oxford: Basil Blackwell.

Schwartz, W. (1979) 'Degradation, accreditation and rites of passage', *Psychiatry*, 42(2): 138–46.

Schwartzman, H. (1989) *The Meeting*, New York, NY: Plenum.

Smith, A.C.T. and Stewart, B. (2011) 'Organizational rituals: Features, functions and mechanisms', *International Journal of Management Reviews*, 13: 113–33.

Strong, P. (1979) *The Ceremonial Order of the Clinic*, London: Routledge & Kegan Paul.

Svennevig, J. (2012a) 'Interaction in workplace meetings', *Discourse Studies*, 14(1): 3–10.

Svennevig. J. (2012b) 'The agenda as resource for topic introduction in workplace meetings', *Discourse Studies*, 14(1): 53–66.

Trice, H. and Beyer, J. (1984) 'Studying organizational cultures through rites and ceremonials', *Academy of Management Review*, 9: 653–69.

Trice, H. and Beyer, J. (1985) 'Using six organizational rites to change culture', in R.H. Kilmann, M.J. Saxton and R. Serpa (eds) *Gaining Control of the Corporate Culture*, San Francisco, CA: Jossey-Bass, pp 370–99.

Van de Luitgaarden, G.M.J. (2009) 'Evidence-based practice in social work: Lessons from judgment and decision-making theory', *British Journal of Social Work*, 39(2): 243–60.

Virkkula, T. (2010) 'Linguistic repertoires and semiotic resources in interaction: A Finnish manager as a mediator in a multilingual meeting', *Journal of Business Communication*, 47(4): 505–31.

Weick, K.E. (1995) *Sensemaking in Organizations*, Thousand Oaks, CA: Sage Publications.

Weick, K.E., Sutcliffe, K.M. and Obstfeld, D. (2005) 'Organizing and the process of sensemaking', *Organization Science*, 16(4): 409–21.

3

How chairs use the pronoun 'we' to guide participation in rehabilitation team meetings

Tanja Dall and Dorte Caswell

Introduction

In social welfare, holding multi-agency meetings in which professionals from similar or different welfare perspectives meet with service users is increasingly seen as a promising way to make decisions about how to solve complex problems. The hope is that this collaboration will increase the effectiveness of interventions and that the service user will be included in the process through their participation in the meeting (see Chapter 2 for a more thorough exploration of these tendencies). Although appealing, however, this ideal is challenged by numerous studies that show a more complex reality in practice. For instance, Hitzler and Messmer (2010) find that a service user's participation in a multi-agency meeting does not necessarily mean that they are included in decision making, while Dall (2020) shows that, even among professionals, decision-making responsibilities may not be equally distributed among participants, even when this is the stated ideal for the meeting.

Similar trends and challenges exist in Danish social welfare, and the interprofessional and multi-agency rehabilitation teams that were introduced as part of the active labour market policy in 2013 are one example of these tendencies. Rehabilitation team meetings are based in the employment services and meant to ensure interprofessional assessment and service user participation in cases where the service user's attachment to the labour market is at risk due to complex health issues, social problems or other challenges. This has proven a challenging task, as several of the professionals present in meetings are unfamiliar with the legislative and organisational context of the employment services (Dall, 2020). Furthermore, for vulnerable service users, the presence of five or more professionals who they have never met before can make meetings and participation in them daunting. In this environment, the role and behaviour of meeting chairs can be critical to collaboration and participation (Angouri and Marra, 2010). The enactment of relational agency – that is, the constant responsive interactions with other professionals and service users (Edwards, 2011; see also Chapter 2) – is crucial in this regard. Through their interactions, meeting chairs have a strong influence over two contrasting aspects in particular: how participants come together around defining and expanding the task at hand; and how boundaries are drawn around participants' knowledge and expertise as well as their roles and responsibilities in meetings. The detailed ways in which chairs allocate speaking time and designate allowable contributions will have substantial consequences for who gets to say what at which times (Asmusβ and Svennevig, 2009).

In speech, personal pronouns are used to distribute authority and responsibility among participants. In this chapter, it will be argued that the chairs' use of 'we' is a subtle way in which they allocate and differentiate participants' roles in decision making as well as manage the task of making 'correct' decisions within this given context. The chapter examines the role of chairs in guiding participation in team meetings by analysing *how chairs use the pronoun 'we' to include or exclude team members and/or the service user* in decision making. The data for this analysis consist of observations and audio recordings of 26 team meetings stemming from a research project on decision making in the rehabilitation teams.

The next section presents the policy and organisational context for the analysis, and this is followed by a conceptual outline of the use of 'we' and the activity role of the meeting chair. Data and the process of analysis are then presented before turning to the analytical section of the chapter. The analysis is presented in two parts: first, a short overview of the four types of the use of 'we' identified in the analysis; and second, a more detailed analysis of the two main themes in the data: the use of the 'exclusive we' in interactions with service users; and the use of the 'inclusive we' in interactions between team members. The chapter ends with a discussion of how these different uses of 'we' function to allocate roles and manage decision making and the implications this holds for collaborative and integrative welfare practices.

Rehabilitation teams in Danish employment services

From 2012 to 2015, the Danish employment services underwent extensive reforms, with the overall aim of getting more people into work, including people with challenges in addition to unemployment (that is, physical, mental or social problems), who are increasingly seen as being capable of participating in the labour market despite these challenges.

One part of these reforms is the introduction of rehabilitation team meetings. The meetings bring together a minimum of four to five professionals from different municipal and regional departments around service users with complex physical, mental and/or social problems. The overall task of the team is to make recommendations about: (a) which supportive measures could facilitate service users' progression towards the labour market; and (b) the financial benefit the service users should receive while the measures are in place. Both the legislation and the pre-legislative work state that recommendations should be interprofessional and take into consideration 'the whole of service users' lives', and list as a goal that service users should take 'ownership' of the recommended plan ('Bekendtgørelse af lov', 2014, §9, subsection 3). The legal and organisational setup, however, makes the rehabilitation team meeting a challenging setting for service user participation and interprofessional collaboration, for several reasons.

First, the decisions to be made are regulated by a complicated set of legal and organisational procedures about which very few service users have intimate knowledge. Second, the meeting itself, with a minimum of four professional representatives facing the service user, may be intimidating for many of them. Similar challenges exist for achieving interprofessional collaboration in decision making. For example, in most meetings only one or two team members represent the employment services and have intimate knowledge of them. The other representatives will have more detailed knowledge of the services and challenges related to other relevant issues, such as health or social problems. As the meetings themselves and the decisions around service users' benefits are rooted in legislation that falls under the remit of the employment services, this gives certain representatives expertise and therefore a decisive role in formulating what is and is not possible in relation to this legislation (Dall, 2020). This authoritative role is further amplified by the fact that all rehabilitation team meetings are led by a chair, who typically represents the employment services. Being a meeting chair means having a legitimate role in allocating speaking time and assessing what is or is not on topic. As will be substantiated throughout this chapter, rehabilitation team meetings in this context contain a clear role allocation in which the chair/employment representative guides and directs both the meeting itself and the decision making more specifically. One way in which chairs manage the collaborative and participatory elements of social welfare in this multi-agency practice is through talk that includes or excludes one or more participants. This can be made explicit to varying degrees, as language works to construct and represent the professional collective (the team) as well as the position of the service user vis-à-vis the professional(s). Collective self-reference is a small but decisive part of this construction.

Collective self-reference and the role of the chair

One of the underlying characteristics of talk-in-interaction is 'action' and the question of what actions the speakers are engaged in as they talk. Speakers make choices and select 'from the alternative ways in which they might have "filled the slot", so as to enact or accomplish particular actions' (Drew and Heritage, 2013, p xxxv). The use of a self-referential term, such as 'we' (as opposed to 'I', for instance) represents an action that has implications for what is accomplished in talk. More specifically, Lerner and Kitzinger (2007, p 527) argue, with reference to Sacks (1992), that the 'selection of a self-reference term is intimately tied to a speaker's situated identity because these terms reveal on whose behalf (or authority), or in what capacity, a participant speaks and thus what stance they are taking up towards the action implemented through their turn at talk'.

Thus, 'I', 'you' and 'we' can be understood as linguistic devices used to denote responsibility and authority in a given situation. The use of collective self-reference terms, such as 'we', is reserved for references to collectives of which the speaker themselves is a member (Lerner and Kitzinger, 2007).

Collective self-references can be inclusive ('you and I') or exclusive ('us, not you'), depending on whether the intended recipient is included in the reference. In multi-agency meetings, the inclusive 'we' may construct a collective consisting of the service user and one or more professionals. By definition, a 'we' will always include the speaker. 'We' can also, however, be used to construct a collective of the team itself or, perhaps, parts of the team. This is particularly relevant when studying meetings with more than two participants, as the number of participants allows for in-group alliances wherein *ad hoc* subgroups may emerge during discussions of a certain topic or decision to be made. That is, alliances may form around the discussion of certain topics and be dissolved or reconfigured around other topics. Kangasharju (2002) finds, in a study of committee meetings between social welfare and health care professionals, that the emergence of an 'opposing alliance' can serve to calibrate and qualify decisions, as the alliance holds potential power that may allow participants to pursue a point against a proposed decision. On the other hand, an alliance between some meeting participants may also create problems for a single participant pursuing their point of view, as the people standing alone against an alliance more easily abstain from resisting a decision with which they have otherwise expressed dissatisfaction (Kangasharju, 2002, p 1468). The use of an inclusive and exclusive 'we' can be one way of constructing such in- or out-groups in meetings, and Kangasharju's study demonstrates how such delineations can influence participation and agreement in concrete ways.

Collective self-references may also be a way to bring wider organisational and social contexts into meetings. According to Lerner and Kitzinger (2007), collective self-reference terms can be relational (for example, speaking on behalf of a family), organisational (speaking on behalf of an agency or professional team) or circumstantial (speaking on behalf of those present at a given time). Organisational self-reference is particularly interesting when dealing with multi-agency meetings, as several organisational affiliations can be made relevant at any given time, as can the team as an organisational unit in itself. Depending on the specific context, these affiliations may lend more or less authority to the speaker, but will, following Lerner and Kitzinger (2007), always be tied to speakers' identity and what they are trying to accomplish through talk.

The role of the meeting chair is tied to a specific organisational identity that carries certain obligations and rights in directing interaction (Asmuβ and Svennevig, 2009; see also Chapter 2). Chairs often hold powerful positions in meetings, as they have a legitimate role in allocating talk among participants, ensuring topic progression and focus and sanctioning inappropriate conduct (Angouri and Marra, 2010; Wodak et al, 2011). Depending on chairing style and the social status of the chair as well as that of the other participants (for example, leader or expert), this involvement can lead to chairs having greater influence over the sense making that goes into decision making (Asmuβ and Svennevig, 2009). As described earlier, in the empirical context studied here, the appointed chairs hold special status due to their intimate knowledge of the legal basis of both the meetings themselves and of the possible decisions to be agreed on, which amplifies the role they have in directing decision making. Discourse analytical studies illustrate how a chair may enact a role as a facilitator of group participation and participatory decision making or take a more authoritative role in directing and controlling the actions of the participants (Asmuβ and Svennevig, 2009, p 11). The choice of self-reference (for example, singular/collective, inclusive/exclusive or relational/organisational/circumstantial, as outlined earlier) can be salient in this regard. Examining chairs' choice of self-reference not only reveals the projected authority and stance of the speaker but also proposes certain participant roles in decision making. Thus, the role of the chair in facilitating agreement means that this person may hold considerable power in directing decision making, and the question of how they enact this power becomes salient.

Data and the process of analysis

Data for the analysis in this chapter stem from a research project examining decision making in rehabilitation teams (Dall, 2017). The extracts are selected from a dataset comprising audio recordings of rehabilitation team meetings concerning a total of 97 service users in three Danish municipalities. The recordings include talk among professionals before the arrival of the service user, as well as talk among professionals and service users. As such, the data include both backstage and frontstage talk (Goffman, 1963; Lewin and Reeves, 2011), and the analysis draws on both these phases of the meetings. All service users and staff gave their consent to be included in the study, and all data have been handled according to the national and university guidelines of ethics and data management.

Through the course of examining the full dataset, an interest arose regarding how the team are discursively constructed as a meeting participant vis-à-vis the service user. From this emerged the specific topic of the use of 'we' and the role of the chair. To make operational a more detailed analysis of the use of 'we', 26 meetings were selected. In these 26 meetings the service user expressed a wish to be recommended for a disability pension, which provides permanent financial support and status as a person unable to return to work. These meetings are of particular interest since disability pensions are a tightly controlled resource in the welfare system, permitting an exploration of how the chair used 'we' as a linguistic device to include or exclude the service user in the decision-making process.

The disability pension is the most tightly controlled benefit in the Danish benefit system and can only be granted when all other measures have been considered. From an organisational perspective, access is therefore restricted both by requiring a thorough professional assessment of service users' abilities and through highly regulated bureaucratic documentation of the case. From the perspective of service users with complex physical, mental and social problems that limit their ability to work, access to a disability pension is often perceived as the only way to maintain their basic living conditions. Therefore these meetings constitute critical cases of the conflict between service user participation and institutional authority in social work meetings. The analysis includes all meetings in which service users want a disability pension but are *not* recommended for one (10 cases) as well as meetings where the service users *are* assessed to be eligible for the disability pension (16 cases).

The first step of the analysis consisted of using the software tool NVivo to code the chairs' use of 'we' as an including or excluding device. In multiparty interactions the determination of whether a use of 'we' is inclusive or exclusive is contingent on the specific language use as well as the analytical lens. When there are multiple intended recipients of an utterance, a 'we' can simultaneously be inclusive of some of the participants (for example, the team members) and exclusive of other participants (for example, the service user). In the data here, where there is talk between professionals and a service user, a chair's 'we' is determined to be inclusive or exclusive of the service user. Where the talk is between two professionals, a chair's 'we' is determined in relation to inclusion or exclusion of the team as a collective. The differentiation between professional–service user talk and professional–professional talk came about inductively, as the coding process highlighted marked differences in the use of 'we' in the two settings. Table 3.1 outlines how the concepts have been operationalised in the data.[1]

Following the initial coding of the four types of 'we', analysis was conducted to examine patterns and differences in how chairs used the pronoun, and what functions those types of use had in relation to the professionals' and service users' participation in the meetings. The results of this analysis are presented in the following section.

Table 3.1: Inclusive and exclusive 'we' in rehabilitation team meetings

Talk	Inclusive 'we'	Exclusive 'we'
Professional–service user	Where chairs reference the service user and the team	Where chairs reference the team or the institution, but not the service user
Professional–professional	Where chairs reference the team as a unit	Where chairs reference the institution (employment services), but not the team

Analysis: four uses of 'we' to guide participation in team meetings

The analysis found that all four types of 'we' are present in the data. Two types were used considerably more frequent than the others, however. These are:

- the exclusive 'we' in interactions with service users;
- the inclusive 'we' in interactions between team members.

We will now briefly illustrate the two least frequent uses of 'we' before moving on to a more detailed analysis of the two most frequent uses of 'we' and their functions in allocating participation in decision making.

The inclusive 'we' in interactions with service users

In this material the inclusive 'we' that chairs use in interactions between themselves and service users contains references to the team and the service user as a shared entity. While it does occur, it is the least frequent use of 'we' in the material and does not occur in all meetings. This inclusive use of 'we' often occurs in relation to the opening of the meeting, when the chair welcomes the service user and outlines the aim and process of the meeting.

Extract 1 illustrates one such instance. The extract begins as the service user enters the room, where the rehabilitation team are already present. Before this, the team members have discussed the case and have been quick to agree that the service user is eligible for the disability pension for which he himself has expressed a wish.

Extract 1: Rehabilitation team meeting A01, service user–professional talk

1. Chair: Yes, let's all just sit down without any extended hand-shaking. Well, welcome, my name is [redacted] and I am the chair today and then I represent the jobcentre in this circle of various departments. We have the health services and social services and employment services – the jobcentre, that's me, and then we have you and your caseworker. We have half an hour. I don't think we are going to need it, as you will learn in a minute, but we do have half an hour together if we need it.

The inclusive 'we' is used throughout turn 1, as the chair invokes a circumstantial 'we' including all present participants ("we have …"). This is done alongside references to the individual participants ("health services", "me", "you and your caseworker") who are implicitly encompassed in this 'we', without – at this point – drawing any demarcations between responsibilities or roles among these participants.

This illustrates how the inclusive 'we' is used in the meetings: that is, as a device that establishes a shared framework for the meeting. In this case the framework is presented in terms of a timeframe, and in other cases the framework may include the purpose and aims of the meeting. As will be detailed later, however, in interactions with service users this inclusive 'we' is often followed by a more exclusive use of 'we' that delegates decision-making responsibilities to certain participants.

The exclusive 'we' in interactions between team members

The exclusive 'we' that chairs use in interactions between themselves and other team members contains references to the organisational background of the chair ('we in the department of …') or to the professional background of the speaker ('as social workers, we …'), although the latter is only rarely used by chairs. It is exclusive in that it does not include the recipient of the talk, whether that be the team as a group or one specific team member.

Extract 2 illustrates the exclusive 'we' in interactions between team members. The extract occurs in a 'timeout' during a rehabilitation team meeting, during which the team members have left the service user in a separate room in order to discuss what to recommend in the case. During the meeting the service user has asked for help getting to and from a psychiatric treatment programme to which she has been referred, because her mental health makes it hard for her to get to the programme offices in a neighbouring city.

Extract 2: Rehabilitation team meeting B22,
professional–professional talk

1. Team member (medical clinic): Now, I don't know what you can do, but I'm thinking it's really important to step in massively in terms of that therapeutic programme, because she is completely right that if she doesn't get there and – she will simply be terminated because there are 20 other people on the waiting list.

2. Chair   But we can't grant taxi transportation, that is the – we
   (Jobcentre): really cannot grant that. That is. We have to teach her to
                go there, then, that's simply ...

The exclusive 'we' is seen in turn 2, where the chair speaks on behalf of the jobcentre and their options for granting transportation for the service user to get to her treatment ("we can't", "we really cannot"). That the 'we' is exclusive is determined in part by the discursive context, in which it is a response to the question of what 'you' can do (turn 1) rather than the team as a unit, and in part by the organisational context, wherein the jobcentre has the authority to (potentially) grant such transportation.

When used in interactions with team members, the exclusive 'we' is often tied to the chair's dual role as both meeting chair and team representative of the jobcentre. As such, this use of 'we' serves to activate the organisational and/or professional status of the chair in discussions with other professionals. As will be illustrated later, this is quite different from the inclusive use of 'we' in interactions between team members, although both uses place emphasis on certain features of the chair's status.

The following two subsections look more closely at the most frequent uses of 'we' in the data – first the exclusive 'we' in interactions with service users and then the inclusive 'we' in interactions between team members – and how these function to allocate and differentiate participant roles in decision making.

The exclusive 'we' in interactions with service users

The exclusive 'we' in interactions between chairs and service users contains chairs' references to the collective of the rehabilitation team and/or the institution of the employment services. The service user is not included in this type of 'we', which is why it is categorised here as an exclusive 'we'. This exclusive 'we' is quite precise in that it is often used to delegate decision-making responsibility by outlining that we-the-team are responsible for making a recommendation (and not you-the-service-user) while also outlining that the final decision-making authority lies with a different institutional body.

Consider the following section from Frank's meeting with the rehabilitation team. Frank is a middle-aged man who has been unemployed for the past nine years. He has severe pain in his back and neck, which he ascribes to his previous work as an unskilled worker in construction, among other things. Furthermore, Frank has been diagnosed with social anxiety (agoraphobia) and alcohol addiction, although he does not himself ascribe his problems to his alcohol intake. Frank's case is being discussed in the rehabilitation team because he has applied for a disability pension and the team are to decide whether they support or recommend against the granting of this benefit. The extract starts early in the meeting, just as Frank has been welcomed into the room and assigned a seat at the head of the table. Frank is accompanied by his caseworker in the employment services and a care worker from a municipal outreach programme with which Frank has regular contact.

Extract 3: Rehabilitation team meeting B07, service user–professional talk

1. Chair: Yes, this meeting is about, that we will introduce ourselves so you know who you are talking to, and then of course, we would like to hear what you have to say, and then we have some questions. We have received all these papers of course, your case files that you have gone through with [caseworker], and read them, but it is always different to be allowed to ask directly, right. And then, of course, you should just say what you feel like saying and if [outreach worker] and [caseworker] want to say something, you do that as well, right. And before time is up, we will take this thing that we call a timeout, so that will be us here in the team that leave the room, then you stay seated with [outreach worker] and [caseworker].
2. Frank: Okay.
3. Chair: And we figure out what we can agree on.
4. Frank: Yes, yes.
5. Chair: You have applied for a disability pension and that is what we will decide upon, whether we will recommend that. We can't make a formal decision, because that is our pensions board who does that, but we have to make a recommendation.
6. Frank: Yes, okay, that's how things are.

The extract contains a fairly consistent use of the exclusive 'we' as the chair outlines the course of the meeting. Starting from turn 1, an exclusive we-the-team is consistently presented opposite you-the-service user ("we will introduce" – "so you know"; "we would like" – "you have to say"; "we have received" – "that you have gone through"). The formulations invite Frank to participate actively ("hear what you have to say"; "just say what you feel like"), but the exclusive 'we' simultaneously allocates decision-making agency with the rehabilitation team ("we have some questions"; "we will leave the room"), which becomes explicit in turn 3 ("what we can agree on").

In turn 5, the chair goes on to make explicit the reason for the meeting ("you have applied for ...") and the aim of decision making ("that is what we will decide upon"). Once again, the exclusive 'we' is separate from 'you-the-service user', which works to establish the team as the decision-making agent. In this turn the chair also outlines the decision-making authority in more detail; the exclusive 'we' "can't make a formal decision", as the final authority lies outside the room, with the pensions board. This use of the pronoun does detailed work in keeping decision making (on the recommendation) within the remit of the team while also distancing the team from the responsibility (and possible blame) for the end result, namely the final decision made by the pensions team. In practice, the recommendation of the rehabilitation team is of great importance to the decision of the pensions team. Thus, in almost all cases, when the rehabilitation team have recommended against a disability pension, the application will be denied by the pensions team. Nevertheless, examining the detailed use of the pronoun 'we' makes visible the chair's role in allocating different roles in the meeting specifically and the decision-making process more broadly. As Frank is new to this type of meeting, these demarcations provide important signals about what he can expect from the meeting, and what is expected of him.

The extract is an information-giving sequence, and Frank does little but receive the information with acknowledging minimal responses. The information given, however, is not just on the process of the meeting but also works to outline Frank's role in the decision making. Thus, Frank is welcome to say what he wants during the meeting, but the decision will be made by, first, the team of professionals (their recommendation) and finally by the pensions board. Frank's role in the decision-making process is established to be one of information giving; he is not part of the 'we' that recommends. While Frank is explicitly invited to participate in the meeting's talk (turn 1), then, he is excluded from participating in the pursuit of agreement (turn 3) and decision making (turn 5) around his eligibility for a disability pension. This role differentiation is illustrative of all the 26 analysed meetings. The roles are rarely challenged by the service users, and Frank's reaction, too, is one of acceptance; "okay, that's how things are" (turn 6).

In the context of collaborative and integrated welfare, it is also interesting that the professionals who accompany Frank into the meeting are equally excluded from decision making. Like Frank, the caseworker and the outreach worker are invited to "say something" (turn 1), yet are not included in the exclusive 'we' who are to "agree" (turn 3) and "decide" (turn 5). As will be the case in many multi-agency settings, a professional is not just a professional on equal footing with other professionals. Rather, each professional becomes a representative of a certain expertise and organisational authority. This representative position influences their participation in both talk and decision making. In this case, the chair sets up the visiting professionals to be potential sources of information (turn 1: "if [they] want to say something") even though they have the closest contact to, and most in-depth knowledge of, Frank and his situation.[2]

The analysis illustrates how chairs' use of the exclusive 'we' in interactions with service users outlines certain participant roles in decision making. Here, team members are identified as the participants among whom agreement is to be reached, while the service user and the professionals closest to him are talked about as excluded from this process in so far as their role is to provide information to the 'we' who decides. Furthermore, the exclusive 'we' serves to place the final decision-making authority outside the meeting itself (with the pensions board) – regardless of the weight given to the recommendation of the rehabilitation team – which creates even more distance between Frank and the decision to be made in his case.

The inclusive 'we' in interactions between team members

This subsection illustrates the other main use of 'we' in rehabilitation team meetings: the inclusive 'we' used in interactions between team members when the service user is not present. This use is inclusive, as it refers to the collective of the rehabilitation team of which the recipient(s) of the talk is considered part. The inclusive 'we' in interactions between team members is less clear and explicit than the exclusive 'we' used in interactions with service users, but it still serves important functions in decision making.

The inclusive 'we' in interactions between team members is illustrated with another section of Frank's meeting (Extract 3). After meeting Frank and discussing various aspects of his case with him and the outreach worker (the caseworker not having participated in the talk), the team retreats to an adjoining room to discuss their recommendation. They agree immediately that he is not eligible for the disability pension

Interprofessional Collaboration and Service User Participation

but do recognise that he has needs that could make other benefits and interventions relevant, if Frank wants to work in that direction. One of the suggested measures is psychological treatment to address his anxiety and alcohol addiction, which prompts one of the team members, a representative from the jobcentre who is also the one writing up the recommendation, to ask for clarification.

Extract 4: Rehabilitation team meeting B07, professional–professional talk

1.	Team member (jobcentre):	Where will the psychological treatment come from? I mean, through you guys, or …?
2.	Chair:	No, but we can't, we just have to recommend on a section 17[3] so we should only recommend –. It would have to go –
3.	Team member (jobcentre):	It was just because you said a resource programme –
4.	Chair	Yes, well, it would have to be presented again if he were to have a resource programme. Then you would have to talk about, you know, then it has to be put forward again.
5.	Team member (social services):	But we could mention it now, that, depending on what the pensions board decides, then you would know that there is an alternative way.
6.	Chair:	Yes, and we believe that we can develop his ability to work by him being part of a resource programme. That is what we will write.
7.	Team member (jobcentre):	Yes, so there are still options for treatment and the ability to work can be developed through a resource programme.
8.	Chair:	Yes.

In turn 1 the team member from the jobcentre poses a question that suggests that she believes that psychological treatment is to be part of the recommendation in Frank's case and asks who should be responsible for that treatment ("where … from", "you guys?"). The chair self-selects as next speaker here, even though the question was likely directed at the team member representing social services and not the chair. This interpretation is supported by the facts that: (a) the option of facilitating psychological treatment falls under the remit of the social services; and (b) the chair is from the same department as the team member posing the question. In her response the chair does not answer the question, but instead outlines the task that comes with this being a section 17 application (turn 2: "we can't, we just have to", "we should"). These are inclusive uses of 'we' in that the chair is talking about the team as a unit, of which the representative to whom she is responding is a formal participant. The repeated use of the inclusive 'we' shifts attention away from who should do what in Frank's actual treatment. Instead, attention is directed to the shared task of the rehabilitation team in making a certain decision. This task and the procedures that follow are further outlined in turn 4, after the team member asks for clarification in turn 3 ("you said resource programme").

Where the use of the exclusive 'we' in Extract 3 with the service user was explicit in the way it allocated decision-making roles, these roles are more implicitly enacted in this extract. The chair uses the inclusive 'we' in turn 2 to draw in a team member who seems to go beyond the team's task at this point. By using the inclusive 'we' the chair signals to the team member from the jobcentre that they too are part of a certain task that is framed by certain regulations ("section 17, so we should …").

The shared nature of the task's fulfilment within the team becomes clear as the other participants engage in a negotiation around how to manage the task at hand. In turn 5, the team member from social services suggests that "we could mention" the resource programme, so the service user would know that this was an alternative. The resource programme is a personalised, interprofessional programme lasting between one and five years, aimed at bringing the service users with complex challenges closer to the labour market. Participation in a resource programme is a prerequisite for being considered for a disability pension, and the example shows how team members other than the chair may also use the inclusive 'we' in the negotiation of what the team will recommend. In this case, some mitigation of the chair's declaration of what to do can be detected. Thus, the chair agrees with the suggestion to mention the resource programme (turn 6: "yes, and …") despite previously outlining a narrow focus on the disability pension (turn 2: "we just have to recommend on a section 17"). Despite this mitigation, the chair's use of 'we' signals the implicit authority to assess what constitutes a legitimate decision through her use of directives (turn 2: "we should"; turn 6: "that is what we will write"), as well as her confirmation of the suggestions of the other team members (turn 6: "yes"; turn 8: "yes"). Some of the directives are *deontic* (turn 2: "should", "have to") in that they pertain to questions about what ought to happen. As deontic rights are tied to authority and power (Stevanovic and Peräkylä, 2012), they can be understood in connection with the social and discursive roles of the chair. Thus, by speaking on behalf of the team (the inclusive 'we') and what they ought to do, the chair is taking the deontic stance of someone having the right to do so. This is met with some negotiation from the other participants, as outlined previously, but is generally accepted. As mentioned earlier, the inclusive 'we' that constructs the team as a unit is used frequently in meetings. Constructing a 'we' that includes team members is one of the ways the professionals prepare for the interaction with the service user. Previous research has shown that when team members work in backstage settings, they may use this as a place to prepare for their onstage performance (Lewin and Reeves, 2011).

In the data, then, the chairs' inclusive use of 'we' in interactions with team members becomes a way of signalling to other team members their role in decision making, as a team with a certain task, and what constitutes the 'correct' way of fulfilling this task: we-the-team should focus on certain things and follow certain procedures. In doing so, the chair simultaneously establishes the 'team' as a unit with certain obligations to which team members must attend and their own role as one with the authority to speak on behalf of the team and assess whether a decision is relevant and legitimate.

Discussion and conclusion

This chapter has illustrated two main tendencies in how chairs use various types of 'we' in Danish rehabilitation team meetings: the exclusive 'we' in interactions with service users and the inclusive 'we' in interactions with other team members. At the linguistic level these uses are different in that they work to either exclude or include various meeting participants in decision making. At the level of content, however, both uses work to establish the professional team as the main unit of authority. These tendencies carry implications for the realisation of collaborative and integrated welfare services in terms of both service user participation and interprofessional collaboration.

Looking first at service user participation, the tendency of chairs to use language that assigns information-giving roles to service users and decision-making roles to the team does seem to be at odds with the aims of collaborative welfare services in which the service user participates in making decisions about their life and activities. While the chairs' use of the exclusive 'we' is not decisive for the role that the service user (and other participants) may actually play in meetings, the chairs' delineation of roles does contain powerful cues to the participants about what are considered appropriate and allowable contributions in this specific setting. This is especially true in the context of social welfare, where professionals hold the formal authority to decide on the eligibility for and relevance of measures that have direct consequences for service users' everyday lives – and in the case of disability pensions, these consequences are immense. In this setting, service users may be hesitant to disagree with professionals. Bearing in mind Kangarsharju's (2002) findings on in-group alliances, they may also find the task of arguing their case daunting when faced with a united front of professional team members. In the data, the use of the exclusive 'we' serves to construct a unified professional authority over the service user, and most often service users readily accept this role allocation, as seen in Frank's case (Extract 3, turn 6: "okay, that's how things are").

While this role allocation is contained within the chairs' use of the exclusive 'we', it is not the exclusive 'we' itself that creates the decision-making asymmetry in this specific context. Rather, ensuring service users' participation in decision making regarding welfare benefits is a challenge inherent in the policy context of which these meetings (and decisions) are part. As policy and legislation place the formal authority to assess eligibility with the professional team, while also regulating these decisions in a complex legislative and organisational framework in which the team are not the final authority, there is a clear limit to how much decision-making power can be given to service users in meetings. Thus, if the chairs were to use a more inclusive 'we' when outlining the process of decision making, they might only serve to disguise the power asymmetries at work without actually being able to have service users participate in decision making. This would result in a kind of 'token participation' (Arnstein, 1969). On the other hand, having service users present and voicing their perceptions of their own challenges and needs might be the first step in allowing them to be involved in decision making. While only a small step, it is an essential one, as it allows for the creation of common knowledge and relational expertise that can foster collaboration in decision making and task fulfilment more generally (Hopwood and Edwards, 2017). Hopwood and Edwards (2017, p 117) conceptualise service user participation as 'a complex, emergent phenomenon located in practices and specific settings, rather than something that can be reduced to procedural prescription'. This becomes particularly salient as the details of how participation and collaboration are done in responsive interaction are explored.

The detailed analysis of how chairs use 'we' both exclusively and inclusively serves to illustrate the detailed work of professionals in implementing policy ideals in everyday practice. When taking into account the policy context of the rehabilitation teams, the chairs' use of 'we' may be understood as a delicate balancing act of trying to invite service users to take an active role in their own assessments by providing information and without denying the asymmetries in play. A more critical interpretation, of course, would be that the use of the exclusive 'we' is in fact a manifestation of these asymmetries and that the construction of a united team ('we') confronting the service user ('you') is part of enacting the institutional power to make decisions independently of the service user's wishes.

A similar discussion could be raised around the policy aim of integrated and collaborative welfare service realised through interprofessional collaboration. When chairs use an inclusive 'we' in their interactions with other team members, it may on the one hand be a subtle way of ensuring that the talk stays on topic and that the decision eventually reached is legitimate in terms of the institutional and legal framework. In doing so, however, the chair simultaneously establishes the team as a unit with certain obligations to which members must adjust. The chair also establishes their own role as one with the authority to speak on behalf of the team and assess whether a decision is relevant and legitimate. Again, this must be understood in the context of both policy and organisation, which in this setting establishes the legal obligations of the employment services as the main purpose of the meetings, thus giving the chair – who in these data is always representing the employment services – the deontic and epistemic status of an expert in this field.

In terms of both service user participation and interprofessional collaboration, the analysis suggests that chairs' use of 'we' places the team in a position of authority, with the chair themselves as a decisive part. This does not mean that service users and other team members have no influence on decision making. It does, however, foreground the salience of the chair's role in ensuring the institutional legitimacy of decisions through – among other features – their use of the inclusive and exclusive 'we'. In either case, the analysis illustrates how the policy aims of collaborative and integrated welfare services are not realised by multi-agency meetings in and of themselves, but that the detailed language use by chairs (and other meeting participants) is an important part of how these aims are implemented in everyday practice.

Notes

1. In coding we have also worked with a fifth category of 'unclear uses of we', which are not analytically determinable as either inclusive or exclusive. For the purposes of this chapter, this category is not included in the analysis.
2. The caseworker has prepared the written report with which the team are presented before the meeting, and both professionals have had regular contact with Frank over a period of time, while the other team members have never met him before.
3. §17 refers to the service user him- or herself applying for a disability pension, whereas §18 takes effect when the employment system initiates the procedure for a disability pension application.

References

Angouri, J. and Marra, M. (2010) 'Corporate meetings as genre: A study of the role of the chair in corporate meeting talk', *Text and Talk*, 30(6): 615–36.

Arnstein, S. (1969) 'A ladder of citizen participation', *Journal of the American Institute of Planners*, 35(4): 216–24.

Asmuβ, B. and Svennevig, J. (2009) 'Meeting talk', *Journal of Business Communication*, 46(1): 3–22.

Bekendtgørelse af lov om organisering og understøttelse af beskæftigelsesindsatsen m.v. [Act on the Organisation and Support of the Active Employment Intervention etc.], no. 1483 of 23/12/2014, Copenhagen: Ministry of Employment.

Dall, T. (2017) 'Decision-making and professional responsibility in complex client cases: an interactional perspective on interprofessional teamwork in a social work setting', doctoral thesis, Aalborg: Aalborg University.

Dall, T. (2020) 'Distribution of responsibility in inter-professional teams in welfare-to-work', *Nordic Social Work Research*, 10(1): 80–93.

Drew, P. and Heritage, J. (2013) 'Introduction', in P. Drew and J. Heritage (eds) *Conversation Analysis*, London: Sage Publications, pp xxi–xxxvii.

Edwards, A. (2011) 'Building common knowledge at the boundaries between professional practices: Relational agency and relational expertise in systems of distributed expertise', *International Journal of Educational Research*, 50(1): 33–9.

Goffman, E. (1963) *The Presentation of Self in Everyday Life*, London: Penguin.

Hitzler, S. and Messmer, H. (2010) 'Group decision-making in child welfare and the pursuit of participation', *Qualitative Social Work*, 9(2): 205–26.

Hopwood, N. and Edwards, A. (2017) 'How common knowledge is constructed and why it matters in collaboration between professionals and clients', *International Journal of Educational Research*, 83: 107–19.

Kangasharju, H. (2002) 'Alignment in disagreement: Forming oppositional alliances in committee meetings', *Journal of Pragmatics*, 34: 1447–71.

Lerner, G. and Kitzinger, C. (2007) 'Extraction and aggregation in the repair of individual and collective self-reference', *Discourse and Society*, 9(4): 526–57.

Lewin, S. and Reeves, S. (2011) 'Enacting "team" and "teamwork": Using Goffman's theory of impression management to illuminate interprofessional practice on hospital wards', *Social Science and Medicine*, 72(10): 1595–602.

Sacks, H. (1992) *Lectures on Conversation*, Oxford: Blackwell.

Stevanovic, M. and Peräkylä, A. (2012) 'Deontic authority in interaction: The right to announce, propose, and decide', *Research on Language and Social Interaction*, 45(3): 297–321.

Wodak, R., Kwon, W. and Clarke, I. (2011) ' "Getting people on board": Discursive leadership for consensus building in team meetings', *Discourse and Society*, 22(5): 592–644.

4

Working within frames and across boundaries in core group meetings in child protection

Christopher Hall and Stef Slembrouck

Introduction

Poor information sharing, communication and coordination between agencies in child protection have been a central concern in the UK since the early 1970s, following a series of public inquiries into child deaths (Parton, 2014a, p 20). In response, government policies have established procedures that require all professionals to share concerns about children and contribute to multi-agency assessments, plans and interventions. Core group meetings (CGMs) were introduced in 1986, responding to concerns about 'poor planning', 'a lack of collated information' and 'a lack of clarity regarding respective roles and responsibilities' (Calder and Horwath, 2000, p 267). They are seen as combining the best features of child protection and family support (Mittler, 1997, p 80), and have been described as the 'control room of inter-agency operations' (Calder and Horwath, 2000, p 268). However, research has questioned how far such ambitions have been realised, with concerns about how different professionals contribute.

This chapter examines CGMs as arenas of multi-agency work in child protection. There is first a review of the development of policy and procedures in child protection in England, including where CGMs fit in. Concepts of framing and boundary work are outlined next to analyse the data. Two main analyses are presented. First, there is an examination of the structuring role of the chair, and second, there is an analysis of how professionals negotiate boundaries of expertise and remit. The conclusion considers how far CGM practice appears to promote multi-agency coordination. The data examined in this chapter were collected in northern England.

Information sharing and coordination in child protection in England

The competence of child protection professionals in England has been the subject of media and government scrutiny as a series of public inquiries into child deaths identified professional and organisational failings (Reder and Duncan, 2003). Professionals were reluctant to share concerns about children or failed to act on crucial information. For example, the inquiry into the death of Victoria Climbié reports: '12 key occasions when the relevant services had the opportunity to successfully intervene in the life of Victoria …. There can be no excuse for such sloppy and unprofessional performance' (Laming, 2003, p 3). Thompson (2016, p 2) observes: 'Working together across multi-agency settings to improve information sharing has now become a moral and political imperative in England and Wales for improving the welfare and the protection of children.'

In response, a series of initiatives was introduced, particularly to regulate professional practices. From the mid-1970s, procedures were developed to manage initial concerns, establish multi-agency assessments and coordinate subsequent interventions. Case conferences were identified as a vital part of the system (Parton, 1985, pp 104–5). Moreover, a broader early intervention approach was developed in the 1990s, aimed at supporting a larger proportion of 'children with additional needs'. As Parton (2014a, p 95) notes, the 1999 version of the procedures, *Working Together*, 'reframed the object of concern away from a narrow, forensically-driven conception of child protection towards a much broader notion of safeguarding'.

Importantly, such developments depend on and enhance 'collaborative and integrated welfare', as outlined in Chapter 1. Both early intervention and formal child protection processes rely on information sharing and multi-agency working through detailed procedures and a range of multi-agency meetings. Furthermore, all professionals are expected to make appropriate contributions. As Appleton and Stanley (2008, p 1) point out, 'safeguarding children is everyone's responsibility'. The metaphor of the jigsaw has been deployed: each professional has some information about a child, which in itself might not be considered important, but when placed together, a fuller picture emerges (Thompson, 2016, p 115). Calder (2001, p 18) considers that the central goal of working together is 'the achievement of some degree of consensus by a group of individuals about a plan of action and its execution'.

Procedures that aim to regulate professional practices are central to risk management practices associated with the move from 'welfarist' to 'neoliberal' approaches in social welfare over the past 40 years (Parton, 2014b, p 2047). Munro (2009, p 1015) notes that a 'strongly regulated child protection system … is expected not only to identify and help the victims of cruelty but also to predict and prevent such cruelty'. Furthermore, a question arises as to how such procedures direct professionals from various agencies to change their work practices, challenging professional discretion; a typical managerialist criticism of the vested interests of welfare organisations (Cummins, 2018, p 14). In 2011, the procedures were revised to reduce what was seen as an 'unnecessary or unhelpful prescription and focus only on essential rules for effective multi-agency working' (Munro, 2011, p 7), but without changing the system of meetings.

Core group meetings: 'the control room of interagency work'

As with much social welfare, there is a shifting balance between support and control in child protection (Slembrouck et al, forthcoming). For cases that enter the formal system, there is an initial multiprofessional investigation and an assessment led by a social worker and the police, leading to a multi-agency meeting – the initial child protection conference (ICPC) (see Chapter 8). The ICPC assesses the evidence provided by the professionals involved with the family and, where appropriate, produces a child protection plan (CPP). The plan outlines a series of expectations on the family to protect the child (for example, to ensure that the child gets to school) and identifies services and professionals to support and monitor the child and family. The CPP is reviewed every three to six months and in between the core group meets regularly to develop and monitor the implementation of the plan.

Recent government guidance (DfE, 2018, p 49) states that the core group should meet within 10 working days of the initial child protection conference and:

- further develop the outline child protection plan, based on assessment findings, and set out what needs to change, by how much, and by when in order for the child to be safe and have their needs met
- decide what steps need to be taken, and by whom, to complete the in-depth assessment to inform decisions about the child's safety and welfare

- implement the child protection plan and take joint responsibility for carrying out the agreed tasks, monitoring progress and outcomes, and refining the plan as needed.

The CGM develops 'the plan into a detailed working plan' (Horwath, 2013, p 88).

CGMs are administrated and chaired by the lead local authority social worker (or their manager) and are attended by those professionals most regularly involved with the child and family – typically a teacher, health visitor, school nurse, support workers, housing support workers, therapists and so on. Importantly, the meeting usually includes the parents/carers, other family members and, where appropriate, the child (no children were involved in the meetings discussed in this corpus). Meetings take place in a variety of settings, often away from social services offices, sometimes in the family home.

Mittler (1997, p 80) outlines four CGM characteristics. They:

- maintain an interagency and interdisciplinary approach;
- work in a more informal way and increase the contributions of all parties to the process;
- provide a framework for detailed negotiations as to what is needed;
- develop relationships to overcome confrontation and support partnerships.

Calder and Horwath (1999, p 64) expect an effective core group to require 'not only commitment to the task but structure, organisation and clarity regarding the way in which its members will work together'. This underlines how the interactional management of the meeting is crucial.

Research suggests that such expectations are not always realised. Calder (2001, p 21) notes the lack of explicit procedure or guidance, with confusion over the role of different professionals. Harlow and Shardlow (2006, p 67) report uncertainty over how social services manage their lead responsibility; some professionals feel that their opinions were not given equal attention. Conversely, they also report that social workers believed that other professionals were reluctant to share information. Horwath (2013, p 98) questions whether the CGM creates 'an environment for meaningful engagement'.

More generally, as identified in Chapter 1, there are questions about information sharing and multi-agency coordination in social welfare. Government and organisational initiatives to promote technical solutions have resulted in rationalist approaches, which see multi-agency coordination as unambiguous, whereas child protection work is often unclear, emergent and constructed. There are concerns as to whether professionals have a 'common language' in order to communicate with other professionals (White et al, 2009). Thompson (2016, p 57) notes how information, formulations and assessments cannot be merely shared, but require translation and revision across organisational boundaries. Lees (2017, p 893) is concerned that 'families' lives are complex, ambiguous and emotionally charged … practitioners must move towards refining, interrogating and framing information in ways that fit into systems for sharing and communicating information between teams and organisations'.

In summary, professionals aim to share information and coordinate professional interventions in CGMs. However, as mentioned in Chapter 2, it is only through an examination of the relational turn in which professionals (and carers/parents) interact face-to-face in meetings that we can understand how multi-agency work is achieved.

Professional framing, frames of interaction and boundary work

Understanding the complexities of multi-agency work in a context such as CGMs invites attention to the management of professional and organisational boundaries that result from working within and across frameworks of action and reference. Boundary work in our analysis applies as each participant has a professional remit. Attention to boundaries comes with having to work within a specific interactional framework, including how this is managed by the chair. Boundary work is manifested in particular ways of proceeding, forms of involvement and engagement as the meeting interaction unfolds: the selection of topics, how they are talked about and the relationship with service users, with other professionals and the chair. It is as much a matter of how things are responded to as it is about who is talking and in what terms. Much interagency coordination may be about preferred scenarios, justifying particular courses of action, claims about one's own role and that of others, whose responsibility it is to address particular concerns, as well as identity work about service users, one's own profession and that of others.

Boundary work can thus be simultaneously connected to ideas of 'framing issues' and 'frames of interaction'. The former depicts multi-agency work as a terrain of competing professional outlooks, whereas the second idea develops a perspective on interagency work being accomplished within the specific boundaries of an interactional framework, the CGM, which in itself counts as an activity type with a purpose, a focus and expected and allowable contributions.

Bucher et al (2016) focus on patterns of framing in the context of field-specific debates that question specific professional boundaries (in their case, health in Ontario, Canada). Attempting a deeper understanding of how field positions are played out in discursive strategies, they examine how professional stakeholders engage in discursive boundary work when they respond to specific policy initiatives for shaping interprofessional practice. Bucher et al's (2016) notion of framing draws on Snow and Bedford's (1988) work on the nature of mobilising activity in (new) social movements. Understood metaphorically, 'to frame' here means to 'to assign meaning to and interpret relevant events and conditions in ways that are intended to mobilize potential adherents and constituents, to garner bystander support, and to demobilize antagonists' (1988, p 198).

Empirically, the authors identify four foci of framing in their analysis of the professions' argumentative documents:

- *framing an issue* (for example, a professional demand in relation to a policy issue, restricting or stretching mandated space);
- *justifying favoured solutions* (for example, supporting claims by referring to an ethical code of conduct or particular reports; justifications can be normative, rational and/or experiential);
- *self-casting of the profession's own identity* (such as signalling capacity and leadership in a particular area of practice);
- *altercasting* or *framing of other professions' identities* (such as ignoring or downplaying other professionals as less capable, or problematising them through claims about unwarranted role assignments).

The analytical mainstay here is related to Bucher et al's (2016) study, but differs. Our interest is to examine how current field-specific positions play out in relation to the child and family, including how CGMs count as arenas for competing interprofessional claims. In addition, we focus on how positions about a specific child, a particular case, a specific issue and so on are established and responded to interactionally in the multi-agency context of CGMs.

As noted earlier, the idea of drawing and guarding boundaries is intrinsic to practices of framing. The same is true for interactional frameworks, when these are understood in Goffman's terms (Goffman, 1974; Slembrouck and Hall, 2014). In fact, it is somewhat surprising that Bucher et al do not refer to Goffman's work, as their perspective also revolves around spatialising metaphors rooted in the observation that 'putting a frame around something' entails 'attention to borders'. While framing in Snow and Bedford's sense is about actively drawing an interpretative frame around an issue so as to steer it in a particular direction, Goffman's notion of frame is about activity being conducted within a common frame of interaction and interpretation. Both senses are underpinned by an activity-oriented and participant-focused understanding of how relevant meaning comes into being and is sustained (Snow and Benford, 1988, p 198).

At the same time, Goffman's account requires attention to the specific group relations that are indexed by communicative conduct (Collins and Slembrouck, 2009, p 22). The key social theoretical underpinning of Goffman's concept of 'frame' is 'co-presence': what interactants do under conditions where they share the same space, perhaps irrespective of social group membership. In his work on frame and footing, Goffman (1974, 1981) examines how interactants collaborate in signalling a shared understanding of a social reality experience that is brought into being and maintained for the duration of a recognisable event (for example, a CGM). Frames are brought into being as accomplished realities that are upheld for their duration, but Goffman recognises the possibility of mismatches, understandings at cross-purposes and even competing perceptions. Yet, he does not examine how the professional or occupational group membership of participants in a shared frame of activity may come with an interactional stake of actively framing the matters talked about in particular terms that are specific to a professional group beyond the space of interaction. This kind of complementarity is needed to shed light on the nature and dynamics of multi-agency work in CGMs: while participants align to the interactional dynamics of the CGM, they remain connected to their own professional worlds. Goffman does, however, provide concepts needed to understand how framing moves in the course of an interaction and is accomplished interactionally.

Boundary work will thus manifest itself in particular interactional alignments. Involvement may be low or high. Participants may take a lead in the centre of the discussion or they may take a back seat when it is not their professional call. Participants may see it as (not) their responsibility to contribute to a particular topic raised. When they do contribute, they may do so with variable degrees of caution/certainty. Which particular claims must one absolutely go on record about, given that one speaks about a case from a particular professional background? Which queries or assertions are beyond one's remit and therefore better left to others? How are claims hedged, when a participant asserts something that, strictly speaking, belongs to the terrain of another profession? How does one manage (dis)agreements within or beyond one's own occupational remit? How do the participants seek to raise or appropriate particular topics and concerns? How much of the framing work is done through the chair? Boundary work will be at stake in answering each of these questions. In examining this, interactional display and professional positioning need to be looked at together.

Data and the process of analysis

The data are drawn from a qualitative mixed-method design case study undertaken in a large local authority in northern England. The methodology was grounded in an ethnomethodological orientation to the socially organised nature of practice (Garfinkel, 1986). The researcher was located in social work teams on a day-to-day basis for more than a year. The 12 core groups that form the basis of this chapter are part of a larger corpus of data that includes observations of practice in key decision-making occasions (supervision meetings, case conferences and so on), 'backstage' case talk, and focus groups and interviews with practitioners and managers from various agencies involved in child protection work.[1]

Ethical approval was granted by Lancaster University and the participating local authority. Parents consented to the study after it was explained by the social worker in the first instance, and then by the researcher. Consent was reconfirmed on a regular basis. Recordings were transcribed and carefully anonymised to protect the identity of all participants while retaining the richness of the interactions.

Informality and structuring of the CGMs

The data are examined in terms of how participants are invited to speak in a CGM and how they frame their contribution through turn-by-turn analysis of conversational activity. The meeting is approached as a sequence of turns-at-speaking, in which each participant responds to the previous speaker, but also attends to prior talk, while cognisant of obligations associated with being a participant in the multi-agency meeting.

The first analysis section explores how the chair structures the meeting, inviting professionals to contribute and attend to the meeting as an occasion to share information and achieve multi-agency coordination regarding child and family. Frequent contact between the professionals and families means that there is often chat and banter, largely absent from more formal meetings. As discussed in Chapter 2, multi-agency meetings are often organised around discrete phases. For example, Hall and Slembrouck (2001, p 149) found that child protection conferences (CPCs) were structured in terms of introductions, information gathering and assessment, discussion and decision making and planning. The

CGM is more constrained as to what topics are available for scrutiny and what decisions can be made. It cannot change the formal status of a case, although it can recommend to the CPC that a case no longer requires child protection status. Sometimes decisions to alter services are made outside the meeting by the home organisation of the professional and are merely reported in the meeting, for example to make a referral for a service (as in CGM 4 – see later in this chapter) or to seek a legal intervention (as in CGM 5 – see later). As previously described, government guidance requires CGMs to monitor the tasks and adjust interventions identified in the CPP. The chair therefore has the delicate task of reviewing the CPP, while managing constraints on the topics available for scrutiny. As noted in Chapter 2, the agenda of professional meetings has to be enacted and attended to, and therefore topics are managed locally (Svennevig, 2012, p 54).

The informality of the CGMs means that there are opportunities to depart from or even subvert some of the formality typically associated with professional meetings. The second part of the analysis therefore examines how participants frame their contributions in terms that promote the efficacy of their profession. Informality also enables openings in which to comment on topics that might normally be seen as beyond their remit.

In the extracts presented in this chapter of turn-taking in the CGMs, SW refers to the lead social worker and chair of the meeting. Other professionals and family members are identified in the extract headings. The 12 CGMs in the corpus have been numbered 1 to 12. Extracts have been numbered consecutively.

Analysis: managing frames and boundaries

The social worker chairs the CGM

Chairing a meeting is both an interactional activity and a mandated identity invested with authority, as noted in Chapter 2. In terms of identity, the social worker is mandated as the designated chair in CGMs, in contrast to the more formal CPCs, which have independent chairs. In this respect, they are both the chair and an actively contributing professional. The rights and obligations of the chair include ensuring a sequential order, especially selecting the next speaker (Boden, 1994, p 86), and monitoring the contributions through their interactional follow-up (Asmuß and Svennevig, 2009, p 11). Accountable chairing cannot be arbitrary: there are likely to be case-specific, meeting-specific or occasioned expectations as to who is the appropriate 'next speaker', such as the worker with most involvement with the family, or the most pressing issue. In terms of boundary work, we can see that the social worker as the chair is likely to draw on a range of resources to monitor the order and scope of contributions, and this is intimately interwoven with the interactional dynamics of invitations to speak next, and introducing and pursuing topics.

Introductions

A formal orientation is evident in the opening of most meetings. For instance:

Extract 1: CGM 3

> SW: OK, if we can start with introductions please. I'm [name], social worker for C and L [names of the children].

In another CGM, SW, while inviting introductions, lays out the expectation on participants to report on the progress of their work:

Extract 2: CGM 6

> SW: OK, well we'll get on. This is the core group for the AB children. If we can all introduce ourselves and see what's been achieved and what's not. I'm [name] social worker for the child protection team and the three children.

In most introductions, the meeting collectively features as a direct addressee. On occasion, the introduction is addressed more directly to the mother. In Extract 3, the mother is new to CGMs.

Extract 3: CGM4

1. SW: OK, we'll start then. Hello everybody. [Mother], we're here today and this is a core group meeting, OK?
2. Mother: Yeah.
3. SW: This is the meeting that we have because we went, we had an initial child protection conference where it was decided that [unborn child] would be made subject to a child protection plan and erm, under the category of at risk of neglect, OK?
4. Mother: Yeah.
5. SW: So these are the meetings we have to have and I'm just going to go round and introduce everyone, all right?

In another meeting, the chair signals the opening by announcing the first topic. The mother is addressed directly:

Extract 4: CGM 1

> SW: I'll start by, err, there's a couple of things been brought to my attention and I haven't been able to catch you in. They were unannounced [visits].

In some meetings, the CPP is established as the focus of the CGM and determines the order in which to proceed:

Extract 5: CGM 10

> SW: OK. I'm just going to go over the child protection plan.

In summary, SW readily takes on the role of the chair by opening the meeting, and structures an agenda and how to proceed. The resources available for the chair include establishing how the parents/carers are to be included, how to invite the professionals' contributions and what might be included, what topics are (dis)preferred, as well as how the discussion is to be organised. Such boundary-marking moves, while voiced informally, share some formal characteristics of larger meetings, for example addressing the meeting collectively, inviting introductions and so on.

The chair controls the interprofessional display in the meeting

The framing activity of the chair is examined in two contrasting CGMs. In our corpus, CGM 6 comes perhaps closest to a formal structure, with the social worker/chair tightly managing invitations to contribute to the meeting and their subsequent responses. After the introductions, there is an invitation to report 'significant events':

Extract 6: CGM 6 (HO = housing officer)

1. SW: Right. Significant events. Does anyone have any significant events to mark down before we start?
2. HO: I have.
3. SW: Oh.

Note how this invitation is posed as a preliminary "before we start" the meeting proper, as well as the chair's surprise ("Oh"), suggesting that HO's bid is unexpected.

Next, each element in the CPP is identified and examined, the first one being domestic abuse:

Extract 7: CGM 6

1. SW: Right. CP plan. Err, domestic abuse. Both parents agreed that [Father] will not stay overnight at the family home. Erm, at last month's meeting, it was evident he was staying overnight at the home. Right, [Mother]. Were you here for the last one?
2. Mother: No. We were at a funeral, getting it sorted.
3. SW: So has he been staying overnight?
4. Mother: No, he just comes in the morning. His mum doesn't like him lying in bed. She goes to work at eight and she wants him out, so he comes round.
5. [7" pause]
6. SW: I've just realised. Do you know who everybody is, [Mother]? Should we do introductions again please? Do you know who I am [laughs].

The topic is introduced and directed at the mother in the form of an accusation: "So has he been staying overnight?" Mother's denial is followed by a seven-second pause and an immediate change of subject. Such moves display strong control of the meeting. The accusation is not interrogated further. The long pause is not posed as a turn transition nor a turn invitation to others, and the immediate change of topic leaves the accusation up in the air.

SW continues to raise the topics outlined in the CPP. The absence of one professional is noted:

Extract 8: CGM 6

1. SW: Right. I'll have to speak to her to find out what's been done. There's work been completed. Do we know what she's saying?
2. Mother: We've done err bedtime and that.

The topic invitation is accepted by Mother, but SW claims the task of checking what work has been completed, displaying the differing epistemic authority (see Chapter 8). The meeting continues in a bounded pattern of dialogue between SW and Mother, with other professionals cast and aligned as onlooking 'overhearers'.

The fifth item concerns housing, which SW directs to HO:

Extract 9: CGM 6

> SW: OK, right, number five on the plan is loss of family home. [Mother] to be supported to work with housing to address rent arrears and the eviction. Right, well, we've just heard some good news about that. Over to you [HO]. Do you want to tell us?

HO explains that agreement has been reached to manage the rent arrears and explains the processes involved:

Extract 10: CGM 6

1. HO: I don't know whether she's had the new notice yet or not. They can take a while.
2. Mother: No.
3. HO: You'll get another one with the revised amount but we need those charges off as well. I need you to bring it to me and I can help you sort that.

This is reported to the meeting as a whole (the alignment is manifest in the use of the third person to refer to the mother), followed by a shift to a second-person address. Note how in the intervening turn Mother responds as if she were addressed directly, and probably this is what prompts the shift to a second-person address, which singles out the mother as addressed more directly than the other participants.

SW next raises the topic of the youngest child starting at nursery:

Extract 11: CGM 6 (NA = nursery assistant)

1. SW: [Youngest child] is at nursery.
2. NA: Five afternoons a week.
3. SW: Happy?
4. Mother: Yeah, brilliant. He loves it. I was well shocked.
5. NA: We did a home visit to [Mother] and [child] and he's doing good.
6. SW: He was a bit iffy about it, wasn't he?
7. Mother: Yeah.

NA describes the attendance, but SW immediately returns the floor to Mother ("Happy?"). Mother's affirmative assessment is echoed by NA as professional evidence in support of the mother's positive report, denoting a joint narrative. SW joins in the success, with a display of prior knowledge of potential problems.

The elements of the CPP having been exhausted, SW invites updates, first from the health visitor:

Extract 12: CGM 6 (HV = health visitor)

1. SW: Right. Update from health please. Anything to report?
2. HV: No, not really ...

Despite initially stating there was nothing to report, there follows a long description of various interventions by HV, at the end of which she raises a concern about the children's diet:

Extract 13: CGM 6 (SN = school nurse)

1. HV: [directed to SW] When I visited last I was a little bit concerned that they weren't having a proper breakfast that particular morning. [Child] said, err. [pause] [directed to the mother] Do they get cereal before they go to school?
2. Mother: Yeah they do. They eat well.
3. HV: It was, yeah, that's true, but according to [oldest child] they'd had crisps and biscuits, so maybe that's a one-off [laughs].
4. [pause]
5. SW: [smiles and looks around the room] OK, anything from school?
6. SN: No, no concern.
7. SW: Right. Last point I think is home conditions.

On two occasions, SW avoids overt alignment with HV's expressed concerns. In the first instance, HV directs her talk initially to SW – "a little bit concerned about ... a proper breakfast" – but SW refrains from comment. There is a pause, indicating that a response was perhaps expected. HV then directs her question to Mother, who counters that the children "eat well". HV adds specificity to the complaint with information from the oldest child – "they'd had crisps and biscuits" – but then downplays the accusation with "maybe that's a one-off". After HV's turn there follows a longer pause. The lack of uptake by SW undermines HV's concern: it is not an issue to consider further. HV's point is silenced. Tacitly, agreement is reached that the children eat appropriately and HV thus relinquishes her concerns. However, note that SW does not openly question or negate HV. Professional relations remain, *prima facie*, intact. SW changes topic and invites SN to contribute and offers no report ("No, no concern"). SW signals the upcoming close of the meeting: "Last point".

The meeting continues with a more open discussion and at one point SW asks: "Has anyone else got any questions?" HV enquires about issues that were mentioned at the last meeting, and makes a suggestion about a referral to a project run by a non-governmental organisation (NGO):

Extract 14: CGM 6

1. HV: Right. The other thing that we haven't mentioned. Err someone gave me some information about [name of NGO]'s doing things for children over the age of five, and they organise outings and that.
2. SW: Oh yeah.
3. HV: We thought it might be all right. If you want a referral doing and you'd have to agree to that really, but they do all sorts of things like football and going out for days, outings as a family or something like that. So, if you want to do a referral, we thought it might be something you'd want to do?
4. Mother: Mhm, yeah.
5. HV: Something nice to do with the kids.
6. Mother: Yeah.
7. HV: I'd support that.

HV's suggestion is tentative but presented as supported by others, possibly her colleagues or others in the meeting ("we thought it might be all right"). The suggestion is not acknowledged by SW. It is not clear who is now responsible for proceeding with a referral, or if this is now an element in the CPP.

Later, in contrast, HO raises an issue about council tax:

Extract 15: CGM 6

1. HO: There's the council tax to sort.
2. SW: Who's going to do that then?
3. HO: We can do it when [Mother] brings in the new bill.
4. SW: Right.

SW immediately acknowledges the issue as the responsibility of HO, thereby endorsing the issue.

SW again summarises the current concerns and asks for further issues, but there are no responses this time. The invitation is interpreted as a closing-down statement.

Extract 16: CGM 6

> SW: Right, so, drug test is outstanding and home conditions remain a concern. Are there any other concerns that anyone feels they need to be, we need to be addressing?

A date for the next CGM is set and the meeting is closed.

This analysis displays the chair structuring the meeting and framing the debate, among other moves, by managing the turn-taking and with it the boundaries of topic development and responses by others. CGM 6 comes closest to a meeting where the chairing results in a tight management of invitations to contribute and subsequent responses. Part of this happens through a management of co-presence: particular dyads are foregrounded and during such displays the other participants are backgrounded. SW is the main conduit between the professionals individually and Mother. Cross-professional interaction does not occur, except where HV reports affiliation from others for a referral. SW manages the turn-taking in terms of separate areas of professional expertise – health, housing, school, nursery and so on. There is no exploration of his own activities. Little direct interaction is enabled between Mother and other professionals. SW occasionally challenges Mother (Extract 7). The meeting is not summarised in terms of actions or a work plan. No formal decisions are made regarding, for example, changes in how the family problems are to be managed in the future or services added to the plan. The CGM enables participants to share information, but there are few attempts to direct participants to alter their service(s). In fact, professional boundaries remain. For example, HV raises the topic of breakfast, but SW does not explore it further; and the suggested referral to the NGO is left hanging in the conversational air (neither endorsed nor refuted), despite the explicit support voiced by HV.

In terms of Bucher et al's (2016) framework, we can say that the social worker as chair is *issue framing* and *justifying* first, by structuring the meeting in terms of the elements in the CPC, and second, invitations are issued for profession-specific contributions. The chair *self-casts* as the formal chair of the meeting with little reporting, and there is no scrutiny of his own professional actions as a social worker. *Altercasting* restricts the reports to the professional remit of the participants, with careful professional management of displayed affiliations with the mother.

The chair relinquishes control of the meeting

Boden (1994, p 99) observes that informal meetings that come closer to conversational patterns of turn-taking allow for more self-selection, topical drift, overlapping turns and possibly interruptions. In contrast with CGM 6, CGM 3 shows much more variety in the exchanges, with less direct management by the chair.

The meeting starts with introductions invited by SW, accompanied by an explanation of the task ahead in a context of longer-term planning:

Extract 17: CGM 3

1. SW: Right. Thanks very much for that. Err, this, err, we've actually got a child protection conference coming up on the 15th as well, so what we'd normally do is discuss after the meeting whether we think there's a child, err, a need for a child protection plan. Err, it may, hh, maybe if we're not quite sure, if we have another meeting perhaps just before. Because I think the 15th takes us to four weeks anyway.
2. Mother: Yeah. I would say have another one then.
3. SW: Yeah. We can do that. OK. What I'm going to do is start with social worker update from the, my contacts, from the last meeting. We'll go round and get updates from everybody and erm, and then we'll look at the actions from last time.

SW raises a key decision for the meeting, whether to recommend the continuation of the CPP at the next CPC, and postponement to the next CGM. This is welcomed by Mother and accepted without discussion. SW then self-selects as the next speaker ("the social worker update") before embarking on a round of updates of the various professionals around the table.

In the exchange leading up to Extract 18, Father raises an objection to part of the social worker's report, but SW stops him from taking a turn (SW: "Father, we will come to you next"). However, Father persists, the issue being whether the child's bedroom is safe and sufficiently separate, as the father's home is a small hotel.

Extract 18: CGM 3

1. Mother: You're doing it now, when I'm trying to talk to you you just dismiss me with the hand hh, this that and the other and even your mum said–
2. Father: Just listen to her, listen to her.
3. SW: One of the things that we can come back to at the end is, quoting you [Father] about nothing being set down in stone, is we can help with that because this is going to prevent a lot of disagreement in the future.

In the extract, Mother joins in the disagreement about the safety of the bedroom, which develops subsequently into a series of disputes between Mother and Father on other topics – new decorations, the child's bedwetting, the father's lateness in collecting the children and so on. As Extract 18 illustrates, SW appears to encourage these digressions, by actively asking questions about these topics. Clearly, the meeting has been allowed to move beyond the considerations of SW's report. Eventually, the dispute becomes an argument, which SW brings to an end.

Next, SW invites the school nurse to contribute. SN reports various interventions with the child and mother, using mainly third-person references for the mother. However, there are also switches to a second-person address to check some details. The headteacher (HT) now interrupts SN:

Extract 19: CGM 3

1. SN: and also–
2. HT: Can I just ask, who's she aggressive towards, just for clarity?
3. SN: Erm, mum and grandma. She's smacked grandma across–
4. HT: Not L [sibling]?
5. Mother: No, no.
6. HT: She's not hit L?
7. Mother: No.

HT seeks permission before requesting clarification: "can I just ask … just for clarity?" (turn 2). HT is respecting professional boundaries by not challenging SN's authority and acknowledges that this is still her turn.

As the meeting develops, the exchanges become more conversational, with Mother, SW, SN and HT all speaking, interrupting and completing each other's sentences and correcting one another:

Extract 20: CGM 3

1. SW: Yeah, previously I'd put it down to her personality. She's always–
2. Mother: Been–
3. SW: Been–
4. HT: Upfront sort of thing–
5. SW: Yeah, but I've noticed a change lately that it's, she's more confrontational lately and she's non-compliant with mum's requests for err–
6. Mother: Anything!
7. SN: And she's not willing to go to school. She's not willing to get dressed.
8. Mother: It's not that she doesn't want to go to school. She just won't do what I'm asking to get her there.
9. SN: Yeah.
10. HT: That's a different issue, isn't it?

Note the affiliative work where Mother completes SW's sentence over "non-compliant with mum's requests for err" (turn 5). Mother's completion – "anything" – upgrades SW's formulation. Boundaries dissolve further, as the exchanges shift without direction between SW/Mother, SN/Mother and HT/Mother.

Over the next 50 turns, SW does not contribute. Instead the parents, SN and HT engage in wide-ranging, collaborative discussions. The parents describe a series of problems at home, and SN and HT attempt to contrast this with the child's behaviour at school and in the context of the changes in the family. During this discussion, SN proposes various interventions about which SW does not comment (referral to a paediatrician, psychological services). She also displays empathy with Mother:

Extract 21: CGM 3

1. SN: It can upset you and then.
2. Mother: Yeah.
3. SN: [Mother] described appropriate strategies, err, how she would deal with the behaviour and I think you might, I think you need a bit more intensive support.
4. Mother: Yeah.

SW does not attempt to constrain the interventions of other professionals. Instead, wide-ranging interaction is enabled between other professionals and the parents/carers, including shared narratives, with SW as an 'overhearer'. Eventually, SW brings the discussion to an end, apologising for stopping the exchange:

Extract 22: CGM 3

> SW: Can we just have a break for a moment and just erm, we've not actually quite finished with C, because we've not heard from school yet and erm, then we'll move on to L. Otherwise it gets really confusing. Is that OK?

In summary, after SW initially structures the meeting in terms of aims, topics and turns, CGM 3 becomes much more conversational in character. Four participants join in a discussion, with little direction from SW as chair. This conversation is informal, with interruptions, overlapping talk, changes of topic and displays of empathy, as well as professional assessment and advice giving. Returning to Bucher et al's framework, the *issue framing* and *justifying* by the chair took place and was initially protected by stopping Father's interruption (see Extract 18). However, the increased interventions of the other professionals mark *issue framing* by others, notably the parents, HT and SN: the boundaries between the different professional experiences are being dissolved. Experiences and concerns are co-articulated across the boundary between service users and professionals. SN and HT make suggestions for appropriate interventions, for themselves (*self-casting*) and in particular for others (*altercasting*), but this tends to be vague (for example: " I think you need a bit more intensive support" in Extract 21).

The alignment of professionals

In the second part of our data analysis, we concentrate on the alignment of specific professionals, in terms of how they engage in *self-casting* and *altercasting* and how particular issues are being framed with or without justifications being added.

The health visitor positions herself as a baby expert

In Extract 23, HV in CGM 7 invites Mother to pass the baby over. The mother has arrived late. The meeting had already started, and the mother prepares to join in. Following the invitation, HV displays knowledge of baby interaction contexts, and of this particular baby, his parents and siblings:

Extract 23: CGM 7

1. HV: Do you want to pass him over?
2. [the mother gets child out of pram]
3. HV: I'll keep him away from [SW]. [laughs – SW has a cold]
4. Mother: He'll probably just go off won't he?
5. Uncle: Do you want me to help with that? [getting baby out]
6. Mother: No, it's all right. I've been rushing. I've not got him changed yet.
7. HV: That's all right. He doesn't have to be flash for us.
8. [The mother laughs]
9. HV: There's only parents that want that.
10. [various comments to baby as he's passed to HV]
11. Researcher: Hello [Mother].
12. Mother: Hiya.
13. HV: He looks like J [sibling].
14. Mother: He is, isn't he? He's getting more and more like him.
15. Uncle: He is, yeah. He's going away from looking like his dad now, he's looking more like you.
16. Mother: Yeah, thank god!
17. [Uncle laughs]
18. SW: We've just been talking about S and ...

The exchange occurs in the frame-restoring space that precedes the interactional return to the meeting proper that was interrupted by the mother's arrival. At the end, in turn 18, SW establishes the connection to the first topic at hand.

HV's displayed alignment is with the mother and the baby. Her interactional conduct is affiliative and mother/baby-focused. She is not only supportive of Mother (by offering to hold the baby while the mother prepares to join the discussion), her authority in handling babies is also demonstrated by example. This is underscored by voiced experiential knowledge about how to handle babies (for example, "there's only parents that want that" in turn 9 and "I'll keep him away from [SW]" in turn 3), and displays of familiarity with this particular family ("he looks like J" in turn 13). The affiliative work and the voiced expertise contribute to assigning a functional role for HV in the meeting. It also anticipates the *justification* of later claims that HV can make during more serious discussion about the family, this particular baby and babies in general. There is *self-casting*, but not *altercasting*: HV positions herself in a role specific to her profession, as an expert about babies and relational with mothers.

The specialist nurse establishes a role through an offer and a permission request

Professionals may struggle to establish a role for themselves. In CGM 4, there are concerns that a pregnant mother who has learning disabilities will not be able to care for her baby. The plan is to remove the baby at birth. A number of agencies have offered support and the meeting is attempting to coordinate the different interventions. In the following extract, a nurse who specialises in learning disability seeks to establish her role.

Extract 24: CGM 4 (SpN = specialist nurse, Ad = advocate)

1. SpN: Could you clarify the plan? Learning disability is not mentioned, you know, where you need us to support. What is that? Various information and what have you.
2. SW: Was it not mentioned?
3. SpN: We need it clarifying.
4. SW: In terms of your involvement [SpN] what err, in terms of your support, what were you thinking?
5. SpN: It's if we need anything perhaps, in a more accessible format and we've got some resources, you know, to do that, to help you understand and look at things in a different way.
6. Mother: Yeah.
7. SW: Like the pre-birth stuff.
8. SpN: Ye[ah].
9. Ad: Mm.
10. SW: And maybe working alongside [support worker]?
11. SpN: I'm not saying that [support worker] hasn't got the resources but there may be [extra]–
12. Ad: [Yeah].
13. SpN: ones and we could team up with that.
14. SW: I mean, yeah. If I put as well that you're to offer support to [Mother] and for any professional to come to you when it's necessary?
15. SpN: Mm, yeah.
16. SW: Because, erm, you know for whatever we're communicating and I know we've had stuff off you before about court process and that. Should I put that one?
17. SpN: Yeah.
18. SW: Leave it open?
19. SpN: Yeah.

SpN introduces the issue of her specific expertise by seeking clarification. She notes the absence of "learning disabilities" in the CPP (turn 1) and requests clarity about her involvement, by formulating an implicit offer (turn 1: "where you need us to support?"). At this point, she does not (as yet) have an established position in the meeting and her role had not been mentioned so far. At the beginning, she introduced herself as "I'm [name], community nurse with disabilities working with Mother" (note the combination, as part of a formal introduction, of having an organisational role and appealing to a working relationship with the mother). In response to the chair's question about what she has in mind, SpN identifies particular resources that she can make available – diagnostic consultation tools (turn 5: "if we need anything perhaps, in a more accessible format and we've got some resources ... to help you understand and look at things in a different way"). *Self-casting* is apparent in this turn, but SpN is careful not to challenge the role of the support workers in turn 11. *Altercasting* occurs here in the form of stressing complementarity – "I'm not saying that [support worker] hasn't got the resources but there may be [extra]" (in turn 11) – and an offer to team up with the support worker (in turn 13). In response, SW adjusts the CPP to include a task item, with a circumstantial role in it, that is, that others may come to SpN "when it's necessary" (turn 14) and "for whatever we're communicating" (turn 16). At the same time, the value of SpN's involvement is underlined in turn 16 by SW's *altercasting* reference to useful services that were provided on earlier occasions ("I know we've had stuff off you before", turn 16). Note particularly the epistemic endorsement inherent in the use of "I know".

A few minutes later, SpN seeks to extend her role by asking to be involved in a planned home visit:

Extract 25: CGM 4 (CPSW = child protection social worker, Mw = midwife)

1. SW: Right, so you'll see [name] next week [pointing to the midwife present in the room] and then you'll be seeing [name of allocated midwife], OK?
2. Mother: Yeah.
3. SW: Lovely.
4. SpN: Can I be at that visit as well?
5. Mw: Yeah.
6. SpN: Thank you.
7. SW: OK, so if I put on here as well then [SpN] you'll support with appointments as well.

8. SpN: Yeah.
9. CPSW: That's better, isn't it?
10. SW: Yeah. It is. OK so, all right, err, so the plan was, the local authority were going to seek legal advice, which we still are doing, OK.

SpN makes a bid for an extended role, offering to accompany Mw on the visit (turn 4: "Can I be at that visit as well?"). It is voiced as a request for permission, but fairly directly ("Can I ..." rather than "Could I suggest that I ..."). The offer is not motivated in the interaction, but accepted straight away by Mw (turn 5), followed by an on-record role addition in the CPP (turn 7, SW: "OK so if I put on here as well then [SpN], you'll support with appointments as well"). Although not mentioned in the interaction, the health remit of the visit probably justifies this. In Bucher et al's terms, an *issue* has been framed successfully as locatable within the remit of a profession without the need for a *justification*. Note how the support worker is left outside the scope of the planned visit.

The headteacher takes over, joined in this by the school nurse

In Extract 26, we return to CGM 3, which we characterised earlier as an instance of a more informally conducted CGM, in which the social worker appears to relinquish some of the control over the interaction. Both parents are present. The topic raised is the daughter's school attendance, which is framed straight away by the headteacher (HT) in the opening turn as "a different issue".

Extract 26: CGM 3

1. HT: That's a different issue, isn't it?
2. Mother: Yeah. It's not that she doesn't want to come to school. She really enjoys school. I mean she didn't want to wear pinafores anymore so I went and bought a skirt, you know. She's quite, err, you know, it's difficult, you know, just getting her to do simple things. She's dressed and then you turn around and you think you're ready to go out of the door and she's, you know, taken something off or she's, I mean we actually, we were late and I had to say it was due to her behaviour, you know, due to this again! I mentioned to you didn't I that she's, you know, late because, you know, a few–
3. HT: She was–
4. SN: Is she like that with you [Father]?

5. Father: I don't. Erm, I'm going to be honest. I don't have to take her out. I mean I try to get to church sometimes but, she likes getting dressed. She has her own wardrobe and she'll hang stuff up, you know, with a bit of direction, you know, she hangs it up herself. And, erm, I got her some pyjamas recently she, I said get dressed and granddad came over and we went to the park and had a really nice time. And then she came back and she wanted to put her pyjamas on, and she does all that herself but obviously I've not got to get anywhere.
6. HT: There's no time pressure.
7. Father: There's no time pressure and I'm being upfront and honest about it.
8. SN: Yeah.
9. Mother: When I mention this, school say her behaviour's fine and, but, I've had this a few times.
10. Father: I'm surprised.
11. Mother: You said she'd been in trouble at school, didn't you?
12. Father: She said something the other day to myself and granddad.
13. HT: It's teeny tiny stuff that really. It's like you're describing two different children here.
14. Father: Yeah.
15. Mother: I think if it's not sorted out just now then school will start to see because it's all new, isn't it?
16. HT: I think it's an issue about boundaries.
17. Mother: And I think she will start to show it at school eventually. It needs–
18. HT: Well, we don't know, do we? All we can say is what's presented at the minute and perhaps because, in my experience, when there's a disparity in behaviour, it largely comes down to where the child feels there's clear boundaries and where there's not. Now in school, there are no issues at all, about behaviour. She's fully compliant. She doesn't challenge and some do. In year R [reception class]! They do [laughs]. We have a naughty cushion, believe me and it's used. She's not displaying that behaviour.
19. Mother: She's said a few times that she's been a shooting star.
20. HT: Absolutely.
21. Mother: She's been on the other star.
22. HT: Yeah. And in fact she seems to buy into the reward systems, so I think that needs mentioning because to me it raises questions about boundaries and her routines and all those things that young children really need.

Mother's observation (turn 2) that it is difficult getting her daughter to do simple things, is contradicted by Father's reported experiences (turn 5). Initially SN, having just interrupted HT, passes the conversational floor to Father in turn 4 ("Is she like that with you?"). The interaction from here onwards is pushed forward by HT and Mother's contributions. HT engages in affiliative work in turn 6, agreeing with Father's observation that the absence of time pressure when she's with him may mean it is easier to get things done. The assessment is echoed by Father, in turn 7. Mother, however, persists in noting the difficulties she experiences (turn 9) and shifts the topic to an incident at school that was reported to her by Father (he confirms the report in the next turn). In response, HT minimises the incident at school (turn 13: "It's teeny tiny stuff that really"), while advancing a diagnosis of different behaviour at school, compared with at home ("it's like you're describing two different children here"). Next, the mother insists that the problem needs attending to (turn 15). At this point, HT volunteers a more explicit diagnosis and explanation (turn 16: "I think it's an issue about boundaries"), while Mother repeats the prediction that the difficulties will soon show at school (turn 17). HT disagrees and elaborates on the effects of clear boundaries in turn 18: the child has no issues at the moment at school and she is compared positively with children who do display problematic behaviours. In turns 19 to 22, HT and Mother continue to disagree. While HT expresses agreement in turn 20 with the child's self-report as a "shooting star", Mother rephrases the characterisation as "being on the other star". In turn 22, HT elaborates her own positive perceptions and continues to pursue her disagreement with Mother: "she seems to buy into the rewards system", a point that needs to be stressed ("I think that needs mentioning") in support of her diagnosis about the importance of boundaries. The point about boundaries is now cast generically as "all those things that young children really need".

In the extract, HT takes the lead in pursuing a particular categorisation that contradicts the perceptions and opinions of Mother. SN joins in, twice – once to allocate the floor to Father, and a second time expressing agreement (turn 8). The social worker-as-chair is notably absent. HT displays experiential knowledge of children at school and of pedagogical principles. The implication from this exchange is that the problem is the mother, rather than the daughter. There is no professional *self-casting* or *altercasting* in this extract, in the sense of explicit attributions or claims to expertise. The exchange is *issue-focused*, oriented to diagnosis (Mother is the problem) and, by implication, solutions. *Self-casting* is implicit in the voicing of issue-focused expertise. Arguably, this counts as a form of *self-casting* beyond one's professional remit, as HT appears to be pursuing the questioning role that typically belongs to the social worker-as-chair, thus directing the meeting's agenda.

Discussion and conclusion

In summary, our analysis has examined interaction in CGMs that displays issues raised by the research reviewed earlier in this chapter. Essentially, we found little evidence of professionals unable to communicate their concerns in CGMs, but the interactional management of frames and boundaries suggests that everyday multi-agency coordination can be compromised.

We first note again the interdependency of the two notions of 'frame': framing issues and that of the interactional frame in which to accomplish this. The capacity to frame issues in relation to a profession depends on the alignments that are afforded and effectively enacted within the interactional frame of a CGM, understood as an activity type. Especially, the interactional management by the chair of the meeting has been noted as determining the scope – or lack of it – for boundary maintaining/dissolving cross-professional engagement, and hence also the possibilities for framing particular issues from the perspective of more than one professional angle. The chair's alignment to the activity-specific frame of a CGM comes with affordances and constraints for the alignments of the other professionals attending.

Second, our analysis suggests that more formal, tightly controlled meetings result in less scope for cross-professional dialogue. Professional worlds are allocated turns, but they largely exist alongside each other. The chair determines uptake. This is a form of gatekeeping vis-à-vis the agenda of the meeting, the CPC and interagency relevance. Tighter chairing restricts the dialogue to the chair, one professional and the parent/carer in the foreground, while others are backgrounded to the position of overhearers. The practice is about 'being informed', rather than 'displaying an active stake in'. A practice of not interfering with professionals' discretion may well come with the expectation that one's own territory is left to oneself. In contrast, it would appear that a less tightly controlling chair provides more scope for cross-professional engagement. In CGMs that are more informally conducted, tentative or hesitant contributions are encouraged by the chair and professionals other than the chair may develop the agenda. In all meetings, there is politeness; professionals are careful not to tread on the toes of other professionals, as might be interactionally expected. Furthermore, it is not clear to what extent CGM practice enables an actively debated, jointly agreed plan, especially as some decisions are made elsewhere and merely reported to the meeting. How do CGM's fare in terms of managing (dissolving?) the boundaries between separate, autonomous organisations and the requirements of effective multi-agency work? Do CGMs provide an explicit script to which all participants are bound? While the more informal CGMs may well foster more interprofessional exchange, this is still largely left to chance without directing participants towards a strong interagency plan. The procedures for the latter would need to direct the various agencies to change their work practices, inevitably challenging professional discretion.

Third, we have considered whether there are hierarchies between professions in the data corpus/extracts. Bucher et al (2016, pp 515–16) contend that framing enables high-status professionals to downplay challenges by using the language of authority associated with their status, and presenting their preferences as the 'natural' order of things, whereas lower-status groups promote boundary revision by self-casting as capable but under-recognised and by problematising higher-status groups as barriers to more open boundaries. Given the tendency for the social worker on the case to chair the CGM and the activity-specific purpose of reviewing the CPP, the other professionals may be ceding to the social worker by default. We have seen the social worker closing down the health visitor's suggestion for referral. Professionals may be reluctant to be seen to disagree with the chair in front of the parent/carer. On the whole, the exchanges do not appear to be competitive and where a professional remit is claimed by reference to capacity (such as the specialist nurse), this is done carefully. In the particular instance, it was voiced as the absence of a role in the meeting thus far. However, while differences in status are not apparent in our corpus, this may well be the case when high-status professionals such as doctors, lawyers or psychiatrists attend the CGM.

A further question is: what constitutes an 'agenda-grabbing move' in the context of a CGM? Do particular professions have an impact where others do not, because they are routinely better adapted to the requirements of interprofessional meetings? A fourth, related point therefore is that we have observed how a key interactional move is for the professional to affiliate with the parent/carer. Such displays of affiliation may count as strong bids for authority and power in the meeting (compare the takeover by the headteacher and school nurse discussed in Extract 26 and the health visitor's 'baby interaction' analysed in Extract 23).

In conclusion, while this study is not an evaluation of the effectiveness of CGMs, our analysis shows that the CGM certainly enables information sharing by those who are present. However, in terms of promoting effective multi-agency collaboration, we have indicated that interactional and organisational constraints mean that the CGM does not necessarily direct participants to adhere to definitive decision-making processes.

Note

[1] We thank the researcher who collected the data, gave us access to this archive and commented on a draft of this chapter.

References

Appleton, J. and Stanley N. (2008) 'Safeguarding children – everyone's responsibility', *Child Abuse Review*, 17: 1–5.

Asmuβ, B. and Svennevig, J. (2009) 'Meeting talk', *Journal of Business Communication*, 46(1): 3–22.

Boden, D. (1994) *The Business of Talk: Organizations in Action*, Cambridge: Polity Press.

Bucher, S., Chreim, S., Langley, A. and Reay, T. (2016) 'Contestation about collaboration: Discursive boundary work among professions', *Organization Studies*, 37(4): 497–522.

Calder, M. (2001) 'Core groups: A review of the literature', *Child Care in Practice*, 7(1): 17–32.

Calder, M. and Horwath, J. (1999) *Working for Children in the Child Protection Register: An Inter-Agency Guide*, Aldershot: Ashgate.

Calder, M. and Horwath, J. (2000) 'Challenging passive partnerships with parents and children in the core group forum: A framework for a proactive approach', *Child and Family Social Work*, 5(3): 267–77.

Collins, J. and Slembrouck, S. (2009) 'Goffman and globalization: frame, footing and scale in migration-connected multilingualism', in J. Collins, S. Slembrouck and M. Baynham (eds) *Globalization and Language in Contact: Scale, Migration and Communicative Practice*, London: Continuum, pp 19–41.

Cummins, I. (2018) *Poverty, Inequality and Social Work: The Impact of Neo-Liberalism and Austerity Politics on Welfare Provision*, Bristol: Policy Press.

DfE (Department for Education) (2018) *Working Together to Safeguard Children: A Guide to Inter-Agency Working to Safeguard and Promote the Welfare of Children*, London: HMSO.

Garfinkel, H. (1986) *Ethnomethodological Studies of Work*, London: Routledge & Kegan Paul.

Goffman, E. (1974) *Frame AnalysisL An Essay on the Organisation of Social Experience*, Harmondsworth: Penguin.

Goffman, E. (1981) 'Footing', in *Forms of Talk*, Oxford: Basil Blackwell, pp 124–59.

Hall, C. and Slembrouck, S. (2001) 'Parent participation in social work meetings – the case of child protection conferences', *European Journal of Social Work*, 4(2): 143–60.

Harlow, E. and Shardlow, S. (2006) 'Safeguarding children: Challenges to the effective operation of core groups', *Child and Family Social Work*, 11: 65–72.

Horwath, J. (2013) *Child Neglect: Planning and Intervention*, Basingstoke: Palgrave.

Laming, H. (2003) *The Victoria Climbié Inquiry: Report of an Inquiry by Lord Laming*, London: Department of Health and Home Office.

Lees, A. (2017) 'Facts with feeling: Social workers' experiences of sharing information across team and agency borders to safeguard children', *Child and Family Social Work*, 22(2): 892–903.

Mittler, H. (1997) 'Core groups: A key focus for child protection training', *Social Work Education*, 16(2): 77–91.

Munro, E. (2009) 'Managing societal and institutional risk in child protection', *Risk Analysis*, 29(7): 1015–23.

Munro, E. (2011) *The Munro Report of Child Protection: Final Report: A Child Centred System*, London: Department for Education.

Parton, N. (1985) *The Politics of Child Abuse*, Basingstoke: Macmillan.

Parton, N. (2014a) *The Politics of Child Protection: Contemporary Developments and Future Directions*, Basingstoke: Palgrave Macmillan.

Parton, N. (2014b) 'Social work, child protection and politics: Some critical and constructive reflections', *British Journal of Social Work*, 44(7): 2042–56.

Reder, P. and Duncan, S. (2003) 'Understanding communication in child protection networks', *Child Abuse Review*, 12(2): 82–100.

Slembrouck, S. and Hall, C. (2014) 'Boundary work', in C. Hall, K. Juhila, M. Matarese and C. van Nijnnatten (eds) *Analysing Social Work Communication: Discourse in Practice*, London: Routledge, pp 61–78.

Slembrouck, S., Hall, C. and Broadhurst, K. (forthcoming) *Communication in Home Visits: Support and Surveillance in Social and Health Care*, Cambridge: Cambridge University Press.

Snow, D. and Bedford, R. (1988) 'Ideology, frame resonance and participant mobilization', *International Social Movement Research*, 1: 197–217.

Svennevig, J. (2012) 'The agenda as resource for topic introduction in workplace meetings', *Discourse Studies*, 14(1): 53–66.

Thompson, K. (2016) *Strengthening Child Protection: Sharing Information in Multi-Agency Settings*, Bristol: Policy Press.

White, S., Hall, C. and Peckover, S. (2009) 'The descriptive tyranny of the common assessment framework: Technologies of categorization and professional practice in child welfare', *British Journal of Social Work*, 39: 1197–217.

5

Alignment and service user participation in low-threshold meetings with people using drugs

Suvi Raitakari, Johanna Ranta and Sirpa Saario

Introduction

Since the 1980s, service user participation[1] has been a widely discussed ideal among politicians, health and social care professionals and service users themselves (for example, Velasco, 2001; Kvarnström et al, 2012; Finset, 2017). Service user movements have highlighted participation as an issue of freedom of choice, human rights and self-determination (for example, Cook and Jonikas, 2002; Raitakari et al, 2015; Lakhani et al, 2018; see also Chapter 1). In general, the concept signifies that service users play an important role in directing health and social care service systems as well as their personal service pathways. Additionally, service users are portrayed as evaluators, informants, consumers, decision makers, experts-by-experience or collaborators in professional encounters.

Western policies emphasise that services and multi-agency collaboration should be pursued in a way that strengthens service user participation (for example, Thomas, 2010; Fox and Reeves, 2015; see also Chapter 1). However, there is conflicting knowledge on how this aim is actually realised in frontline practices of health and social care (for example, Kortteisto et al, 2018; see also Chapter 1). Multi-agency collaboration is a challenging way to realise participation because it requires various competencies, such as the capacity to express oneself, to consider the stances of other parties and to cross potential barriers, such as poor communication and lack of respect (Hopwood and Edwards, 2017; Naldemirci et al, 2018).

In this chapter, service user participation is examined through interprofessional interactions in multi-agency meetings in Finnish low-threshold substance use services. The aim is to scrutinise interactional practices that strive to collaboratively strengthen the service user participation of vulnerable groups.[2] Hence, our approach differs from previous studies that have constructed various conceptualisations of service user participation[3] (Arnstein, 1969; Hickey and Kipping, 1998) or barriers in service pathways that service users experience (for example, Borg et al, 2009). Some studies have examined service user participation in multi-agency working exclusively in theoretical terms (Fox and Reeves, 2015), in conjunction with service user interviews (Thomas, 2010; Kvarnström et al, 2012) or through analysing interactional data from multi-agency meetings (Juhila et al, 2015; Koprowska, 2016), as is done in this chapter.

Collaboration requires sufficient sharing of institutional agendas and decisions, and aligning with one another's views and aspirations in interactions. Collaborative participation can thus be distinguished from participation that is based on acting as an individual consumer or advocate within services. In the analysis section of this chapter, how collaborative service user participation is bound to particular interactional activities is considered, especially alignment. More precisely, it examines: (a) how the participants of multi-agency meetings align themselves and others as collaborators; and (b) how service user participation is thus potentially realised in agenda setting and decision making via alignment during meeting interactions.

The chapter proceeds in the following way. First, it introduces the context and standpoints of vulnerable clients. Second, it explains how acts of alignment are approached as indicators of collaboration and the related possibilities for service user participation. Before the analysis and discussion and conclusion sections, it elaborates on the use of data and the process of analysis. The focus throughout the chapter is on 'doing' collaborative service user participation while setting the agenda and making decisions in low-threshold meetings with people using drugs. The multi-agency meetings studied are *ad hoc* review meetings in the sense that they are arranged when they are deemed beneficial for managing the service user's service pathways. They are not routine fixtures in the service organisations, as weekly team meetings would be (see Chapter 2 for organisational routines and integration ceremonies).

Low-threshold substance use services and vulnerable status

Substance use services in Finland have undergone a major shift towards increasing multi-agency collaboration and a stronger drive towards service user participation. For example, the law on substance abuse (41/1986, §9) states the importance of collaboration between various services, ranging from health and social care to housing and employment authorities. Furthermore, the obligation to enhance service user participation is articulated in the policy documents of the Ministry of Social Affairs and Health (2009) and the National Institute for Health and Welfare. This has increased opportunities for people using drugs to become more powerful actors in shifting institutional contexts (see Ranta, 2020).

However, the illegality of drug use and its everyday risks, along with discrimination and marginal societal status, may limit service users' opportunities and competency to act as active and independent decision makers in their own lives. It is known that people in marginalised positions 'may have such severe experiences of oppressive and violating encounters with other people and societal institutions that their self-trust and autonomy competencies have gradually diminished. Feminist scholars talk about reduced self-trust in these kinds of circumstances' (Juhila et al, 2020, p 3; see also Dodds, 2000; McLeod and Sherwin, 2000). Potential violations of one's autonomy and low self-trust may also have a significant influence on one's ability to act as a collaborator in multi-agency meetings. Accordingly, the assumption is that active drug use creates constraints for assuming a position of strength in multi-agency meetings, and when aspiring to collaborative service user participation, these constraints need to be taken into consideration.

A weakened ability to function also makes people using drugs structurally vulnerable (McNeil et al, 2016), as they can face different kinds of 'treatment barriers' in health and social care (Notley et al, 2012). Low-threshold services, which are the context of this study, are one way to overcome obstacles in receiving support from the 'mainstream' service system. These services reach citizens who are hard to reach in other health and social care services (Notley et al, 2012). The concept 'low-threshold' also refers to client-centred and easily accessible services with no bureaucratic obstacles or a requirement for abstinence. It is assumed that multi-agency working between low-threshold services and other service providers can promote participation and mitigate the vulnerable position of people with multiple service needs. For instance, low-threshold services can operate as gateways to services with stricter requirements, thus enabling appropriate transitions in personal service pathways. In sum, the upcoming analysis makes visible the possibilities and limitations of collaborative service user participation among people whose competence is compromised, whose societal status is vulnerable and who have difficult life experiences, including rejections by welfare services.

Service user participation – shifting alignments

The presumption of the analysis is that taking a particular position in interactions may either advance or hinder the degree of service user participation realised in collaboration. Thus, collaborative participation is understood as a negotiable, 'elusive' and fluid process where participants take various shifting positions, such as 'teller' or 'knower'. Participation also appears when participants align with others to get acceptance for their stances or to influence others' views. When collaborative participation takes place, alignment occurs in such a manner that service users can, at least to some extent, obtain active and valued positions in interactions, as well as influence agenda setting and/or decision making. Alignment and mutuality can be seen as core elements of collaboration (Edwards, 2017).

From this it follows that collaboration and related opportunities for service user participation are understood as acts of *alignment*. According to Juhila et al (2014, p 119), alignment refers to 'mutual cooperation among professionals and service users, where both are oriented to similar institutional tasks and interactional agendas'. Hall and Matarese (2014, p 85; ref. Stivers, 2008, pp 34–5) define alignment as 'displays of support of the hearer and endorsement of the teller's conveyed stance'. Affiliation is thus *emotionally realised alignment*, for example by displaying empathy (Steensig, 2013, pp 1–2; Kykyri et al, 2019, p 3). Affiliation entails reciprocity, engagement and intersubjectivity. The definition of the concept of 'alignment' used in this text comprises affiliation, that is, an 'affective level of cooperation' (Stivers et al, 2011, p 20; see also Stivers, 2008, p 53; Kykyri et al, 2019, p 3).

One way to express alignment is to position oneself and others in a particular manner in an interaction. *Positioning* is a discursive achievement, which is constrained and made possible by moral expectations and cultural discourses perceived relevant by the participants. A position is a moral stance that includes expectations of one's rights, restrictions and responsibilities as an actor in the interaction (Wetherell, 1998; Selseng and Ulvik, 2018). Language use reveals how one is positioning oneself and others in a given interactional situation. For instance, one may take a position of a 'bystander', 'leader', 'expert' or 'accused one'. When analysing the data, it is identified markers, such as positive, minimal responses like 'yeah', that display potential (emotional) support for the service user's or professional's viewpoint. The service user may strengthen their position as a collaborator by going along and supporting the professional's views, or the professional equally may support the service user's position by going along with the service user's views. In general, markers of aligned positioning make the interaction flow in a like-minded cooperative direction at the given moment.

Data and the process of analysis

The data in this study comprise nine audio-recorded naturally occurring multi-agency meetings from two Finnish low-threshold services targeted at people using drugs.[4] In the first setting, an outpatient clinic (seven meetings), the focus is on comprehensive psychosocial support. This includes both one-to-one supportive discussions and collaboration with other services, such as housing support, adult social work and psychiatric services. The other setting, a floating support project (two meetings), aims to reduce individual and societal risks due to drug use and increase the participation of people injecting drugs. The focus is especially on housing and avoiding the risk of homelessness. Hence, the work entails doing home visits and collaborating particularly with the local housing company, adult social work and the Social Insurance Institution.

In both research settings, a common way for collaboration to occur is to arrange multi-agency meetings whenever they are deemed useful to steer the service user's often-complex life situation and service pathways. The meetings involve several institutional tasks, such as reviewing the service user's current (problematic) situation, making service choices and preparing for the service user's transition to a new service or housing arrangement. The themes discussed are related to drug use, housing, financial matters, mental health and other everyday issues. The participants know each other in advance – the low-threshold professionals especially have well-established relationships with the service users. When the participants know each other, the meetings have more informal features, for example turn-taking more often resembles everyday conversation (see Chapter 2). The meetings do not have a named chair with a clear role to steer the meeting encounter or a strict, pre-written agenda (which differs for example from Care Programme Approach meetings in England; see Chapter 7). As a result, the participants themselves can select the next appropriate speaker and potentially change the topic (see Chapter 2), hence, in the following analysis, agenda and topic are used as parallel terms.

According to Peräkylä and Ruusuvuori (2007), it is crucial that participation is realised in each phase of the service user encounter. They present five different components of patient participation, including patients' 'contribution to direction of action', 'influence in the definition of the agenda of the consultation' and 'influence in decision-making' (2007, pp 167–9). Other research argues that agenda setting, decision making and choice are crucial, yet complex elements of service user participation (Matthias et al, 2012; Juhila et al, 2015).

In the first phase of the analysis, using the ATLAS.ti program, the whole dataset was worked with to code all instances where either *the agenda for the meeting* or *decisions concerning the service user's current or future situation* were discussed. The coding confirmed that the structure of the meetings was not linear but 'spiral', due to their informal nature (see Chapter 2 for structures of meetings). This spiral informality was manifested in, for example, shifting topics that were re-discussed several times during each meeting. It also emerged that the position of the leader moved between professionals according to the topic under discussion. The professional who took the lead had the greatest expertise concerning the particular domain. In addition, instead of distinct 'decision-making' sequences, decisions could be made during different phases of the meetings. Decision-making sequences refer to instances where participants concluded everyday matters, such as when the service user could fill in social benefit forms or what topics would be addressed next. Living arrangements or future service choices were also negotiated. Sometimes it was left open whether a decision had actually been made, in that the decision was tentative and partial in nature (see Chapter 2 for a distinction between decisions and the decision-making process).

Ultimately, it was discovered that service user participation was chiefly accomplished by setting the agenda and making decisions collaboratively. The meetings allowed and required the participants to align in striving for collaborative service user participation. It seemed that in these particular low-threshold settings, professionals were committed to strengthening service users' abilities to act as collaborators during the meetings and thus potentially mitigate their vulnerable positions. Service users did not participate in the meetings by, for example, 'exiting' the services, complaining or taking the position of a 'consumer' (for the distinction between exit and voice in participation, see Pickard et al, 2006). The professionals' drive to align with the service user and their support for collaboration can be recognised from expressions where, for instance, they:

- accept the service user's initiative regarding the topic;
- ask the service user's opinion regarding practical arrangements;
- express affiliation.

Examples of these discursive practices are discussed later in the chapter.

In the second phase of the analysis, four theoretically relevant data extracts were analysed by utilising the analytical concept of 'alignment'. We concentrated especially on the discursive markers of alignment as they are displayed in the data. In addition, we paid attention to professional and institutional factors that may set limits and explain particular types of alignment, and through that, participation. The first two extracts display agenda setting and the latter two show decision-making sequences.

Analysis: doing collaborative service user participation while setting the agenda and making decisions

Service users cannot be active by themselves in institutional settings, as an interactional space and encouragement given by the professionals is required (see Ranta, 2020). Thus, service users' abilities to influence the meeting agenda and decision making are dependent on professionals' interactional competence and practices. However, service users' competencies and interactional moves are significant factors that influence how professionals conduct their institutional task-based work. Thus, the following analysis approaches service user participation as an interactional achievement.

Defining the agenda and the course of interaction

Extract 1

> Adam is currently homeless and has been visiting the outpatient clinic for several years. Before the multi-agency meeting, Adam met the outpatient clinic's social worker, and they discussed how to proceed with his housing issues. Adam (A), the municipal adult social worker (ASW), the outpatient psychiatrist (OP) and the outpatient social worker (OSW) are having a meeting concerning Adam's situation. The data extract is from the beginning of the encounter.

1. OP: How are you, Adam?
2. A: It's like from one state to another. My mood kind of worsened when I saw my big brother after a really long time when he got back from [name of the place where he had completed national civilian service], and he told me about this thing that I remembered when

I was five or six years old, that rape thing that I remembered. So, he told me that it wasn't a one-off case. That it happened when I was three years old, but it was another person at that time. This person was my cousin.
3. OP: How much older was s/he then than you, this cousin?
4. A: About 10 years.
5. OP: Yeah, okay, a definite act then. So, how are you dealing with it now? Have you been thinking about it a lot, or how?
6. A: Well, I mean, occasionally some things have come into my mind, but I don't want to get into it.
7. OP: It's completely okay. We're dealing with present-day issues here.
8. A: Present-day issues.
9. OP: Just one thing, Adam. We raised your Concerta dose ((medication for ADHD)) last time we met. Did you notice any changes in your condition?
10. A: Well, I mean, yeah. I can function better in the evenings.
11. OP: Good, so it worked as it was meant to.
12. A: Yeah.
13. OP: Good, that's good. So we can probably orient to your social]
14. OSW: [Yeah, and to your everyday life, how it's going. Yeah. Last time we talked about this homelessness issue with ((name of the landlord of local housing company)). Adam hasn't had a flat to live in for six months, a bit more than six months, right?
15. A: Mm.
16. OSW: It was very moving when you described what it means when you're trying to find a place to stay at night.
17. A: Yeah. Few nights back, I slept in an accessible toilet at the railway station, as I couldn't find a place to sleep, and my phone didn't work either. So, I slept there.
18. OSW: There would certainly be places that are more comfortable.
19. A: Yeah. There would. (5) A home of my own would be the best, but.
20. OSW: There's this contradiction or difficulty then, as you said that it would be a bit terrifying for you to live alone?
21. A: Yeah. I'm afraid that I'm kind of losing control. And then my own home, especially keeping it clean and maintaining the things and stuff, it's a lot of trouble.
22. ASW: I agree with that, we have tried that.
23. OP: Right.
24. ASW: And already back then, you were also afraid of moving in on your own. And then it turned out that it didn't, that you couldn't handle it, living alone.

The OP uses the opening turn to ask Adam how he is doing, encouraging him to speak. In this way, he invites lay experience talk and shows that he is interested in Adam's meaning making. Adam is positioned as a teller with relevant knowledge and experience that will be heard first in the meeting. Adam aligns with these expectations and the agenda by describing his feelings and traumatic childhood incidents. He expresses competence in narrating his experiences in a multiprofessional interaction and by directing the agenda towards therapeutic issues. The OP supports this by asking for additional information (turn 3) and validates Adam's account by stating that what had happened really was a rape, "an act" (turn 5). He also expresses emotional alignment by showing that he cares and is thus interested in hearing how Adam is coping with the burden. The turn-taking fits well with institutional-professional expectations of a psychiatrist's position and expertise. Next, Adam states that he wants to change the agenda (turn 6). The OP aligns in an empathic way with him and accepts the topic change (turn 7). He gives Adam the right to set boundaries concerning discussions about his life.

The topic shift is indicated when the topic of "present-day issues" (turn 7) is formulated by the OP. Adam aligns with it by repeating the new agenda (turn 8). The chosen topic seems to fit all participants. It can be assumed that handling present-day issues is in line with the institutional task of the clinic and the current meeting. The OP continues in the leading position by choosing medication as the next topic of discussion (turn 9). From there, an alignment sequence starts (turns 10–13), during which both Adam and the OP express positivity, and they support each other's views and interpretations. They both have privileged access to psychiatric knowledge, yet only Adam has personally experienced the medication change. This makes him a valuable informant and collaborator (see Chapters 7 and 8 concerning epistemic rights), and he is thus capable of interacting according to the expectations related to this position. Next the OP gives space to social issues by suggesting a topic change (turn 13).

The OSW overlaps and takes a turn immediately; interpreting that topic change back to everyday issues requires her to take the lead (turn 14). She reports Adam's homelessness history, which she verifies with Adam by giving him an opportunity to reflect on her description. Adam seems to accept the OSW's interpretation with a minimal response (turn 15) and she continues by displaying alignment and expressing emotional support for Adam's demanding life situation (turns 16 and 18). She also shows that she remembers and values the stories Adam has told (turn 16). These interactional acts make it possible for Adam, first, to take a position of a valuable reporter of his homelessness history (turn 17), and second, to position himself as a service user who can express his own wishes (turn 19).

It is notable that the social workers do not support Adam's position as 'dreamer of a home of his own'. Instead, they choose to shift the topic to the difficulties anticipated in Adam having his own home. Both the social workers and Adam jointly make a problem formulation concerning the difficulties of living independently (turns 19–24). Adam expresses a "but" in his wish for independent living (turn 19), and thus creates an opening to discuss the difficulties related to his housing. The social workers align with this change from hopeful future talk to problem talk. In turn, Adam accepts the social workers' interpretations of his contradictory feelings, difficulties and fears and is competent in describing them in detail (turn 21). A strong marker of alignment is the ASW's agreement with Adam's problem formulation (turn 22). Turn-taking also reveals how the social workers have previous knowledge of problematic issues. Hence, they can share the difficult experiences with Adam and take the position of 'problem formulators' (see Chapters 7 and 8 concerning epistemic rights). Adam is jointly positioned as someone with personal difficulties that hinder him from exiting homelessness. The positioning in this trouble-talk sequence may reflect the social workers' institutional task to recognise potential risks in the service user's life, and the expectation for the service user to be open about his troubles.

The extract implies a degree of collaborative working between the professionals and the service user, who is in a strong position to make topic changes and problem formulations. The professionals align with the service user by accepting his views and showing emotional support, while the service user aligns with topic changes made by the professionals as well as their interpretations concerning his constraints. It can be concluded that participation is realised through mutual alignment and collaborative agenda-setting practices, yet the professionals take the leading position in selecting topics as part of their professional-institutional roles.

Extract 2

> Alex has experienced long-term and recurrent homelessness during the course of his life. Before the multi-agency meeting was arranged, he had just learnt that he had been allocated a flat by the Housing Support Unit. Alex (A), the outpatient clinic's social worker

(OSW) and the housing support worker (HSW) are discussing Alex's situation together.

1. HSW: We ((A and HSW)) talked a bit about the thoughts that have come up about getting a flat from ((a name of the Housing Support Unit)), and I was thinking if you'd like to tell ((us)) about your own thoughts now.
2. A: Well, no. (4) Perhaps it causes a bit of pressure about do I manage to keep it. Not major pressure, just some thoughts.
3. HSW: So, it's more like being worried about whether you can do it.
4. A: Yeah.
5. OSW: Do you remember when the last time was that you had a flat of your own? It was probably there (2). Did you live in ((name of the neighbourhood)) back then?
6. A: Yeah.
7. OSW: It was quite a number of years ago.
8. A: It was, yeah.
9. OSW: Do you remember how long?
10. A: Four or five ((years)) ago, possibly.
11. OSW: Yeah, since then, you've been homeless and lived in all kinds of housing arrangements. I checked; I tried to search on our computer for the kinds of issues there have been, and I checked that you visited us here in the outpatient clinic for the first time in 2002. This probably describes, how would you say it, like, the difficulty or complexity of your situation from the point of view of the authorities, probably not your own view, but for the authorities. Alex's treatment is being tossed back and forth within our services ((refers to the NGO)) as well. And you've occasionally been in ((the outpatient clinic for people using alcohol)), and occasionally in here ((outpatient clinic for people using drugs)), and it's like 'eeny meeny miny moe', which place is responsible for your treatment, and who is responsible in the end. It's been something like that, hasn't it?
12. A: Yeah.
13. OSW: And you've occasionally asked if you could move to the ((outpatient clinic for people using alcohol)) and then they've moved you back here. So, this is, I sort of wished that ((name of municipal's commissioner service)) was here, to see that this kind of fragmentation of substance use treatment is happening here ((in the NGO)) as well. Even though we are part of the same organisation, we are still searching for the ((right)) place for the person to be treated. Somehow, there has always been this question of what your primary intoxicant is.

14. A: Yeah.
15. OSW: And has the drug use always been secondary and the alcohol use is primary? Isn't that how it is?
16. A: It has been pondered and thought over, I guess.
17. OSW: Yeah, what do you think about it today?
18. A: It is alcohol that comes first now.
19. OSW: Yeah, that's how I've seen it all the time. And when it begins, the drinking, other issues arise.
20. A: Mm.
21. OSW: But it all starts from drinking then, after it gets going then.
22. A: That's how it starts, yeah.

The HSW opens the meeting by referring to a discussion she has previously had with Alex and gives Alex the opportunity to talk about his thoughts in more detail (turn 1). Alex is addressed as a knowledgeable participant capable of expressing his feelings related to the housing transition, the main agenda of the particular meeting, and in this way, of directing how the topic is formulated and handled together further on. Alex first hesitates and refuses to take the leading position in the interaction. However, after a long pause, he uses the offer being made to take the next turn to talk. (Conversation analytical work has previously demonstrated that delays in an interaction indicate hesitation and trouble; see for example, Stivers et al, 2011, p 22.) Alex defines the current housing transition as causing "pressure" resulting from the uncertainty related to his ability to sustain his housing (turn 2). The HSW aligns with Alex's problem formulation by repeating it in a slightly different form, and in this way, is checking that she has understood it correctly (turn 3), which Alex then verifies (turn 4).

From then onwards, the OSW takes a strong leading position: she begins to put Alex's sense of pressure in context, and in this way, makes it more understandable and acceptable. She asks Alex about the duration of his homelessness history and his last home (turns 5, 7, 9 and 11). The OSW and Alex's joint homelessness narration changes the topic from present-day pressures to past homelessness pathways. The OSW is in the positions of 'narrator' and 'questioner', and Alex aligns with this by taking the positions of 'verifier' and 'answerer'. Alex's participation is realised by only using minimal responses and scant descriptions. This can be interpreted in many ways: minimal responses can indicate a client's passive resistance, a 'voiceless' and powerless position both in the meeting and in society. Minimal responses can also mean that Alex trusts the OSW's competence to talk on his behalf. Although in a minimal way, Alex goes along with formulating the topic in the professional-led question–answer turn-taking format (turns 6, 8 and 10) (for more on question–answer sequences, see Peräkylä and Ruusuvuori, 2007, p 169; Chapter 2).

The OSW continues contextualising Alex's situation in an understanding way as she describes difficulties from the point of view of the authorities and service systems (turns 11 and 13). She constructs Alex's past treatment pathway as fragmented, including confusion about responsibilities and thus bouncing Alex back and forth between alcohol and drug treatment services. He is positioned as a 'victim of the system' and the blame is directed at others. In this way, the OSW implies that she understands the reasons for Alex's situation and avoids blaming the service user. She sets herself in the position of a professional who knows the existing problems in the service system and has followed Alex's transitions between different services for a long time. Thus, she seems to have a mandate to explain possible obstacles to his receiving proper treatment. However, she checks that Alex shares her views on the topic (turn 11). Alex seems to align with the problem formulations by using minimal responses (turns 12 and 14), yet these responses are difficult to interpret in an unambiguous way.

The next agenda change is marked by the question about Alex's primary intoxicant (turn 13). The OSW's question shifts the discussion from the service system to Alex's alcohol and drug use and the relationship between them (turns 13–22). She strongly suggests that drug use has been secondary for Alex and alcohol is the primary issue. She asks for Alex's view about this by using a leading and fixed-choice question (turn 15). Interestingly, Alex does not take a clear stance, but replies in the third person, positioning himself as a 'bystander' and an 'outsider' (turn 16): it is something that has been thought over by others. The OSW may have recognised this passive positioning as she repeats the question, asking Alex for his own opinion (turn 17). After this insistent interactional act, Alex formulates alcohol as the problem that "comes first" (turn 18). The OSW strongly supports and aligns with this opinion and displays a causal account, that it is the alcohol that triggers other troublesome issues (turns 19 and 21). In turn, Alex verifies this and goes along with this interpretation (turns 20 and 22), so the problem formulation is not disputed but accepted by both participants. However, a critical question can be asked about whether it becomes too demanding for the service user or the HSW to resist and disagree with the professional when she is controlling the topics and stating her opinion so strongly.

In sum, the extract demonstrates professional-led collaborative service user participation that is based on the professional's expert position and long relationship with the service user. Participation is potentially advanced when the professional narrates the service user's problematic service pathways in a respectful way and the service user confirms professional conclusions by using minimal responses. The professional's 'narrating work', that is, talking on behalf of the service user (see also Chapter 7), may be seen as helping the service user to formulate his case (see Naldemirci et al, 2018). Alignment is expressed by using positive responses that imply like-minded thinking. However, reflecting critically, as the professional is the more powerful participant, she may potentially override the service user's (as well as the HSW's) voice and rely too much on what she knows about the service user's reality. She is aware of institutional preconditions that set limits on the service user's treatment and housing options. The service user's meagre responses may not indicate agreement so much as a vulnerable and passively resistant position in the welfare system and in the current meeting.

Making decisions and choices

Extract 3

> Max has been living at his mother's place due to homelessness, and he has been looking for a flat together with the floating support workers. The floating support workers (FSW1 and FSW2) have invited Max (M) and a landlord from the local housing company (HC) to discuss Max's housing situation. During the meeting, the landlord and Max discuss the new flat and the rental contract. The participants are making final decisions.

> 1. HC: Good. We'll just wait ((until the new flat is available)). But I assume you'll take the flat?
> 2. M: Yeah, there's no problem, of course.
> 3. HC: Let's book it for you then, so it's promised. The booking day is today, so it's all done now.
> 4. M: Yeah.
> 5. HC: Let's put it on the computer.
> 6. FSW1: Okay. How are we going to proceed with the rent security deposit issue then? Would you like to?
> 7. FSW2: An electronic ((application)) for the Social Insurance Institution is needed, now rather than later.
> 8. FSW1: Do you, would you like to start to do it now?
> 9. M: Yeah, I, whatever suits me.

10. FSW2: It's, but the bank statements. They should be printed from the online bank service.
11. M: Is it better that the disability pension has been paid to my account or worse that it has not been?
12. FSW2: It doesn't]
13. M: [I just received the pension.
14. FSW1: Your pension income doesn't matter.
15. FSW2: It is not that meaningful, as you don't (2). The application is for 1,100 ((euros)), that is the rent security deposit. After 1,100, you should have 500 left that you are entitled to, the spending money.
16. M: Does it matter whether we do it today or tomor]
17. FSW1: Are you up to it ((now))?
18. M: Yeah, I mean]
19. FSW1: [But we're here tomorrow, what day is it today? Wednes]
20. M: Wednesday.
21. FSW1: Aren't we here tomorrow? Yeah. So, it's up to you, what's your own ((opinion))?
22. M: Well, it would of course]
23. FSW2: [If you have the energy to do it, let's do it right away.
24. M: We can do it, yeah.
25. FSW2: It's only]
26. M: [I should have the bank's user name and password and stuff.
27. FSW2: Takes quarter of an hour]
28. FSW1: [And then it's done.
29. M: It would be better of course if it was done.

HC outlines the next steps in the housing pathway and asks Max to make the first decision: whether to take the flat being offered or not (turn 1). Max is thus put in the position of a choice maker in the interaction. He goes along with HC's assumptions and accepts the offer (turn 2). It can be anticipated that Max has only limited options, and as a result, is in a vulnerable position in local housing markets. This may be why he seems so sure about taking this particular flat. HC decides to make the booking arrangements on site via a computer during the conversation (turns 3 and 5), which Max seems to support with a minimal response (turn 4).

As the decisions to rent the flat and make the booking arrangements have been made, the floating support workers take the leading position and change the topic to the bureaucracy of getting income support for paying the required rent security deposit. During the conversation, Max is given an opportunity three times to decide how and when to proceed with the application process (turns 6, 17 and 21), yet both floating support workers strongly suggest taking care of the matter immediately (turns 7, 23, 27 and 28). The questions display empathy and emotional alignment towards probably an exhausted Max, who needs to get through the bureaucratic process. Max is hesitating about whether to fill in the application right away or later (turns 9 and 16). He positions himself as a consulting collaborator: he will proceed with the application as it is deemed best in his situation. The participants seem to conclude that it is better to write the application right away, and in this way, they direct Max's decision making. The decision about when to make the application is a major one in this particular context. It can be assumed that the professionals are aware that if it is not done immediately, there is the risk that the service user will forget about it – and it is their task to ensure that the service user obtains housing.

To conclude, the extract displays the professionals' institutional task of securing housing by giving resources, support and advice. The extract reveals how everyday decisions, like how and when to fill in the application form, can be challenging for people in vulnerable positions, and how concrete support is needed. Collaborative participation is realised by approaching the service user as a choice maker. However, the professionals express their preferences strongly as well, and in this way, they support and direct the service user's decision making. Asking questions that imply sensitivity and respect is an important discursive device to engage the service user in the discussion and strengthen his position as a self-governing participant. However, interactive activities that enhance the service user's position as a participant also comprise the risk that they might be directed too forcefully and in a close-ended way, potentially resulting in missing the service user's views. For all participants, participation is carried out by being involved in advice giving, decision making and choice making as well as taking a consultative and flexible stance. Emotional alignment is conducted by expressing awareness that the situation is potentially tiring for the service user, and not wanting to 'push' him to his limits. The service user aligns with these tasks by consulting the professionals and taking into account what matters to them in a particular process and shows competence in creating common knowledge (see Chapter 1).

Extract 4

> Sam has recently detoxified himself from drugs and alcohol. The participants of this multi-agency meeting are Sam (S), the social worker

from the outpatient clinic for drug addictions (OSW), the social worker from the outpatient clinic for alcohol addictions (ASW), the psychiatrist and the psychologist from a psychiatric outpatient clinic. Despite Sam's detox, they made a decision earlier to continue treating Sam in the low-threshold outpatient clinic for people using drugs. Thus, the outpatient social worker asks:

1. OSW: What would you think if I booked you an appointment quite soon, or are you now in ((a hurry)), do you want to focus on finding a flat?
2. S: Yeah, I mean, that keeps me busy, but I won't be visiting ((the local housing company's office)) for, like, eight hours a day, so.
3. OSW: Be on call.
4. S: It's enough to visit there once a day; they'll call me from there, or the worker who I ((talked with)) told me that they'll call me immediately from there. I need to check that ((other local housing company)) also.
5. OSW: Could you come on Friday at 12?
6. S: Yeah, I could.
7. OSW: Yeah, I'd have an appointment for an hour there. So, we would do a concrete plan and check these ((issues)), so they are then clear to us. So that when the flat is found, it'll be possible to focus on that.
8. S: Yeah.
9. OSW: Yeah, and I'll write it down here, and it's 18th May at 12.
10. S: Yeah.
11. OSW: Okay. But I don't think there's anything unclear in this situation; now it's just the plan and other options can still be thought about, but they'll work out, one by one.
12. S: Yeah, they tend to work out.
13. ASW: One by one.
14. S: Yeah, so.
15. OSW: Yeah.
16. ASW: Do you have any questions yet about the ((outpatient clinic for alcohol addictions)), anything to do with that or other issues that you have wondered or thought about, or—?
17. S: I haven't really.
18. ASW: They'll work out.
19. S: I've visited there a few times or, well, the last time I was there was last autumn.
20. ASW: Okay.

The OSW asks Sam in a sensitive way for his opinion about booking his next appointment quite soon (turn 1). She expresses awareness and empathy about demands on Sam's time and aligns with the view that Sam may not now have the time and energy to visit the outpatient clinic for drug users. The institutional aim is to support detoxification, and this is carried out by taking into account Sam's timetable. Sam supports the idea that he is occupied with finding a flat, yet not so occupied that he would not have time for anything else. In this way, he signals that he is willing to engage with the clinic's support (turns 2 and 4).

After Sam's positive response, the OSW is able to make a straightforward suggestion for an appointment time that Sam accepts (turns 5 and 6). A joint decision has been made. The OSW brings up that she will then have time to plan and clarify the options in Sam's current life situation together with him (turns 7 and 11). During these turns, the OSW also strengthens positive thinking: there is nothing unclear about the situation and things will work out well. By using inclusive 'we' terms (see Chapter 3 about the use of the 'we' term), the professional discursively aligns with the challenges and successes Sam is experiencing in sustaining his housing and life without drugs. Sam seems to confirm her reasoning and specific suggestions by using minimal responses (turns 2, 6, 8, 10 and 12).

The ASW is involved in the discussion by clarifying that if Sam has anything to ask concerning the clinic for alcohol addictions that she is available. Thus, the ASW sets herself in the position of 'customer service personnel' (turn 16). However, Sam is not in need of additional information as he does not have anything to ask (turn 17), and he has occasionally visited the service before (turn 19). Next, the ASW aligns with the other participants by sharing the OSW's positive thinking (turn 18) and accepting Sam's view (turn 20).

It is seen also in this extract that asking questions in a sensitive, empathic and respectful way is a predominant discursive device to give the service user space to express their views and choices. This professional-led interaction supports collaborative service user participation, yet it sets the service user in a position to give answers to pre-set questions and to make choices from pre-set options. As in Extract 3, the service user is in a central position in deciding 'when' to do the tasks that are required. Sam also decides what information is helpful for him. In this way, the service user's previous knowledge is respected and aligned with, yet it is also influenced and directed. The professionals have a strong and leading position in negotiating the service user's access to various services. At the same time, the service user expresses competence in formulating his views and preferences. Thus, engagement requires addressing and persuading the service user's free will and decision-making power. Worth noticing is the professionals' efforts to align emotionally with the service user's reality, and how they express belief in his capability to manage future challenges. The professionals also signal that he will not be left alone, but 'we' together will ensure that things will work out.

Discussion and conclusion

The aim of this chapter has been to analyse the interactional practices of collaborative service user participation. In all the extracts, the participants strive for collaborative participation by aligning more or less with one another, using the various interactional devices listed below:

The service user:

- talks about their thoughts, and others accept this agenda (Extracts 1 and 2);
- negotiates with professionals about what would be the best course of action and timing from their and the institutions' points of view (Extract 3);
- holds a strong position in asking questions and setting boundaries to deal with their personal experiences, and others encourage this (Extract 1);
- shifts the agenda in a way that all participants agree on (Extracts 1 and 3);
- goes along with question–answer sequences and expected positioning (all extracts);
- uses constructive and expected (minimal) responses (all extracts).

The professional:

- shifts the agenda in a way that all participants agree on (all extracts);
- acts as a 'teller' by constructing the service user's problems and speaking on their behalf – the professional checks that the constructed reality is in line with the service user's interpretations, which involves the service user in the discussion and gives them the opportunity to align or misalign with the professional's views (Extracts 1 and 2);
- expresses emotional support and empathy towards the service user's troublesome experiences (all extracts);

- asks questions to give the service user the position of a decision maker and a choice maker and expresses a willingness to align with their will (Extracts 3 and 4);
- asks sensitive questions concerning the service user's strengths, yet also directs their decision making by making suggestions – the professional thus displays alignment with the demands the service user is facing in the service and recovery pathways (Extracts 3 and 4);
- keeps up hope via positive utterances and thus supports and aligns with the service user's efforts (Extract 4);
- sorts out practical issues for the service user and enables them to engage with the services (Extracts 3 and 4).

To do collaborative service user participation requires the participants' constant reflection on interactional devices that would best enhance alignment in a given situation. Steensig (2013, p 5) makes an important point when stating: 'But pointing out what is alignment and affiliation cannot be an aim in itself. The concepts have analytical relevance only if they contribute to understanding how social cooperation (or the opposite) is done.' This has been exactly the purpose of using the analytical concept of 'alignment' in this chapter (see also Kykyri et al, 2019).

Despite these markers of alignment and collaboration, the extracts also include turn-takings that display topic control, persuasion, passive resistance and minimal uptake. These interactional devices can be interpreted as alienation from mutual and symmetrical collaboration. They also indicate how professionals have the responsibility to lead the interaction and get on with the institutional agenda. The service user holds the power to passively resist and control their own narration. Collaborative participation is thus always shaped and limited by institutional-professional hierarchies, various boundaries and power issues that are in play in multi-agency interactions.

It seems that questions addressed to the service user are the most common triggers for them to participate, but this is often done through minimal responses. This makes noticing and interpreting minimal responses an essential part of doing collaborative participation in action – they can be as critical and informative as narratives. Professionals also take a leading position and choose certain topics by asking specially formed questions. Furthermore, asking questions is a pivotal device to achieve alignment, because it indicates a willingness to give the decision-making power to the other person. Questions can comprise expressions of emotional support, empathy and togetherness, and leave space for decision making and topic changes.

Each professional asks questions concerning topics important to them, and in this way, governs the particular knowledge-power domain. Questions asked by the service user reveal what is important to them in each situation. Recognising what matters and to whom is an important point of departure in multi-agency working towards collaboration and common knowledge (Edwards, 2017; Hopwood and Edwards, 2017). It can be concluded that the person who asks the questions is in a powerful position to direct the meeting interactions. For service user participation, an essential difference is whether the service user initiates or merely responds to questions (Peräkylä and Ruusuvuori, 2007, p 169; Matthias et al, 2012). Collaborative working requires developing interactional competencies in multi-agency communication – developing additional 'relational expertise', that is, 'a capacity to work with others to expand the object being worked on' (Hopwood and Edwards, 2017, p 108).

Accomplishing collaborative participation among people in vulnerable positions requires, as Juhila et al (2020, p 4) argue, 'strengthening clients' self-trust and capacity so that clients become gradually more confident that they have rights to present personal wishes, are allowed and able to assess their own needs and make responsible choices, and are treated by others respectfully as responsible agents' (see also Benson, 2000, p 82; McLeod and Sherwin, 2000, pp 261–2). For instance, a great number of minimal responses may imply weakness either in the service user's self-trust or in their position in particular sequences of interaction. Alignment can be used as an interactional device to strengthen the service user's capacity to participate. More generally, multi-agency meetings may have a role in mitigating the vulnerable position of service users in services and society, if they are constructed and experienced as integration ceremonies (see Chapter 2). Unfortunately, the data do not allow access to the participants' thoughts concerning their experiences in the multi-agency meetings – or their views on the ability of the meetings to enhance their integration into welfare networks and the community.

D'Agostino et al (2017, p 1248) stress that '[p]rovider-patient encounters are interactive and reciprocal'; thus, all participants have responsibilities in communication. Yet, it has also been argued that, due to their professional skills and powerful position, professionals have greater responsibility than the service user to work towards alignment, communication and collaboration in institutional settings (Naldemirci et al, 2018). This is put into practice in our data, for instance by being sensitive to service users' self-determination, their potentially harsh life circumstances and their limited competencies to function. Difficulties in everyday life and in communication challenge the ideal of an active, narrating and self-governing service user, calling for professionals' strong support in doing collaboration. Yet, there is a risk that the greater power of professionals results in restricting the service user's ability to participate, for example by using too fixed questions or talking too much on behalf of the client.

It has been well documented how professionals may have difficulties realising service user participation, as this requires handing over (at least partly) the decision-making power to the service user, who may have limited abilities to function (Kortteisto et al, 2018). Additionally, the service user may struggle to present their 'case' in multi-agency settings. There can also be situations and issues where someone is not able or willing to participate (Hickey and Kipping, 1998; Fox and Reeves, 2015; Carey, 2019; Chapter 1). In other words, collaborative working may not always be the best choice. Service user participation can also be reflected on critically as implying 'a complex form of governance and ideological control, as well as a means by which local governments and some welfare professions seek to legitimise or extend their activities' (Carey, 2019, p 1691). These critical findings demonstrate how collaborative participation is never completely but partially achieved and at risk of failing. Hence, to accomplish collaborative participation requires uncompromising critical reflection together with the active pursuit of interactional changes via discursive devices, such as alignment.

Notes
[1] The concept has many parallel terms, such as client/patient/consumer participation/involvement (Velasco, 2001; Thomas, 2010).
[2] As Virokannas et al (2018) state, 'vulnerability' is a contested term that is often categorised either by people's 'natural' characteristics, such as age, sex or disability, or by situational aspects, such as social, economic, health and living conditions. In this chapter, the concept of 'vulnerability' refers to the latter categorisations.
[3] Service user participation is commonly also understood in terms of individual or collective participation (Chapter 2 in this book). At the individual level, it is considered important that service users are active in setting goals, defining measurements and making choices concerning their personal service pathways (Cahill, 1996; Hickey and Kipping, 1998). At the collective level, the emphasis is on giving service users more say in planning, providing, assessing and researching services (Beresford, 2002; Carey, 2019; Chapter 2 in this book). In the text, service user participation is approached exclusively from the individual level.

4   When studying 'naturally occurring' substance use service encounters in community settings, ethical principles such as anonymity, self-determination, voluntariness, and avoidance of harm to participants require special consideration. The research followed the guidelines of the National Advisory Board on Research Integrity, which defines ethical principles of research in the humanities and social and behavioral sciences (Finnish National Advisory Board 2020). Both professionals and service users were informed about the study and both oral and written consents were obtained.

References

Arnstein, S. (1969) 'A ladder of citizen participation', *Journal of the American Institute of Planners*, 35(4): 216–24.

Benson, P. (2000) 'Feeling crazy: Self-worth and the social character of responsibility', in C. Mackenzie and N. Stoljar (eds) *Relational Autonomy: Feminist Perspectives on Autonomy, Agency and the Social Self*, New York, NY: Oxford University Press, pp 72–93.

Beresford, P. (2002) 'User involvement in research and evaluation: Liberation or regulation?', *Social Policy and Society*, 1(2): 95–105.

Borg, M., Karlsson, B. and Kim, H.S. (2009) 'User involvement in community mental health services: Principles and practices', *Journal of Psychiatric and Mental Health Nursing*, 16(3): 285–92.

Browne, G. and Hemsley, M. (2008) 'Consumer participation in mental health in Australia: What progress is being made?', *Australasian Psychiatry*, 16(6): 446–9.

Cahill, J. (1996) 'Patient participation: A concept analysis', *Journal of Advanced Nursing*, 24(3): 561–71.

Carey, M. (2019) 'Some limits and political implications of participation within health and social care for older adults', *Ageing & Society*, 39(8): 1691–708.

Cook, J.A. and Jonikas, J.A. (2002) 'Self-determination among mental health consumers/survivors: Using lessons from the past to guide the future', *Journal of Disability Policy Studies*, 13(2): 87–95.

D'Agostino, T.A., Atkinson, T.M., Latella, L.E., Rogers, M., Morrissey, D., DeRosa, A.P. and Parker, P.A. (2017) 'Promoting patient participation in healthcare interactions through communication skills training: A systematic review', *Patient Education & Counseling*, 100(7): 1247–57.

Dodds, S. (2000) 'Choice and control in feminist bioethics', in C. Mackenzie and N. Stoljar, N. (eds) *Relational Autonomy: Feminist Perspectives on Autonomy, Agency and the Social Self*, New York, NY: Oxford University Press, pp 213–35.

Edwards, A. (2017) 'Revealing relational work', in A. Edwards (ed) *Working Relationally in and across Practices: A Cultural-Historical Approach to Collaboration*, Cambridge: Cambridge University Press, pp 1–24.

Finnish National Advisory Board on Research Integrity (TENK) www.tenk.fi/en.

Finset, A. (2017) 'Patient participation, engagement and activation: Increased emphasis on the role of patients in healthcare', *Patient Education & Counseling*, 100(7): 1245–6.

Fox, A. and Reeves, S. (2015) 'Interprofessional collaborative patient-centred care: A critical exploration of two related discourses', *Journal of Interprofessional Care*, 29(2): 113–18.

Hall, C. and Matarese, M. (2014) 'Narrative', in C. Hall, K. Juhila, M. Matarese and C. van Nijnatten (eds) *Analysing Social Work Communication: Discourse in Practice*, London: Routledge, pp 79–97.

Hickey, G. and Kipping, C. (1998) 'Exploring the concept of user involvement in mental health through a participation continuum', *Journal of Clinical Nursing*, 7(1): 83–8.

Hopwood, N. and Edwards, A. (2017) 'How common knowledge is constructed and why it matters in collaboration between professionals and clients', *International Journal of Educational Research*, 83: 107–19.

Juhila, K., Caswell, D. and Raitakari, S. (2014) 'Resistance', in C. Hall, K. Juhila, M. Matarese and C. van Nijnatten (eds) *Analysing Social Work Communication: Discourse in Practice*, London: Routledge, pp 117–35.

Juhila, K., Hall, C., Günther, K., Saario, S. and Raitakari, S. (2015) 'Accepting and negotiating service users' choices in mental health transition meetings, *Social Policy & Administration*, 49(5): 612–30.

Juhila, K., Ranta, J., Raitakari, S. and Banks, S. (2020) 'Relational autonomy and service choices in social worker-client conversations in an outpatient clinic for people using drugs', *British Journal of Social Work*, published online 26 February 2020, DOI: 10.1093/bjsw/bcaa011.

Koprowska, J. (2016) 'The problem of participation in child protection conferences', *International Journal of Child and Family Welfare*, 17(1/2): 105–22.

Kortteisto, T., Laitila, M. and Pitkänen, A. (2018) 'Attitudes of mental health professionals towards service user involvement', *Scandinavian Journal of Caring Sciences*, 32(2): 681–9.

Kvarnström, S., Willumsen, E., Andersson-Gäre, B. and Hedberg, B. (2012) 'How service users perceive the concept of participation, specifically in interprofessional practice', *British Journal of Social Work*, 42(1): 129–46.

Kykyri, V.-L., Tourunen, A., Nyman-Salonen, P., Kurri, K., Walström, J., Kaartinen, J. and Seikkula, J. (2019) 'Alliance formations in couple therapy: A multimodal and multimethod study', *Journal of Couple & Relationship Therapy*, 18(3): 189–222, published online 9 April 2019, https://doi.org/10.1080/15332691.2018.1551166.

Lakhani, A., McDonald, D. and Zeeman, H. (2018) 'Perspectives of self-direction: A systematic review of key areas contributing to service users' engagement and choice-making in self-directed disability services and supports', *Health & Social Care in the Community*, 26(3): 295–313.

Law on substance abuse [Päihdehuoltolaki] 41/1986.

Matthias, M.S., Mitchelle, P., Salyers, A., Rollins, L. and Frankel, L.M. (2012) 'Decision making in recovery-oriented mental health care', *Psychiatric Rehabilitation Journal*, 35(4): 305–14.

McLeod, C. and Sherwin, S. (2000) 'Relational autonomy, self-trust, and health care for patients who are oppressed', in C. Mackenzie and N. Stoljar (eds) *Relational Autonomy: Feminist Perspectives on Autonomy, Agency and the Social Self*, New York, NY: Oxford University Press, pp 259–79.

McNeil, R., Kerr, T., Pauly, B., Wood, E. and Small, W. (2016) 'Advancing patient-centered care for structurally vulnerable drug-using populations: A qualitative study of the perspectives of people who use drugs regarding the potential integration of harm reduction interventions into hospitals', *Addiction*, 111(4): 685–94.

Ministry of Social Affairs and Health (2009) *Plan for Mental Health and Substance Abuse Work: Proposals of the Mieli 2009 Working Group to Develop Mental Health and Substance Abuse Work Until 2015*, Helsinki: Ministry of Social Affairs and Health.

Naldemirci, Ö., Lydahl, D., Britten, N., Elam, M., Moore, L. and Wolf, A. (2018) 'Tenacious assumptions of person-centred care? Exploring tensions and variations in practice', *Health*, 22(1): 54–71.

Notley, C., Maskrey, V. and Holland, R. (2012) 'The needs of problematic drug misusers not in structured treatment: A qualitative study of perceived treatment barriers and recommendations for services', *Drugs: Education, Prevention & Policy*, 19(1): 40–8.

Peräkylä, A. and Ruusuvuori, J. (2007) 'Components of participation in health care consultation: A conceptual model for research', in S. Collins, N. Britten, J. Ruusuvuori and A. Thompson (eds) *Patient Participation in Health Care Consultations: Qualitative Perspectives*, Maidenhead: McGraw-Hill Education, pp 167–75.

Pickard, S., Sheaff, R. and Dowling, B. (2006) 'Exit, voice, governance and user-responsiveness: The case of English primary care trusts', *Social Science & Medicine*, 63(2): 373–83.

Raitakari, S., Saario, S., Juhila, K. and Günther, K. (2015) 'Client participation in mental health: Shifting positions in decision-making', *Nordic Social Work Research*, 5(1): 35–49.

Ranta, J. (2020) 'Reducing harms through interactions: Workers orienting to unpredictable frames in a low-threshold project for people injecting drugs', *International Journal of Drug Policy*, 82: 102828.

Selseng, L.B. and Ulvik, O.S. (2018) 'Talking about and interpretative repertoires in stories about substance abuse and change', *Qualitative Social Work*, 17(2): 216–35.

Steensig, J. (2013) 'Conversation analysis and affiliation and alignment', in C.A. Chapelle (ed) *The Encyclopedia of Applied Linguistics*, Oxford: Wiley-Blackwell, pp 1–6.

Stivers, T. (2008) 'Stance, alignment, and affiliation during storytelling: When nodding is a token of affiliation', *Research on Language & Social Interaction*, 41(1): 31–57.

Stivers, T., Mondada, L. and Steensig, J. (2011) 'Knowledge, morality and affiliation in social interaction', in T. Stivers, L. Mondada and J. Steensig (eds) *The Morality of Knowledge in Conversation*, Cambridge: Cambridge University Press, pp 3–24.

Thomas, J. (2010) 'Service users, carers and issues for collaborative practice', in K.C. Pollard, J. Thomas and M. Miers (eds) *Understanding Interprofessional Working in Health and Social Care: Theory and Practice*, Basingstoke: Palgrave Macmillan, pp 171–85.

Velasco, I. (2001) *Service User Participation: Concepts, Trends and Practices*, Edinburgh: Scottish Council for Single Homeless.

Virokannas, E., Liuski, S. and Kuronen, M. (2018) 'The contested concept of vulnerability: A literature review', *European Journal of Social Work*, DOI: 10.1080/13691457.2018.1508001.

Wetherell, M. (1998) 'Positioning and interpretative repertoires: Conversation analysis and post-structuralism in dialogue', *Discourse & Society*, 9(3): 387–412.

6

Sympathy and micropolitics in return-to-work meetings

Pia H. Bülow and Monika Wilińska

Introduction

One of the key tenets of this edited volume is that the study of communication patterns during multi-agency welfare meetings is pertinent to the understanding of current social policies and their implementation and practices in everyday life. In this chapter, multi-agency return-to-work meetings are explored with a focus on the emotional underpinnings of institutional practice assembling various parties of the rehabilitation process. In particular, attention is paid to alliances and the ways in which various alliances may or may not reflect sympathy towards service users and their troubles. To this end, the chapter leans on the concept of 'sympathy' as an emotion that bonds, especially in difficult times. However, as Candace Clark (1997) elaborates, sympathy or rather its lack thereof can magnify differences between those who are better off and those who are worse off. The aim is to discuss the context of multi-agency welfare meetings via the prism of sympathy and the role of alliances between service users, professionals and employers in promoting or discouraging spells of sympathy during such meetings.

The following section sheds light on the context of the Swedish work rehabilitation process and the institutional as well as emotional character of return-to-work meetings. Thereafter, the theoretical grounding based on the work of Candace Clark and her concept of 'sympathy' is presented. Following the presentation of methods is an analysis of several situations from two return-to-work meetings and a discussion about the place of sympathy and alliance in the institutional context.

The institutional and emotional landscapes of multi-agency welfare meetings

The introduction of multi-agency return-to-work meetings in 2003 is written into wider changes regarding the social insurance system and the work rehabilitation of people on sick leave in Sweden. Critics conceive of it as an extension of the 'intensified work-line strategy' (Junestav, 2009), which brought an increased emphasis on activation and self-sufficiency among sick-listed persons and the tightening of sick leave entitlements (Melén, 2008). In parallel, the public discourse regarding sickness absence has changed. In contrast to previously being dominated by work conditions, stress and burnout as the reason for long-term sick leave, the media coverage has now become dominated by stories of the overuse and abuse of the generous social insurance system (Johnson, 2010). The changing political landscape and citizen regime implied that the responsibility for rehabilitation became shared between the Swedish social insurance agency (SSIA), employers, health care and the individual on sick leave (Wilińska and Bülow, 2020).

The return-to-work meeting is a multi-party, cross-institutional encounter involving the service user as well as relevant stakeholders. The stakeholders consist of the employer or an employment officer, various health care professionals and an officer from SSIA who summons and chairs the meeting. This implies that several kinds of logic, agenda and even different laws coexist and sometimes compete. This is, for example, visible in the diverse ways of understanding the concept of 'workability' that return-to-work meetings aim at assessing (see Ståhl et al, 2011; Seing et al, 2012). Critics argue, however, that what unites the meetings' stakeholders is a conviction that workability relates to sick-listed persons' strengths, capacities and high motivation levels to improve their own situation (for example, Ekberg, 2011). It is therefore common for service users to experience those meetings as an interrogation and as a threat to their moral worth when their claim to be ill is questioned. Thus, to a great extent, such meetings may be exemplary of degradation ceremonies, as discussed in Chapter 2.

While including professionals from different agencies as well as the employer and the service user, the return-to-work meeting resembles some kind of case conference, such as child protection conference in the UK, and the parental participation in these (Hall and Slembrouck, 2001; Hall et al, 2006; see also Chapter 8). As such, it can be described in terms of both interprofessional discourse and professional–lay discourse (Linell, 1998) since the presence of the service user is a necessity. This implies that institutional discourse is agenda driven

(Johanson et al, 1996) or, from time to time, orchestrated (Aronsson and Cederborg, 1994), in that someone (usually the official from SSIA) allocates turns and decides when and how the meeting participants can speak (see Chapter 2 on turn-taking and turn allocation).

However, the return-to-work meeting is more than a mere assemblage of various, institutionally defined parties of the work rehabilitation process. It is rather an example of relational practice (Hunter, 2015) constituted by interacting actors who are influenced by and who influence the institutional agenda. The position that the individual participant takes or is assigned is something that is constantly negotiated in the interaction. In a group with many participants, competition for space more often arises and it can be difficult to take and to hold the floor. At the same time, it becomes easier to choose the role of silent listener, without major demands for active participation. Importantly, these processes are emotional not only because different feelings are involved, but also because of the productive engagement of emotions (Hunter, 2015; Fortier, 2016). This makes the return-to-work meeting highly emotional for all parties involved, but mainly for the service user.

This chapter therefore suggests that the 'institutional' and the 'emotional' contents of return-to-work meetings become not only embedded, but also indistinguishable under the current sociopolitical and economic circumstances. From a social perspective, emotions aid us in the process of sense making and they also reveal our attachment to certain issues. Emotions also become an indication of the ongoing process of judgement and moralising. In the context of the work rehabilitation process, the duty to work is one of the key underlying norms that shine through institutional practices. The duty to work, understood as paid labour, is an indisputable norm in contemporary welfare states that is also strongly connected to identity (and normality) (Patrick, 2012). This duty is a given when referring to groups who stay out of work due to their disability and/or illness and who are subjected to numerous welfare interventions. A return-to-work meeting is underpinned by reasoning about work morality and moral worth in relation to the labour market. The norm of duty to work could limit the service user's ability to negotiate their place in the conversation by taking into account, or being reminded by others, what obligations the person who is on sick leave has to return to work. In such a context, the notions of sick leave and illness are far from simple. For example, Flinkfeldt (2017) introduces the concept of 'sick leave legitimacy' to designate the collaborative and interactional process of establishing the right to stay away from work. Being out of work is therefore not a simple consequence of illness; it is rather an achievement conditioned upon the use of 'rights' arguments that can convince all parties of the work rehabilitation process that claims to stay sick off work are legitimate.

Within the institutional setting, certain emotions may therefore bind people together, but they may also impede some forms of dialogue or collaborative work. This may lead to changes in the institutional setting and institutional practices. When people are moved by and with emotions, so institutions and forms of institutional life move along. To emphasise that emotionally loaded character of institutional interactions, the term 'emotion ability' was introduced to designate the importance attributed to an ability to feel what one is expected to feel (Wilińska and Bülow, 2020). Emotion ability becomes visible in the increasing focus on evoking the 'right' feelings and attitudes in ensuring that service users are not only following institutional recommendations, but also, above all else, that they demonstrate positive appreciation of those. With this, the affective task, or rather the affective dimension of the institutional meeting, conditions the fulfilment of the institutional task. This chapter therefore moves away from a view conceiving institutional interaction as facing a dilemma regarding the need to balance the institutional task of solving the problem at hand with the affective task of showing compassion and understanding (for example, Ruusuvuori, 2001, 2005), to propose that institutional context is full of life and emotions (Wilińska and Bülow, 2020).

Micropolitics, social place, sympathy and alliances

According to Clark (1990, p 305), 'micropolitics, as all politics, has to do with the creation and negotiation of hierarchy', and to getting hold of and maintaining what she calls a (social) place. In contrast to the concept of 'social status', 'a place is a less well defined, micro-level position' that gives the involved participants feelings about being in a position to say or act in a certain way – or not to do so. Thus, social place is about the relations each person has regarding everyone else in a particular interaction and encompasses aspects such as power, prestige and face-to-face status (1990, p 306). This means that social places are situational and changeable and that places may overlap during an ongoing interaction (1990, p 306). Thus, as Clark argues, people 'constantly monitor the shifting micropolitical balance' (1990, p 305). These shifts in micropolitical balance may reflect emerging alliances between and among participants of multi-agency welfare meetings.

Kangasharju (1996) asserts here that each multi-agency conversation creates a possibility for creating various collectives and these substantially affect participation frameworks. In the context of multi-agency welfare meetings, this means that, for example, an alliance between professional actors may potentially threaten the position of a service user, while an alliance including a service user may shift the focus from professional expertise to, for example, shared experiences or history. The existing research on alliances in multi-agency meetings usually makes a distinction between alignment and affiliation. While alignment is considered to designate structural and behavioural levels of cooperation, affiliation has to do with emotional aspects, such as empathy (Kykyri et al, 2019). In elaborating on that distinction, Stivers et al (2011) add that affiliations are much more social in their character, by involving not only affection but also action-oriented elements.

Since social place is a relational position, emotions play an important role in maintaining, claiming and negotiating one's place. Emotions such as awe, shame or pride work as place markers, and by expressing various emotions people make claims on a certain place in relation to others. The relational character of social place means that one participant in a multi-agency meeting could occupy a higher place, which includes more esteem and privileges, while others take or give the position of follower or victim. One of the key emotions that Clark has worked with extensively is sympathy. Sympathy, in the words of Clark, is an emotion that bonds, that brings people together and functions as a type of 'social glue' (Clark, 1997, p 5). In explaining sympathy as a social process in everyday life, Clark maintains that sympathy is not only about emotional reaching to the other person, but also draws on cognitive and physical dimensions. With this, she distinguishes three elements constitutive of sympathy: empathy, sympathy sentiment and display. Empathy, according to Clark, may involve various levels of closeness to or distance from the subject or object of empathy. Ranging from cognitive (the most distant form of empathy), via physical to emotional empathy, empathy signifies the process of 'taking the role of the other' (Clark, 1987, p 294). In contrast, sympathy sentiment can be a feeling either *with* or *for* the other. That feeling may lead to a concrete action, which then turns into a sympathy display. Following the distinction between empathy and sympathy, Ruusuvuori (2005) furthered Clark's theorisations by demonstrating how both phenomena are practically accomplished in the context of talk. Notably, while Clark's reasoning about sympathy was based on everyday interactions, Ruusuvuori conducted her research in the context of institutional talk, emphasising in this way that even though institutional constraints for displaying various emotions cannot be ignored, emotions are not out of place in institutions.

In exploring sympathy as a social process, Clark also draws attention to the various rules and roles that can be distinguished in the sympathy process. For the first, each sympathy process must include at least two persons who take the role of a sympathizer and sympathizee. While sympathy is said to connect and bond a sympathizer and sympathizee, the interesting feature of that connection is that it is inherently asymmetrical. Clark provides two reasons for this: first, the sympathizee always starts from a position of a trouble or a problem that they experience; second, in receiving the gift of sympathy, the sympathizee enters into a situation of debt – they are expected to repay the received gift. Thus, while creating cohesion, sympathy is also a force maintaining or reinforcing stratification (Clark, 1997, p 229). Sympathy processes and interactions provide an insight into the micropolitics of various situations, because, to some extent, the questions of social place and power are always present when sympathy claims are made, and sympathy gifts are received. As much as sympathy can be given strategically to strengthen one's position in the situation, a gift of sympathy can be strategically rejected to preserve one's standing in the situation.

Taken to the context of the work rehabilitation process, illness and related inability to work, as well as the reduced financial wellbeing that often follows, may provide morally and cultural accepted grounds for sympathy. As Clark (1997, p 22) emphasises, sympathy is 'a morality constructing act' and 'sympathizers are moral gatekeepers'. The legitimacy of sympathy claims is assessed not only via their content but also via the ways in which they are made. Here, Clark discusses four rules that seem to regulate sympathy claims in everyday life. First, sympathizees are not to make false claims for sympathy. This not only destroys the ground for present connection, but also ultimately erases the possibility for future bonds. Second, sympathizees should make their claims in moderation, that is, not too often and not too much. Although the exact limits of sympathy claims may vary from situation to situation, there are clear limits when too great and too frequent sympathy claims produce contradictory results to those intended by a sympathizee. Third, sympathy claims are needed to maintain relations between people, with the members of a particular collective who make no such claims tending to be viewed as overly passive. Fourth, gifts of sympathy are to be reciprocated either by gratitude or by giving sympathy back to the sympathizer.

In the following, Clark's concept of 'sympathy' is applied to the context of return-to-work meetings to shed light on the position of service users and their potential role as sympathizees. Further, considering the micropolitical grounding of sympathizing, the ways and extent to which various institutional roles and positions change/shift and how sympathizing is accomplished via the formation of alliances are explored.

Data and the process of analysis

This chapter is based on an analysis of eight return-to-work meetings that were observed and video-recorded between January and April 2013 (for more details about the video recordings, see Wilińska and Bülow, 2017). The regional ethics board in Linköping, Sweden, approved the study (Dnr 2012/82-31). The meetings lasted on average 34 minutes and 30 seconds (range 15–48 minutes) and concerned five men and three women, all sick-listed for a considerable time due to conditions such as depression, anxiety, tiredness or pain. Five of the sick-listed persons worked in low-skilled jobs, two worked in the service sector and one was a highly skilled professional. In all the meetings, the sick-listed person (SL), an official from SSIA and a doctor participated (see Table 6.1). In addition, a rehabilitation coordinator (RC) participated in all but two meetings. RCs are employed by health care and are typically occupational therapists, medical social workers or physiotherapists.

In total, between four and seven people were involved in each meeting. In five meetings, the employer participated and in three of these meetings, the employer was accompanied by a human resources (HR) representative from the company. For various reasons, no employer took part in three of the meetings. In two meetings, the sick-listed person was accompanied by a relative (husband or wife). When the employer and/or the sick-listed person asked someone to join them for the meeting, it was an indication that the meeting felt challenging in some way.

The verbal conversations were transcribed verbatim by professional transcribers who worked according to the principles of denaturalised transcription: while aiming to provide as accurate a transcript as possible (see the Transcript key towards the end of this chapter), details such as accents and non-linguistic sounds were omitted (Oliver et al, 2005). After the meeting, follow-up interviews with meeting participants were conducted. The interviews were recorded and transcribed verbatim.

The analysis began with a search of emotionally loaded episodes. To define 'emotionally loaded' episodes, the interaction view of emotions was applied. Emotions were thus seen as situated and embodied

Table 6.1: Participants in the studied meetings

Meeting	SL	SSIA	GP	RC	Other health professional	Employer	Human resources	Relative	Number of participants
1	Yes	Yes	Yes	Yes	No	No	No	No	4
2	Yes	Yes	Yes	Yes	No	Yes	Yes	Yes	7
3	Yes	Yes	Yes	No	No	Yes	No	No	4
4	Yes	Yes	Yes	Yes	No	No	No	No	4
5	Yes	Yes	Yes	Yes	Yes	Yes	Yes	No	7
6	Yes	Yes	Yes	Yes	Yes	Yes	Yes	No	7
7	Yes	Yes	Yes	No	No	Yes	No	No	4
8	Yes	Yes	Yes	Yes	No	No	No	Yes	5
Total	8	8	8	6	2	5	3	2	42

practices that could be studied through attention to a variety of bodily actions, implying that 'an explicit emotion vocabulary is not necessary for a powerful display of emotion' (Goodwin and Goodwin, 2000, p 49).

Such practices can therefore be observed either via an attention to the 'notable talk occurring about emotions' (Wetherell, 2012, p 97) and/or the perspective of the body and its movements, 'where the body has been more intrusive than ordinarily'. The audio and visual material enabled a focus on language and bodily displays and their role in constructing emotionally loaded situations. Subsequently, 'emotionally loaded' episodes included: (a) participants who verbally described their feelings or used emotional language; (b) sudden changes in bodily positions, for example, a doctor almost nudging a sick-listed person, and two participants mimicking each other's body movements; and (c) participants displaying emotional responses, such as crying or laughing.

The analysis centred on the instances of sympathy claims made by the service users and the ways they were received. In this, the process of sympathy as comprised of claiming, receiving, giving, accepting, rejecting and/or denying sympathy was explored. Both verbal and non-verbal signs of sympathy and the messages they communicated were analysed. Previous research on cooperation and alliances in talk has found that while verbal and non-verbal devices co-occur when forming alliances (for example, Oben and Brône, 2016), they may not always be congruent with each other (for example, Kykyri et al, 2019). Further, Goffman's concept of 'participation framework' and specifically his concept of 'footing' (Goffman, 1981) was used to analyse sympathy claims within the multi-agency return-to-work meetings.

In the analysis process, attention was paid to:

- words and pauses (silences);
- turn-taking;
- the direction of gaze, gestures and bodily movements/actions;
- the closeness/distance between participants.

The following section is based on an analysis of several sequences from two different meetings. The first meeting presented is one of two meetings with very vivid emotional displays during which the sick-listed person began crying. The second meeting represents one of the few meetings that, on the surface, were devoid of clear emotional displays. What connects the meetings is that both sick-listed persons experience similar difficulties in being understood by their employers.

Using the language of sympathy, their troubles constituting grounds for sympathy are thus quite similar. In the following analysis, verbal and non-verbal ways of claiming and receiving sympathy are demonstrated and the place sympathizing has in the institutional context is discussed.

Analysis: alliances and sympathizing in status meetings

Typically, a return-to-work meeting consists of several distinct phases during which various parties are given an opportunity to talk. Following small talk, it is the SSIA officer who opens the formal meeting by outlining the aim of the meeting and presenting a summary of the case so far. In the second phase, the sick-listed person is invited to talk about their current condition (see Chapter 2 for the organisation and structure of the meeting and the role of the chair). After that, the SSIA officer turns to the doctor to ask about the medical status of the sick-listed person. In the fourth phase, work ability and the possibility of returning to work are discussed. If the employer is present, sometimes accompanied by an HR manager, they are invited to describe preparations for work adjustments or their thoughts about how to support the sick-listed person's return to work.

Although most status meetings are both emotionally and morally charged, the participants show a common endeavour to adhere to the meeting order and to show politeness (see Chapter 2). The formality of the meeting is also seen in the emotional and physical constraints placed on the meeting participants. Typically, such meetings are conducted in conference rooms, where participants' bodily movements are very restricted. Further, the institutional character of the meeting is reflected in the ways in which various parties presents themselves; they attend the meeting in their professional roles, such as representatives of an authority, a profession or a company, or in the case of the sick-listed person, as a service user, a patient or an employee. Because of this, it is not uncommon that the sick-listed participants are brought to tears or show signs of grief, resentment, despair and disappointment. Similarly, situations where the other actors show clear signs of emotional acting and reacting to the feelings of the sick-listed person tend to be accommodated into the institutional meeting frame.

Claiming sympathy

The first example of *sympathizing* concerns a meeting that involved seven people: the sick-listed person (SL); an official from the SSIA

Sympathy and micropolitics

Figure 6.1: The seating arrangement in meeting no. 5

(SSIA); a therapist from a special programme for rehabilitation outside ordinary health centre work (T); the rehabilitation coordinator (RC); the general practitioner (GP); and the employer (Emp) who was accompanied by someone from the HR department (HR). The presence of HR is an indication that the employer regarded the meeting as a potentially complex or difficult case. Lastly, present in the room, was one of the researchers, sitting behind the video camera.

Each meeting participant entering the room can freely choose their seat. It is noteworthy that while SL and T sit next to each other, all other participants sit on the other side of the table, with Emp and HR sitting exactly opposite SL (see Figure 6.1). The last person to enter the room is the official from SSIA who places herself in the middle between T and HR.

SSIA opens the meeting by acknowledging all the people she knows from previous meetings or contacts, and also welcoming the two newcomers – HR representative and T. After this, SSIA turns towards SL and invites her to tell everyone about how she feels and what had changed since the last return-to-work meeting. SL immediately accepts and describes her improving condition, which she mainly attributes to the stress management training she has attended. While SL is narrating her story, T is looking at SL and keeps nodding. SSIA also looks attentively at SL, making notes at the same time. After approximately two minutes, SL summarises her experiences:

Extract 1: Meeting no. 5, time 02:58–03:31

1. SL oh it has been really good
2. SSIA yes.
3. SL well I try to get back to that calmness. (.) today I'm not particularly calm I [must say.
4. Xx   [mm
5. Xxs no
6. **((several participants talking simultaneously while nodding and smiling at SL))**
7. GP no of course that-
8. Emp that's understandable
9. SSIA that's so many people.
10. GP here we sit all (.) (these) people.
11. SSIA yeah but exactly, this is a very special situation.
12. Xxs mm mm ((several voices simultaneously))
13. SL precisely so it is a bit tough though.
14. GP mm mm
15. SSIA yes
16. SL ehm cause you are sort of- feel a bit exposed
17. Xx mm
(1.0)
18. SSIA at the same time as- as we are all around you and want-
19. SL yeah. I know.
20. SSIA hehe ((with laughter in her voice)) and want what's best for you so to speak. and so.
21. **((SSIA turns to T))**

In turn 3, SL continues the story about her improvements until she begins describing the current situation, stating that "well I try to get back to that calmness", and adding: "today I'm not particularly calm I must say". That utterance is interpreted as an evaluation of the ongoing meeting and thereby as a claim for sympathy. Following that, a gift of sympathy is unanimously offered by everyone. Not only are various voices heard saying that it is understandable, but also everyone looks at SL with a smile to demonstrate their closeness and to emphasise that they sympathize with her troubles.

Then in turn 13, SL looks around and repeats the claim for sympathy by elaborating on the feeling of having a hard time. This time, SL's claim receives only minimal response tokens from GP (turn 14) and SSIA (turn 15). However, SL continues claiming sympathy for the third time in turn 16. The third claim is met with only one minimal response token (turn 17, impossible to hear/see who is doing that), and then after a one-second pause, SSIA provides an account for all the others and their collective engagement with SL ("at the same time as- as we are all around you and want-", turn 18). The first part of SSIA's statement "at the same time as" might be interpreted as almost a "but", and thereby as an objection to the claims that SL is making. In this, SSIA marks the boundary between an accepted and unaccepted amount of sympathy that could be claimed. Such an interpretation is confirmed by SL's action when she promptly interrupts SSIA to confirm SSIA's words by saying "yeah. I know" (turn 19). Following that, SSIA's laughter in turn 19 could be seen as part of mutual work to repair the situation when too much sympathy is claimed. SSIA then ends the episode by summing up and declaring that "we" as professionals and employers want the best for SL and by changing the topic and inviting the external therapist (T) to talk about the rehabilitation programme.

While the beginning of the episode demonstrates that SL's claims for sympathy are legitimate and there appears to be common ground for understanding the difficulties that she is facing, the second part of the episode shows that SL breaks some rules regarding sympathy claims. This could either be explained by her claiming too much or presenting one claim after another without acknowledging the first sympathy gift she received. Further, that the three sympathy claims differ in terms of the moral grounds on which they are established. Given the prompt response to the first sympathy claim, it could be noted that everyone in the meeting experiences some form of nervousness or anxiousness about how the meeting will progress. Sharing similar experiences, the meeting's participants find it relatively easy to sympathize with SL. The second and third sympathy claims are made in relation to much more personal and intense experiences and these are not received so easily. The deeper emotional content of these two sympathy claims does not seem to create the moral ground needed to trigger the gift of sympathy.

Unmet sympathy claims

In the same meeting, about seven minutes later, an episode begins in which SL makes verbal and non-verbal sympathy claims. That episode follows a rather tough discussion between SSIA and SL and in which SSIA in a consistent way focuses on work and work-related plans and disregards SL's attempt to explain her feelings and difficulties. However, in the following extract, SL is given some space to explain

Interprofessional Collaboration and Service User Participation

her difficulties related to the emotions arising when approaching, or even going near, the physical environment of her workplace.

Extract 2: Telling about difficulties (meeting no. 5, time 10:32–11:15)

1. SL ehum I hm I have been- now I have been around there and I have been out and had lunch with ***((SL begins moving her palm on the table))*** my colleagues from work,
2. ***((SL keeps on drawing circles with her hand on the table))***
3. SSIA hmm
4. SL at least I have done tha- and now we will go out and have lunch ***((SL begins knocking her palm at the table))*** again after Easter, I have asked for that.
5. ***((SL keeps on knocking at the table))***
6. SSIA hmm
7. SL because I try, I mean (.) but eh (.) I think ***((SL places both palms in her lap))*** it would be a total flop if I went to the workplace to do that.
8. ***((SL wipes her nose and eyes with her hand several times))***
9. SSIA yeah
10. SL though it's strange because I liked working there and everyone was nice, and so
11. SSIA yes ehm
12. (5.0) ((SSIA makes notes))
13. SSIA then, I'm wondering about the medical view now ((to GP))

While SL is talking, SSIA provides only minimal response tokens such as hmm, mm, yeah and yes. The physical acting that SL performs simultaneously as she talks is of importance here. First, SL puts her right hand on the table and begins drawing small circles on the surface of the table. Second, a few seconds later she instead starts knocking her palm repeatedly at the table before eventually placing her right-hand fingers on her lips. Third, she then wipes her nose and eyes with her hand several times. Although her hand movements may be less or more conscious, they are very visible to other participants as acts signifying emotions such as sadness, despair and perhaps resignation, which may be heard and seen as sympathy claims. The overall atmosphere in the room becomes very serious, but no one reacts. It takes as long as five seconds from the moment that SL ends her story to SSIA's change of topic in turn 13. While SL is presenting her story, GP, RC and Emp are alternately looking at SSIA/SL and taking notes. T is looking at SL and occasionally nodding. HR's gaze is entirely fixed on SL. Interestingly, when the other meeting participants begin shifting their gaze from SL to SSIA during the five-second pause, HR keeps looking at SL and moves her head only when SSIA begins speaking.

Following the earlier, more intense exchange between SL and SSIA, it becomes evident that in Extract 2 other members of the meeting assume the role of audience who do not interrupt. They are actively following the conversation with their gaze and some of them are taking notes, but no one actively responds either verbally or non-verbally to the sympathy claims made by SL. Furthermore, even SL looks almost entirely at SSIA, in that way directing her claims to one person. SSIA with her frequent nodding and word continuers receives SL's story but does not invite any uptake after turn 7. Further, with her "then" in turn 9, she seems to treat it as a finished act that does not necessitate any other intervention. SL is thus left alone with her unmet sympathy claims.

Non-verbal sympathy gift

The next extract starts where the previous one ends. It is important to notice how SSIA shifts focus, which also means that the formal meeting now continues between GP and SSIA. It is typical for return-to-work meetings that a large proportion of time consists of the SSIA officer talking to the other participants one by one or, when it makes sense, as a pair. This will leave those who are not addressed as audience or in the background. In the following example, it is what happens in the background which is of special interest.

Extract 3: Interaction in the background (meeting no. 5, time 11:15–11:40) (see Figures 6.2–6.4)

13.	SSIA	I'm wondering a bit about a <u>medical view</u> now ***(to GP))***
14.	GP	mm
15.	SSIA	how do you assess SL's situation in all that? because she has now undergone-
16.		***((SL rubs her chin, HR follows her with gaze))***
17.	GP	mm (see Figure 6.3)
18.	SSIA	I mean I understand that these weeks have been intense and it meant a lot of work
19.	GP	mm

Interprofessional Collaboration and Service User Participation

20. *((HR bends down to her right side and begins looking for something in her handbag while repeatedly gazing at SL))*
21. SSIA   with oneself and then where does where is she now so to speak?
22. GP   yeah but it's it's has all taken (.) ehu (.) it has taken much more time than expected at the beginning. that's why it happens that one thinks that things got better with depression= (see Figure 6.4)
23. *((HR, smiling to SL, stretches her hand across the table to hand a tissue to SL, SL accepts the tissue with audible "thank you"))*
24. GP   =and then one gets back to the (same) and it can happen that. but now it's become much better. it has become
    ((continues))
25. *((SL wipes her eyes with the tissue))*

In the first part of the episode, it is SSIA and SL who talk, and in the second part, it is SSIA and GP, while all the others assume the position of audience. However, at the same time as verbal exchange between SSIA and GP proceeds, an interaction almost without words occurs across the table when HR continues to gaze at SL who is displaying signs of sadness and tears (Extract 3). HR seems to feel sorry for SL and as an act of sympathy, she offers SL a tissue. The whole (almost) non-verbal interaction between HR and SL takes place simultaneously as SSIA and SL's GP are talking and can be seen as what Goffman (1981)

Figure 6.2: Extract 3: Interaction in the background (meeting no. 5, time 11:15–11:40)

Figure 6.3: Subordinate and dominant communication

Figure 6.4: Sympathy gift

terms 'subordinate communication' in relation to the dominating communication between SSIA and GP. Yet HR's offer makes her lean forwards and stretch her arm over a rather wide table and, by that act, she crosses the turn between the two opposite parties – the employer's side and the employee's (Extract 3, Figure 6.4). Following sympathy rules, SL not only accepts the tissue but also recognises the sympathy given to her and, although quietly, she voices a word of gratitude.

The process of claiming, giving, receiving, rejecting and denying sympathy is imbued with various meanings depending on the context in which it occurs. Although sympathizing is always about bonding, Extract 3 shows that this bonding may happen on various levels and it may touch only some but not all roles that individuals hold. While SL seems to direct her sympathy claim to SSIA, it is HR who performs a sympathizing act towards SL. However, that sympathy gift is given to a fellow human, not an institutional role of a sick-listed person. The sympathizing act here therefore does not interfere with the actors' institutional roles as a representative of the employer and as the sick-listed employee. HR is ratified as a meeting participant but in this particular episode/situation, she is not acting from her institutional role but showing her human fellowship. This episode might be seen as a kind of footing (Goffman, 1981) within the frame of the meeting but with a changed role towards SL. Thus, the sympathizing act as well as the response do not affect the course of action or subsequent turns and topic of conversation in the dominant communication. The formal meeting proceeds as if nothing has happened. Although almost entirely silent, the sympathizing act occurs across the table and because of that, the act is quite conspicuous in showing the human fellowship that bonds people even in the context of institutional talk. Still, following Cromdal and Aronsson (2000), footing here is exploited by ratified participants to conduct unofficial business as a subordinate interaction among bystanders.

Building moral ground for sympathy claims

Meeting number 2 serves as another example of how sympathy can be claimed, given and received. However, in this example, the sympathizing is clearly related to the institutional positions of employer and employee. This return-to-work meeting concerns a man in his 50s who has been on sick leave for more than a year due to depression, and seven people are present. Apart from the SSIA officer (SSIA), the sick-listed man (SL), his doctor (GP) and his employer (Emp), who is accompanied by a person from the company's HR department (HR), the sick-listed man's wife (W) and a medical social worker (SW) also participate. See Figure 6.5 for the seating arrangements.

As discussed earlier, the sick-listed person in a return-to-work meeting is in an exposed position. Such a position can make it difficult to display strong emotions, such as crying or anger, yet at the same time, conditions such as depression and anxiety affect the emotions. In this return-to-work meeting, SL – sitting straight in the chair – appears a bit tense. Occasionally he uses his hands for gesturing but most of the time he sits with his hands clasped in his lap with his gaze

Figure 6.5: The seating arrangement in meeting no. 2

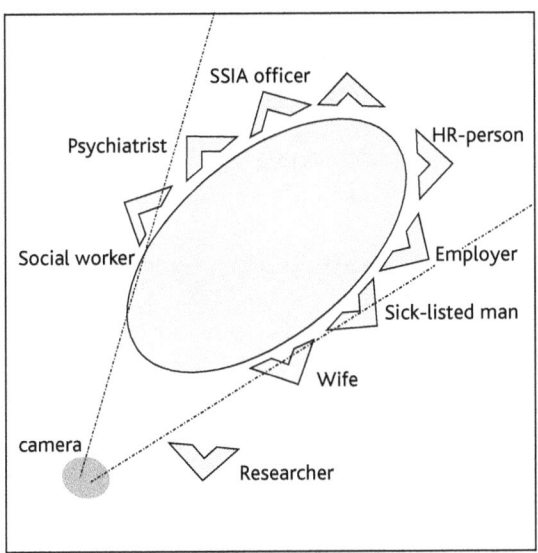

directed straight ahead. At the same time, he is quite active verbally during the whole meeting, and he often corrects information about medication or time on sick leave when GP or SSIA summarise what has happened. And when asked to tell his own story, SL does so in a clear manner, describing his difficulties and recounting his contacts with various doctors. However, when SSIA, Emp and HR are discussing what kind of work adjustments could be made at the company, HR declares that the company has little opportunity to move SL to another kind of work, but that they usually manage to arrange training periods for sick-listed employees as a process for returning to their previous work. At that moment, SL, still sitting straight and facing GP and SSIA, begins to accuse Emp as a company about the unsuccessful attempt to get him back to work nearly a year before.

Extract 4: The accusation (time 27:49–28:22)

1. SL   yes but then I hope it will be eh (.)
2. **((SL is looking down; HR gazes at SL and leans towards him))**
3. SL   it's solved differently from the last time I tried.
(.)
4. SL   we went through- and then we came (to) that I would do what was the easiest. then it took two days, then a supervisor came out and said now you must do something completely different.

5.	((SL briefly turns to HR who nods))	
(.)		
6.	SL	and do it later. ((gaze straight forward))
7.	SSIA	no, things like [that should be avoided. abso[lutely.
8.	HR	[.hm [mm
9.	((HR is nodding repeatedly while SSIA is talking))	
10.	SL	so it <u>didn't</u> feel good. it was as if (.) someone pulled the rug out from
11.	((SL looks down while tilting his head towards Emp and HR))	
12.	SSIA	mm
13.	SL	and I tried to fight and then,
(1.0)		
14.	SSIA	yes you fell apart completely.
15.	SL	I fell completely and I think I tried eh to work for about a week on the new thing and then I was,

The fact that the accusation is not directed towards Emp or HR personally, but is aimed at an anonymous supervisor at the company, may help SL to establish some common ground that everyone can relate to. Instead of starting to defend herself and the company, HR, who turns her body to face SL, displays an active listening style, bending her head and leaning forward as if trying to hear SL better. When SL very briefly turns his head towards HR, HR makes a pronounced nod in response. All this marks, if not sympathy, at least interest and the willingness to listen. And when SSIA confirms that that kind of behaviour is unacceptable, and therefore supports the accusation, HR aligns with them by repeated nodding. The accusation is therefore acknowledged as a proper topic for the meeting.

Generally, an accusation may not be the most appropriate form of sympathy claim, but it may serve as a useful strategy for establishing moral grounds for claiming sympathy. The beginning of the sequence indicates SL's drive to create a frame according to which some actions and practices are clearly identified as wrong. Very clear confirmation from SSIA (turn 7) emphasises that SL has succeeded in achieving this. Encouraged by this, he then provides a more personal account of himself as a fighter who, despite Emp's morally wrong action, tried to keep up with the unreasonable work demands. Through this, SL gains an ally in SSIA who completes his story by making the point that he "fell apart completely" (turn 14), an interpretation that SL accepts and echoes. More than that, SSIA's response can be seen as a form of empathetic role taking that constitutes one of the elements in the process of sympathy giving.

Picking up on this, SL continues with his accusations, but this time directs them at the health care professionals. According to him, his worsening condition is partly due to the mistakes and inconsistencies observed in the ways his case was handled by the medical staff. Rather than focusing immediately on himself and his own experiences, SL keeps on presenting his condition as a direct outcome of things either done to him or things that should have been done but were not. The end of this story is presented in Extract 5.

Extract 5: Telling about a tough time (time 28:55–29:35)

1. SL then she ((GP)) referred (me) to psychiatry.
2. **((SL is lifting and flipping both arms from one side to the other))**
3. SSIA precisely.
4. SL and then it took time before- so the whole summer [(.) so I felt=
5. SSIA [and autumn.
6. SL =the first week (.) after I stopped working, yes the whole summer is <u>ruined</u>. I just felt- I just dropped, I couldn't stop it.
7. **((SL firmly bangs palms on the table; HR nods))** (.)
8. SL and then as I said then I had to take (xx) ((tranquillizers)) and to calm me down and (it) stopped. then I also took sleeping **((SL is briefly flipping his arms up in the air))** pills for a while as well.
9. SSIA°. hyeah°
10. **((HR nods and turns her head away from SL and towards the doctor))**
(1.0)
11. SL so that was a tough period. yes, it was.
(1.0)
12. **((HR gazes at SL))**
13. HR but if you look at the employer, you could do a proper <u>planning</u> **((places both hand in front, palms directed inwards as if cutting an imaginary box in the air))** [there may not have been any proper planning.
14. SL   [yeah.
15. **((HR stretches her open left hand with palm upwards towards SL))**

In the second part of the episode, SL continues his story of experiences with the health care professionals. In this part, he holds the floor entirely with only a few word continuers from SSIA. HR keeps her pose and gaze directed to SL most of the time. The longer SL goes into the story, the more vividly he presents his experiences and emotions by using his hands to amplify the severity of his story. SL marks the end of the story about his hard times with a coda "*so that was a tough period. yes, it was*" (turn 11), which summarises and characterises his experiences.

The way SL tells his story about the tough times due to illness and various circumstances can thereby be heard as claims for sympathy. However, except for HR nodding a couple of times, and SSIA who confirms the story by the use of reinforcing words, such as '*precisely*' and 'h*yeah*', none of the other participants verbally endorses the emotional meaning of the story conveyed by the words and gestures. Instead, HR returns and responds to the former accusation and criticism of the company, pointing out how this can be done differently and admitting that the last time the case might not have been handled very well. HR uses the Swedish word 'man', which is more like 'one' in English, in both cases of 'you' in turn 13. This is a convenient and very commonly used pronoun, which does not point at anyone in particular but might include a number of people or only the speaker themselves. However, in a subtle way, this might be read as an act of sympathy in which HR verbally and non-verbally unites with SL in attributing some responsibility for his troubles to the company in which she works.

HR's open hand stretched towards SL in turn 15 can be contrasted with instances when she speaks about the company, the planning and the formal procedures applied to supporting employees on sick leave. During such episodes, she tends to move her hand as if following straight lines drawn in the air and dividing the space in front of her into smaller and larger boxes. Her stretched hand with palm directed upwards can thus be seen as an important offering (Kendon, 2004), a gift of sympathy that she offers to SL. That sympathy gift appears to connect two people from the same company who recognise the misconduct happening at their workplace. In that moment, HR perhaps steps outside her role as an employer's representative, which also changes the nature of alignment between SL and herself. A few seconds later, HR goes back to her ordinary role and 'ordinary' gestures (cutting the air into narrow strips) showing how the future work plan could look. However, very quickly (five turns later), HR makes a new shift (footing), which renews the alignment with SL.

Extract 6: Employer–employee alignment (time 29:42–29:57)

1.	HR	the only thing that could change that is that we don't have that transport. [that they just take it=
2.	SL	[yes
3.	HR	=away, ((*flings her arms about*)) [you never know=
4.	SL	[yeah
5.	SSIA	=that [but-
6.	SL	[no, but of course, I understand that=
7.	HR	yes [you know that
8.	**((HR stretches left hand with palm upwards towards SL))**	
9.	SL	[=(xx) that there must be a job that is adapted so that you don't invent a job.
10.	HR	yeah
11.	SL	that is not the point either.
12.	HR	no
13.	SSIA	mm

Immediately after the description of a possible work return strategy, HR shifts tone, gestures and gaze when turning to SL with a smile, a friendly tone and sweeping gestures with her hands. She is now talking about the "*only thing that could change*", the plan (turn 1). Instead of acting as an employer, as she did the second before, she again aligns with the employee against someone else who might threaten the stability of the plan: "that they just take it away" (turns 1 and 3). SL accepts and elaborates on this alignment by emphasising that he would like to have an ordinary job, not an invented one.

Extract 7: Displaying sympathy (time 29:58–30:08)

1.	HR	no. but then it may be possible to do better than we did then.
2.	**((stretches the left open hand towards SL and bends her neck))**	
3.	SL	yes
4.	HR	so it is.
5.	SSIA	mm
(1.0)		
6.	Dr	I feel that as long as we have no answer=
7.	HR	no. ((*nodding*))
8.	Dr	=it's too early to plan anything.

In the last part of the whole episode, which follows directly after the alignment of HR and the employee (SL), HR once more relates to the accusation made by SL about two minutes earlier. This time she includes herself, as a representative of the employer, when admitting that the rehabilitation process could be accomplished in a better way "*than we did then*" (turn 1). While saying this, HR stretches her open left hand towards SL as if again offering him sympathy and then she bends her neck in a way that might be interpreted as a bow. With his "yes" in turn 3, SL appears to accept the gift. As if ending the process, HR offers a summarising "*so, it is*" that is recognised by SSIA. Interestingly, after a short pause, GP steps in as if breaking the alliance built between HR and SL by indirectly emphasising that what they have discussed so far has no legitimacy because SL's condition does not allow for making any return-to-work plans yet. Thus, GP's turn can be regarded as an attempt to put the whole meeting back on track again, that is, to concentrate on the tasks for the return-to-work meeting. The episode of sympathy claims and sympathy giving can therefore be regarded as a parenthesis in the meeting, only considering relations between participants and not dealing with the tasks at hand. That HR is the first to agree verbally and non-verbally with GP could mean that she realises that her actions were outside the planned frame and she promptly uses the opportunity to get back on track.

Discussion and conclusion

The starting point of this chapter was the understanding of multi-agency welfare meetings as imbued with emotional and moral dilemmas that are equally important to the institutional tasks at hand. The focus was on the place of sympathy in such meetings and the ways in which sympathizing interacts with various alliances built between the health and welfare professionals and service users.

The analysis demonstrates that sympathy is not alien to the institutional context; the same rules, the same processes of sympathy that have been recorded in other contexts (mainly concerning everyday interactions), also appeared in the context of the multi-agency welfare meetings analysed here. The institutional context, however, brings particular limitations on how, by whom and when sympathizing may occur to ensure that the meeting proper remains intact. Institutional meetings are task-oriented, asymmetrical and each participant has a prescribed role to fulfil. In contrast, sympathizing is about emotions and relations. To recognise the service user's sympathy claims may therefore be seen as a potential threat to the ordinary structure of the institutional meeting as well as to the institutional roles assigned to the various meeting participants – unless other roles are activated during such occurrences.

The instances of offering sympathy gifts analysed here demonstrated the subtle ways in which the institutional actors in multi-agency welfare meetings activated their diverse roles, stepping in this way outside the one-sided institutional role prescribed by the meeting's frame. Consequently, sympathizing acts did not cause any changes in the course of the ongoing formal meeting since it did not affect any of the institutional roles. Instead, the sympathizing only connected two persons on the basis of their humanity. This was achieved through footing and the change of alignment that the speaker initiated between themselves and the others present at the meeting. In cases when the sympathizing could be seen as part of the dominant communication of the meeting (meeting no. 2), other participants seemed to disqualify those instances from being sympathy acts inscribed in the institutional context, instead treating them as something outside the frame of the proper meeting. Thus, HR in meeting no. 2 might sympathize with SL from the position of her professional role as one employee to another employee, but not necessarily from the institutional position of an employer. Forming institutional bonds through sympathizing acts seems hard to achieve in a multi-agency meeting such as a return-to-work meeting since such acts not only change the asymmetrical 'balance' between stakeholders and the service user, but also threaten to change the whole meeting and thereby the balance between various stakeholders. Changes in footing that involved assuming a different role vis-à-vis the service user and distancing oneself from the formal role of the meeting seemed to be a way for stakeholders to handle sympathy claims in the meeting.

The application of the concept of 'sympathy' to an analysis of institutional meetings provides another set of lenses through which to critically scrutinise the micropolitics of such meetings and to discuss the power relations underpinning them. Sympathy and the process of sympathizing are not about equality and the equal distribution of power. On the contrary, sympathy may magnify existing power imbalances and stratification as evident in various situations. Multi-agency return-to-work meetings are supported politically through the notions of participation, shared responsibility and collaboration, while everyday practice indicates that those meetings are anything but that. The acts of sympathy analysed in this chapter demonstrate the subtle ways in which service users' troubles make them into dependent meeting participants whose voice may or may not be granted the space they would wish. Clearly, references to illness and personal difficulties tend to be dismissed as legitimate grounds for sympathy acts. Service users are reminded in this way that their key worry is lack of work, not their poor health. Further, the examples presented here also demonstrate that when sympathizing coincides with alliances, the formal structure/content of the meeting can be affected. The relations created outside the meeting room and their histories therefore have a prominent place in determining the situational dynamics. What is remembered from before and how it is remembered has consequences for crafting present situations. By the same token, when sympathy does not coincide with an alliance, then it becomes 'just' an act of humanity. It still, however, has its place in the institutional setting, but its power to effect the meeting proper is very limited if it has any at all. By using Goffman's (1981) concept of 'footing', this could be understood as a way of temporarily changing individual stakeholders' roles within the overall institutional meeting frame.

This chapter also problematises the boundaries drawn between institutional and emotional worlds. Emotions are inherent to the institutional setting. This does not mean that institutional meetings are like everyday encounters, but rather that the institutional frame of the meetings is produced by interacting actors who, while negotiating the formality of the meeting, resort to their various positions, make judgements and create new meanings. All this is underpinned by emotions understood as ways of relating to others. The process of constructing and responding to emotions is above all else a bodily process and it is through bodily movements and changes that emotions become readable. Within the institutional setting, certain emotions may therefore bind people together, but they may also impede some forms of dialogue or collaborative work. The focus on sympathy and sympathizing allows us to trace the ways in which that bonding occurs and the grounds on which it is based. Above all else, this chapter highlights the multidimensional roles and perspectives assumed by institutional actors that, in addition to professional codes of conduct, are deeply embedded in the emotional life of each and every one. Multi-agency welfare meetings expose the interdependence of various subjectivities and positions that may sometimes require more or less emotional work than usually but are never entirely devoid of emotion. Health and welfare professionals are therefore tasked with recognising that, by definition, the institutional agenda is always an emotional agenda.

Transcript key

The following symbols have been developed by Gail Jefferson (Hutchby and Wooffitt, 1998).

((wipes her nose))	non-verbal activity such as gestures and gaze recognised as turns or part of turns
((comment))	transcriber's comments on contextual or other features
[	start of overlapping talk
?	questioning intonation
.	a conclusive fall in tone
,	a 'continuing' intonation
(.)	short pause
(1s)	pause 1 second or longer
=	indicates 'latching' between utterances of the same speaker
(xx)	inaudible word or words
(guess)	transcriber's best guess at an unclear utterance
-	sharp cut-off of the prior word or sound
underlined	speaker's emphasis

References

Aronsson, K. and Cederborg, A.-C. (1994) 'Conarration and voice in family therapy: Voicing, devoicing, and orchestration', *Text*, 14(3): 345–70.

Clark, C. (1987) 'Sympathy biography and sympathy margin', *American Journal of Sociology*, 93(2): 290–321.

Clark, C. (1990) 'Emotions and micropolitics in everyday life: some patterns and paradoxes of "place"', in T.D. Kemper (ed) *Research Agendas in the Sociology of Emotions*, New York, NY: State University of New York Press, pp 305–33.

Clark, C. (1997) *Misery and Company: Sympathy in Everyday Life*, Chicago, IL: University of Chicago Press.

Cromdal, J. and Aronsson, K. (2000) 'Footing in bilingual play', *Journal of Sociolinguistics*, 4(3): 435–57.

Ekberg, K. (2011) 'Arbetsförmåga och anställningsbarhet i teori och praktik' [Workability and employability in theory and practice], *Socialmedicinsk Tidskrift*, 88(5): 399–407.

Flinkfeldt, M. (2017) 'Wanting to work: Managing the sick role in high-stake sickness insurance meetings', *Sociology of Health and Illness*, 39(7): 1149–65.

Fortier, A.M. (2016) 'Afterword: acts of affective citizenship? Possibilities and limitations', *Citizenship Studies*, 20(8), 1038–44.

Goffman, E. (1981) *Forms of Talk*, Philadelphia, PA: University of Pennsylvania Press.

Goodwin, M.H. and Goodwin, C. (2000) 'Emotion within situated activity', in N. Budwig, I.C. Uzgris and J.V. Wertsch (eds) *Communication: An Arena of Development*, Stamford, CT: Ablex, pp 33–53.

Hall, C. and Slembrouck, S. (2001) 'Parent participation in social work meetings – the case of child protection conferences', *European Journal of Social Work*, 4(2): 143–60.

Hall, C., Slembrouck, S. and Sarangi, S. (2006) *Language Practices in Social Work:. Categorisation and Accountability in Child Welfare*, London: Routledge.

Hunter, S. (2015) *Power, Politics and the Emotions: Impossible Governance?* New York, NY: Routledge.

Hutchby, I. and Wooffitt, R. (1998) *Conversation Analysis*, Cambridge: Polity Press.

Johanson, M., Larsson, U.S., Säljö, R. and Svärdsudd, K. (1996) 'Addressing life style in primary health care', *Social Science and Medicine*, 43(3): 389–400.

Johnson, B. (2010) *Kampen om sjukfrånvaron* [The battle of sick leave], Lund: Arkiv Förlag.

Junestav, M. (2009) 'Sjukskrivning som politiskt problem-sociala normer, institutionell förändring och det politiska språket'[Sick leave as a political problem – social norms, institutional changes and the language of politics], *Arbetsmarknad and Arbetsliv*, 15(4): 9–27.

Kangasharju, H. (1996) 'Aligning as a team in multiparty conversation', *Journal of Pragmatics*, 26(3): 291–319.

Kendon, A. (2004) *Gesture: Visible Action as Utterance*, Cambridge: Cambridge University Press.

Kykyri, V.-L., Tourunen, A., Nyman-Salonen, P., Kurri, K., Wahlström, J., Kaartinen, J., Pentonnen, M. and Seikkula, J. (2019) 'Alliance Formations in Couple Therapy: A Multimodal and Multimethod Study', *Journal of Couple and Relationship Therapy*, 18(3): 189–222.

Linell, P. (1998) 'Discourse across boundaries: On recontextualizations and the blending of voices in professional discourse', *Text*, 18(2): 143–57.

Melén, D. (2008) *Sjukskrivningssystemet: sjuka som blir arbetslösa och arbetslösa som blir sjukskrivna* [The system for reporting sick: sick become employed and unemployed become sick], Lund: Lund University.

Oben, B. and Brône, G. (2016) 'Explaining interactive alignment: A multimodal and multifactorial account', *Journal of Pragmatics*, 104: 32–51.

Oliver, D.G., Serovich, J.M. and Mason, T.L. (2005) 'Constraints and opportunities with interview transcription: Towards reflection in qualitative research', *Social Forces*, 84(2): 1273–89.

Patrick, R. (2012) 'Work as the primary "duty" of the responsible citizen: a critique of this work-centric approach', *People, Place and Policy Online*, 6(1): 5–15.

Ruusuvuori, J. (2001) 'Looking means listening: Coordinating displays of engagement in doctor–patient interaction', *Social Science and Medicine*, 52(7): 1093–108.

Ruusuvuori, J. (2005) '"Empathy" and "sympathy" in action: Attending to patients' troubles in Finnish homeopathic and general practice consultations', *Social Psychology Quarterly*, 68(3): 204–22.

Seing, I., Ståhl, C., Nordenfelt, L., Bülow, P. and Ekberg, K. (2012) 'The policy and practice of work ability: A negotiation of responsibility in organizing return to work practices', *Journal of Occupational Rehabilitation*, 22(4): 553–64.

Ståhl, C., Svensson, T., Petersson, G. and Ekberg, K. (2011) 'Swedish rehabilitation professionals' perspectives on work ability assessments in a changing sickness insurance system', *Disability and Rehabilitation*, 33(15–16): 1373–82.

Stivers, T., Mondada, L. and Steensig, J. (2011) 'Knowledge, morality and affiliation in social interaction', in T. Stivers, L. Mondada and J. Steensig (eds) *The Morality of Knowledge in Conversation*, Cambridge: Cambridge University Press, pp 3–24.

Wetherell, M. (2012) *Affect and Emotion: A New Social Science Understanding*, London: Sage Publications.

Wilińska, M. and Bülow, P.H. (2017) '"We are on air now": the visibility of video-recording in the institutional setting', *International Journal of Social Research Methodology*, 20(4): 343–55.

Wilińska, M. and Bülow, P.H. (2020) 'Emotion ability – practices of affective citizenship in the work rehabilitation process', *Critical Policy Studies*, 14(1): 38–66.

7

Negotiating epistemic rights to knowledge concerning service users' recent histories in mental health meetings

Kirsi Juhila, Lisa Morriss and Suvi Raitakari

Introduction

Face-to-face interactions between professionals and service users are central to mental health services. Participants jointly seek, gather, produce and assess knowledge about concerns, risks and troubles that need to be addressed, for example, mental health, financial and interpersonal issues. Social work and health care are often conducted in multi-agency settings and meetings where professionals from different disciplines and service users address each other. In multi-agency meetings, mental health service users are both talked to and talked about, and they also describe their own situations and experiences. This creates a sensitive interactional task for professionals. Professionals need to express such knowledge about the service users that they deem relevant to tackle the issues at hand and make judgements in situations where service users are co-present as listeners, yet also co-producers of knowledge. Producing and using knowledge is bound to epistemic rights, to the 'distribution of rights and responsibilities regarding what participants can accountably know, how they know it, whether they have rights to describe it, and in what terms' (Heritage and Raymond, 2005, p 15).

This chapter studies how knowledge of service users' recent histories and their experiences is produced, presented and used in statutory Care Programme Approach (CPA) meetings in England. The participants in the meetings are service users, their care coordinators, housing support workers and psychiatrists. The analysis displays which participants in this multi-agency interaction epistemically own knowledge about the service users' recent past. What makes the ownership of this knowledge interesting is that despite dealing with service users' personal histories, at times it is the professionals who hold this knowledge based on their previous interactions with a particular service user. Thus, in analysing the meetings, we are interested in how professionals present themselves as knowledgeable about the service user's history, and how service user participation is realised or not on these occasions.

The Care Programme Approach

The Care Programme Approach (CPA) was introduced in 1991 as a statutory framework for people requiring support in the community for more severe and enduring mental health problems (Department of Health, 1990). The framework has four main requirements:

- a systematic assessment of the service user's health and social care needs;
- the formulation of a care plan to address these identified needs;
- a named key worker (now called a care coordinator) to coordinate the care plan;
- regular reviews to ensure that the care plan still meets the needs of the service user.

The CPA was modernised (Department of Health, 1999) with a focus on integrating the CPA and care management, more consistent implementation of the CPA nationally, streamlining the CPA process to reduce the burden of bureaucracy and achieving a proper focus on the needs of service users. Carpenter et al (2004) interviewed 260 mental health service users on CPA registers in four districts in the north of England. The majority of these participants (230) were then re-interviewed six months later. During the first interview, approximately half of the service users knew that they had a written care programme. Most participants who knew of the care plan held positive views; approximately 90% agreed with their care plan, and thought it was clear and comprehensive and addressed their needs. In terms of the CPA review, more than half of the users in Districts A and D but only a third of the users in Districts B and C attended such meetings.

The Department of Health published a consultation paper in 2006 with the aim of enhancing the effectiveness of the CPA process. The paper acknowledged concerns that instead of enabling real engagement with people, the process was rigid, inconsistent and a managerial 'tick-box' tool. In addition, mental health service users felt that they were not involved as partners in the process, and the emphasis was on problems, risk and treatment, rather than a strengths-based approach towards recovery (Department of Health, 2006). Following this, the CPA was revised in 2008 to refocus on people in contact with secondary mental health services with 'complex characteristics' (Department of Health, 2008, p 11). These 'characteristics' are set out in a table in the 2008 guidance and include:

- a severe mental disorder with a high degree of clinical complexity;
- current or potential risk(s), including a risk of suicide, self-harm and harm to others;
- a current or significant history of severe distress/instability or disengagement.

A person with one or more of the 'characteristics' has a named care coordinator and an initial comprehensive multidisciplinary, multi-agency assessment to formulate a care plan, which is then reviewed at least once a year at a formal multi-agency CPA review meeting. This care plan should include explicit crisis and contingency plans, and support for any physical health needs. In this revised form, the CPA resonates with the prevailing policy of collaborative and integrated care that is expected to respond to service users' complex problems and needs with a comprehensive care plan that is regularly reviewed in multi-agency meetings (see Chapter 1). It also seems to rely on the idea of relational agency, emphasising that interactions among various professionals and service users produce solutions to complex problems that are more than just a combination of individual professionals' and service users' expertise and interpretations of problems (Edwards, 2011; see also Chapter 1).

The new guidance included a Statement of Values and Principles (Department of Health, 2008, p 7), stating that this approach to individuals' care and support 'puts them at the centre and promotes social inclusion and recovery'. However, Gould (2013) found that CPA care plans predominately emphasise clinical outcomes, medication and risk. Indeed, Tew et al (2012, p 455) argued that there needs to be a fundamental paradigm shift where an individualised 'treatment-oriented' approach such as the CPA is replaced by a recovery-oriented approach, 'in which working with family and friends, and promoting social inclusion, are no longer optional extras'.

Finally, the 2016 National Community Mental Health Survey undertaken by the Care Quality Commission (2016) had responses from 13,200 adults receiving specialist care or treatment for a mental health condition. Of these adults, 29% had their care coordinated under the CPA. In terms of knowing who was in charge of organising their care and services, 88% of the CPA respondents had been given this information. Only 52% of the CPA respondents had 'definitely' agreed with the mental health services about the care they would receive, 82% said their care had been reviewed in the previous 12 months and 80% knew who to contact out of office hours in a crisis. Fewer than half of the CPA respondents (43%) answered that they had had help with or advice on finding support for physical health needs in the previous 12 months, and only 43% 'definitely' received help with or advice on finding support for financial advice and finding or keeping work. Lastly, only 38% of the CPA respondents had 'definitely' had support from mental health services to enable them to engage in a local activity. To conclude, according to various reports, it appears that the CPA process still has problems from the point of view of service users and in terms of their participation.

Furthermore, research on how the CPA is accomplished in interactions between service users and professionals is lacking. Hence, there is a need for a detailed study of frontline practices of the CPA. This chapter deals with one of the core CPA practices, namely the multi-agency meetings (CPA meetings) where service users' situations and future steps in their care pathways are reviewed and discussed. In analysing these meetings, special attention is paid to knowledge production. What and whose knowledge is in focus and considered valuable is consequential in generating 'common' knowledge in these meetings. In particular, how service users are treated as participants in creating knowledge concerning their own lives is reflected in whether the meetings resemble degradation ceremonies or integration ceremonies (see Chapters 1 and 2).

Epistemic access and rights to service users' recent histories

This chapter asks how knowledge of service users' recent histories is produced, presented and used by the participants in their interactions in CPA meetings. Specifically, the focus is on which participants seem to epistemically 'own' this knowledge by displaying themselves as having direct and primary access to it and also having rights to present and use it as 'experts' (on epistemic rights in conversations, see Heritage and Raymond, 2005; Raymond and Heritage, 2006; Heritage, 2012). 'Owning' knowledge is connected to participants' epistemic statuses in interactions. According to Stevanovic and Peräkylä, (2014; see also Rautajoki, 2010):

> The term epistemic status refers to the position that a participant has in a certain domain of *knowledge*, relative to his/her co-participant(s). It is one facet of the participants' momentary relationship. It is based on the participants' common personal history, while being shaped by the cultural and institutional expectations of who should know what, and about what. Importantly, however, epistemic status is continuously modified in the turn-by-turn sequential unfolding of interaction, as participants share their knowledge with each other. (Stevanovic and Peräkylä, 2014, p 189, emphasis in original)

Epistemic statuses in the CPA meetings are thus displayed and modified in turn-by-turn sequential interactions. However, there are some cultural preconceptions about who is assumed to have access and rights to certain domains of knowledge. In everyday conversation, participants are treated as having privileged access to their own past experiences and the associated right to knowledge claims about these experiences (Pomerantz, 1980; Sacks, 1984; Heritage and Raymond, 2005, p 16). In professional–service user interactions, service users are also supposed to have epistemic authority ('ownership') of their own inner thoughts and experiences as well as knowledge of their personal life histories, whereas people in the medical, psychological and social work professions, among others, are expected to possess knowledge because they have educational qualifications based on these domains of knowledge. In the course of (inter)professional–service user interactions, participants usually orient to these assumed epistemic authorities. For example, in a social worker–service user interaction in mental health, a worker can say, 'How are you feeling?' and in this question format, cedes the ownership of inner feelings and their assessment to the service user themselves (see Heritage and Raymond, 2005, pp 21–2). Alternatively, the service user can orient to the worker's epistemic authority by asking, 'Do you think I need some therapy in order to overcome this crisis?' Ekberg and LeCouter (2015) give an example of the differences between assumed epistemic authority in therapy settings:

> Making proposals for behavioural change may inadvertently create a dilemma for therapists. Although they carry the authority of a professional perspective, therapists only ever have secondary access to knowledge about a client's life and situation, based on what the client has shared within the therapy session. Clients will always have the ultimate epistemic access to how situations have played out in their lives, and how their behaviour may affect their situation in the future. (Ekberg and LeCouter, 2015, p 13)

However, in the CPA meetings, epistemic authority regarding the service users' personal life histories and related experiences appears to be shared with some of the professionals present, as care coordinators and housing support workers may orient to this knowledge and thus display that they have access to it. The professionals indicate in their turns that they have had direct access to the referent states of the service users' recent personal histories. The professionals' knowledge and right to make statements concerning the service user are then based on the assumption that they have been present, and seen and experienced the service user's reality.

Data and the process of analysis

The material in this chapter consists of three CPA meetings that took place in England. The meetings were audio-recorded with the consent of all the participants and then transcribed as part of a larger project examining service user–professional interactions in mental health in England and Finland.[1] The participants present in the CPA meetings are the service users and their care coordinators, the support workers from the service users' current supported housing services and psychiatrists. Psychiatrists act as chairs in two meetings, with a care coordinator chairing the third meeting, as the psychiatrist was unable to attend.

CPA meetings are organised in a question–answer format based on an official form that the chair follows in order to thoroughly discuss all the required topics and assess the possible risks, thereby fulfilling the pre-specified organisational purposes and institutional task of the meetings. In this sense, the meetings have a rather formal and ritualistic structure (see Chapter 2). Overall, the participants in the meetings seek to coordinate the services, assess the past, and plan forthcoming steps and interventions in the service users' pathways and future lives in general.

The analysis of the three CPA meetings was commenced by highlighting the sequences where the service users and professionals refer to the recent histories of the service users. Such sequences were present in each of the three meetings. In total, 41 sequences of this kind were identified. These mostly began with a question posed by the chair to the service user. For example, the questions invite the service user to describe what they have done recently, how they deal with everyday affairs (for example, cleaning and money matters), what kinds of close relationships they have, how well they have felt mentally and physically, what medicines they take and whether their services are appropriate for them.

As the questions from the chair involve the service users' personal matters, the service user should be ceded epistemic authority in having privileged access to the information and the associated right to answer the questions. However, professionals, especially the support workers but the care coordinators too, also often present themselves as knowledgeable about the service users' recent personal matters. Based on this core finding, a key research question of the study is: How do mental health professionals produce, present and use knowledge whose epistemic rights can be regarded as belonging to the service user? Following Heritage and Raymond's (2005, p 34) proposal to identify 'a variety of practices that are deployed in managing these epistemic claims', six devices were identified through which the professionals produce, present and use knowledge of the recent histories and past experiences of the service users. They were present in all three CPA meetings. These devices are:

- confirming service users' personal knowledge;
- adding some knowledge to service users' personal knowledge;
- fishing for personal knowledge from service users;
- producing positive assessments of service users;
- producing knowledge on behalf of service users;
- challenging service users' personal knowledge.

In the next section, four illustrative extracts from the CPA meetings are analysed. The extracts demonstrate the six devices and the ways in which the professionals use them in producing knowledge of the service users' recent histories, thus displaying that they have some epistemic authority for this knowledge. In analysing the extracts, attention is also placed on whether the talk on the service users' recent histories is discussed jointly among the professionals and the service users or not.

Analysis: displaying epistemic rights regarding service users' recent histories

'Aligning talk' about positive changes in the service user's recent life

The first extract is taken from the meeting with Tim, a man in his 20s and currently living in supported housing. The sequence begins when the chair asks Tim if he has any "worrying debts".

Extract 1

1. Chair: Okay, do you have any worrying debts that you?
2. Tim: No, I don't at all. I always pay my bills on time.
3. Housing support worker: Brings me the receipt every two weeks.
4. Tim: Just going back to ((previous unit)), a lot of people were always asking me for money and pressuring me for money as well, like abuse, financial abuse and that, and actually, I don't get that right now at ((present supported housing unit)), so I've always got my money to myself now. Do you know what I mean? So, that's even better. They were just using me for money all the time, always asking, knocking on my door at two o'clock in the morning asking for a fiver, and you're saying, away man. Do you know what I mean?
5. Care coordinator: So that is something.
6. Housing support worker: And this is one of the things that concerns us.
7. Care coordinator: That we always talk about because, Tim, you don't like to say no to people, but it's not been an issue at ((present supported housing unit)).
8. Tim: The concern is to get my own place; I don't get involved with people that take smack or drugs and that, but like I say, with my own place, I'll obviously get support off you lot. I know that, yeah, but like otherwise my mum and stepdad and Eric ((unclear)), I'm not going to have loads of lads in now, have like a drugs sesh, I'm not like that.
9. Housing support worker: I know you're not.
10. Care coordinator: But you made that change, you cut the people out of your life that could have caused that to happen again. You don't see them, do you?
11. Tim: Yeah, that's because what it was when I was poorly back in '06, I wanted to be in hospital because I wanted the help. When I was on heroin, yeah, I was on it for about, just about three and a half weeks, and the majority of the time, I did have some, and when I went to hospital, I went to ((hospital)) because I went a bit mad in the head, and I got withdrawal symptoms for a couple of days, and after that, I was clean and I haven't touched it since then. So, I've been clean seven years of heroin plus like smoking, I stopped smoking as well, like, as you know about other drugs. Don't drink that much now, go to work, get out and about, and just keep well to my medication.
12. Housing support worker: He is.
13. Tim: So, I feel better now because this is where I wanted to be.

14. Chair: Well, you've actually achieved a very good recovery and you're sustaining it okay, and you're very, very mindful about what might trigger a relapse, which is obviously drugs and alcohol.

Tim responds to the chair's question by using extreme formulations ("No, I don't at all. I always pay my bills on time"; see Pomerantz, 1986), thus offering reassurance that there are no worries regarding debts. The housing support worker *confirms* Tim's response and simultaneously produces a *positive assessment* of Tim's ability to take care of his financial matters by *adding* concrete evidence to it: "Brings me the receipt every two weeks" (turn 3). While applying these two devices, she displays herself as knowledgeable about Tim's money matters. After this, Tim starts recounting his experiences when he was living in another housing unit (turn 4). He presents his previous self as a victim of abuse, as "a lot of people" were continuously asking him to give them money and were pressuring him to do so. He was not even safe in the unit, since "people" could come to his door at any time. Notable in Tim's turn is that it contains the narrative of an identity change. He used to be a victim of 'financial abuse' in the past but is not anymore: "I've always got my money to myself now." This short turn can be interpreted as a recovery narrative: in terms of financial matters, he has moved towards living more independently. Right after Tim's narrative, the care coordinator and the housing support worker start talking almost at the same time. In their turns (5–7), they display knowledge of Tim's past as a victim and the changing situation in the current unit, and thus *confirm* the narrative. However, they also seem to slightly *challenge* the narrative by producing some concern and hint that the problem of Tim's inability "to say no to people" is perhaps not yet totally resolved.

Tim continues that the key to solving the problem is to get his "own place" (turn 8). It is difficult to interpret whether he disagrees with what the professionals have just said about the concern. Tim continues 'change talk', as he assures the professionals that he will not be involved with the 'wrong kind' of people any more, especially if he gets support from the professionals and his family members. Admitting that he continues to need support, however, indicates that he remains in a recovery process. Here again, the housing support worker and the care coordinator join the conversation with *confirming* and *positive assessments* about the change that Tim has made in his life (turns 9 and 10). Furthermore, the care coordinator still *fishes* from Tim the assurance that he does not see certain 'abusive' people anymore (turn 10). Tim responds to this fishing not just by simply saying no, but by creating another recovery narrative, starting from the time when he still used drugs and ending with the situation where he stopped using heroin and smoking (turn 11). In the last sentence of this turn, Tim presents himself as a person whose governance of life is rather good in comparison with the past: "Don't drink that much now, go to work, get out and about, and just keep well to my medication." In turn 13, he makes a positive self-evaluation on this current state: "So I feel better now because this is where I wanted to be." The housing support worker's comment between Tim's turns – "he is" – can be interpreted as *confirmation* of Tim's talk on the positive changes (turn 12). Finally, after hearing the conversation between Tim, the housing support worker and the care coordinator, the chair concludes that Tim has "achieved a very good recovery". He talks directly to Tim, thus showing that Tim is the main character in the recovery process.

To conclude, in this conversation about Tim's history, Tim has epistemic authority. The chair poses his opening question directly to him and concludes the conversation by treating him as a core recipient. Tim is active in describing the processes of change in his recent history, thus displaying himself as an owner of this knowledge. The housing support worker and the care coordinator mostly confirm Tim's talk and make positive assessments of the changes that Tim speaks about making in his life. While doing this, they show themselves as partly knowledgeable about Tim's recent history, having access to it as professionals. This is predominantly an example of aligning and joint talk about the service user's recent history, with a slight note of non-aligned talk regarding whether the concern about letting 'abusive people' take Tim's money has been completely resolved.

'On behalf of talk' about the service user's recent support needs

Susan, the service user in the second extract, is a middle-aged woman who lives in a supported housing unit. Very early on in the CPA meeting, the chair asks Susan to outline the support she receives in the supported unit.

Extract 2

1. Chair: Can you tell us a little bit about what support you get?
2. Susan: They help us cleaning up in the flat. And they take us out places and that.
3. Chair: Yeah, okay, and how much help do you need?
4. Susan: How much help I need?

5. Chair: Yeah, some people need a little bit and some people need a lot. Where are you at?
6. Susan: I don't (..)
7. Chair: Okay, may I ask ((housing support worker)) about what her view is about how you manage?
8. Susan: Yeah.
9. Housing support worker: Susan has support from myself most days, and we've also now got a personal budget worker involved, and that's an extra nine hours a week.
10. Chair: On top of the support that you?
11. Housing support worker: On top of the support that she gets from myself and our support assistant. Susan's saying she's good at present, but in the last fortnight, Susan's been phoning the crisis team because your mood had dipped and you had thoughts of self-harm.
12. Susan: Yeah.
13. Housing support worker: And going to the shop and buying tablets. And when it was discussed you couldn't really say why, you just say it comes over you and it happens. But Susan, her life skills, if we don't see her daily, then it lapses, it really dips, and what we've done is we work off kind of timetables, Susan, don't we?
14. Susan: Yeah.
15. Housing support worker: We sit down and we have a plan of even when she eats because she forgets to eat.
16. Chair: Do you? Oh, right.
17. Housing support worker: So, we do menu planning. And we have pictures of breakfast and lunches just to give Susan ideas. We have a timetable for showering, cleaning and socialising. And Susan also has a daily journal where she writes down what she does daily, and this helps with her functioning.
18. Chair: Okay. It's quite highly structured, isn't it?
19. Susan: Yeah.
20. Chair: And how do you find that? Do you find it helpful or do you find it a bit intrusive?
21. Susan: Helpful.
22. Chair: You do, okay. So, you welcome the support do you, okay? Without that support, what do you think you would do?
23. Susan: I don't know.
24. Chair: Would you do your cleaning up, would you do your washing, would you do your cooking?
25. Susan: Well, I'd do my washing, yeah.

26. Chair: Yeah, oh okay, but it's nice to have somebody around just like a little supporter really just to make sure things get done. What about paying your bills?
27. Susan: I pay them.
28. Chair: Yeah? Is that going okay?
29. Housing support worker: Susan is fantastic at paying her bills.
30. Chair: Are you? Right, okay.
31. Housing support worker: And brilliant with her medication and even brilliant with the washing; they're her three good skills.
32. Chair: So, you've got some skills that you're perfectly in charge of, haven't you really, but some that you need a bit of support on.

Susan associates "support" with "help" and replies that she gets help with cleaning and with going out (turn 2). The chair then reframes this by asking "how much help do you need?", which Susan simply repeats, demonstrating that she does not understand what is being asked (turns 3–4). Even though the chair rephrases this by quantifying this as "a little" or "a lot", Susan still does not provide an adequate response (turns 5–6). The chair, thus, asks Susan if it is okay for the housing support worker to give her perspective (turn 7). By asking permission for this, the chair recognises that turning to another person in this matter violates Susan's epistemic rights to assess her own everyday life and the help she needs in it. Susan's acceptance "yeah" (turn 8) gives the housing support worker a kind of permission to violate Susan's epistemic rights. She also uses this right by answering the chair and producing information about the amount of support *on behalf of* Susan (turn 9).

The chair seems to question whether Susan is receiving extra support of nine hours per week through a 'personal budget' (turn 10). Recognising the inherent questioning, the housing support worker confirms by repeating the chair's phrase "on top of the support that" and continues with a justification. In doing so, she directly *challenges* a positive evaluation Susan made earlier in the meeting about her own situation, that "she's good at present". This challenge is produced by *adding* new knowledge as evidence: "Susan's saying she's good at present, but in the last fortnight, Susan's been phoning the crisis team because your mood had dipped and you had thoughts of self-harm" (turn 11). The first half of this statement is directed at the chair, referring to Susan in the third person, but it then moves to addressing Susan directly through "your" and "you had". By this direct addressing, the housing support worker invites Susan to confirm this knowledge, to which they both have access. Once Susan has affirmed this, the housing support worker continues by introducing further personal knowledge *on behalf of* the service user ("going to the shop and buying tablets", turn 13). Again, she starts by addressing Susan as "you", and then part way through the reply, she directs her answer to the chair, before again moving back to Susan to ask a direct *fishing* question: "don't we?" Here, adding the tag question makes a positive yes answer conditionally relevant (Heritage, 2010), which Susan duly supplies. The use of rhetorical questions shepherds service users towards particular responses (Jingree et al, 2006).

In her following turns (15 and 17), the housing support worker provides the chair with extensive detailed knowledge relating to Susan's recent daily routines and life. The chair's reply is prefaced by the particle "Oh" (turn 16). "Oh" reveals that the chair finds the previous turn in some way problematic (Heritage, 1998), and she goes on to describe it as "highly structured" (turn 18). The *fishing* tag question, "isn't it?" again makes a yes answer preferable here, which Susan supplies. The chair then asks Susan: "Do you find it helpful or do you find it a bit intrusive?" (turn 20). It is notable that the chair chooses Susan as the recipient in turns 16 and 18, which emphasises her epistemic rights in the matters under discussion concerning her personal life. Overall, questions are marked by 'recipient-titled epistemic asymmetry', but they also contain presuppositions and agendas (Hayano, 2012, p 400). In turn 18, the chair seems to imply that this highly structured timetable is rather controlling. However, Susan does not agree with this implication as she repeats the word "helpful", which shows slight alignment with the housing support worker's descriptions about the support that Susan needs in her everyday life (turn 21). In her next utterance, the chair asks a more general question (turn 22), which Susan is unable to answer (turn 23). Thus, the chair asks three specific questions related to cleaning up, washing and cooking (turn 24). Susan only answers one of the questions (turn 25); the "well" preface may indicate that she is contesting the answerability of the chair's questions (Heritage, 2015).

The chair minimises the support that she previously alluded to as "intrusive" by describing it as: "just like a little supporter really, just to make sure things get done" (turn 26). Here, the chair is reframing the situation by decreasing the extent to which Susan is moving forwards with her recovery. She then asks Susan about paying her bills and gets a positive answer from her (turns 26 and 27). After that, she asks the housing support worker to endorse Susan's answer that she pays them: "Is that going okay?" (turn 28). This checking positions the chair as doubting Susan's answer, which, in turn, positions Susan as not having exclusive epistemic rights to knowledge of her own situation. The housing support worker *confirms* Susan's answer and produces a *positive assessment*, stating: "Susan is fantastic at paying her bills" (turn 29). The chair again seems doubtful by again questioning Susan (turn 30). However, the housing support worker continues to display her knowledge of Susan's everyday life by making a *positive assessment* of her other two skills: taking her medication and washing (turn 31). This assessment leads the chair to conclude that Susan has some skills but needs "a bit of support" in other areas (turn 32).

To sum up, the conversation in this extract contains a lot of talk on Susan's behalf. The chair puts her first questions directly to Susan concerning the support she gets. Susan responds to the questions in a hesitant way, and soon, the chair asks her permission to turn to the housing support worker regarding her support. The housing support worker responds by producing a lot of detailed talk on Susan's behalf about the support she gets and needs. The chair directs a couple of questions to Susan, who gives short or hesitant answers. The housing support worker talks in a way that shows her to be very knowledgeable about Susan's recent history and personal everyday life. Susan does not resist this, but lets the housing support worker talk on her behalf. In this sense, the talk between Susan and the housing support worker is more joint than non-aligned.

'Disagreeing talk' about the service user's memory of services he is entitled to

The third extract is again taken from Tim's CPA meeting. The chair asks Tim about '117 aftercare'. Since this information is required on the CPA form, the extract demonstrates how the talk is structured around the completion of the form.

Extract 3

1. Chair: Are you aware that you're entitled to 117 aftercare?
2. Tim: I've not heard of this before.
3. Chair: Most people haven't heard of it.
4. Care coordinator: We actually spoke about it last time, and Anna talked to you about it, about how certain things get paid for when you're on 117 because you'd been on a section of the Mental Health Act in the past.
5. Tim: Yeah, Section 3, yeah.
6. Care coordinator: Can you remember us talking, you can't remember us talking about that?

7.   Tim: I can't honestly. I know you did, like I'm not saying you didn't, but I just can't remember.
8.   Chair: We've got a leaflet there, but basically, it's one of the better things about being detained under the Mental Health Act.

It is notable that in her opening question, the chair makes an implicit assumption that Tim would understand her reference to the legal term '117 aftercare'. As Tim's care coordinator goes on to partly explain, the chair is referring to Section 117 of the Mental Health Act 1983 (turn 4).[2]

For the chair's first question on his awareness of 117 aftercare, Tim replies that he has not heard of it before (turn 2), which the chair confirms is quite common (turn 3). By normalising this unawareness, the chair saves Tim's face (Goffman, 1967). However, after that, the care coordinator interjects and produces knowledge *on behalf of* Tim and *challenges* Tim's knowledge (turn 4). The use of the word "actually" is significant, as Oh (2000, p 254) points out; it has a distinct function in talk, indicating that 'the speaker is engaged in a particular speech act, especially of a face-threatening type, such as contradicting, correcting, or disagreeing with the previous speaker'. Further, Oh (2000, p 266) argues that the use of 'actually' signals unexpectedness and 'tends to be associated with a denial of expectation, and thus often produces contrastive meaning'. Here, the care coordinator is contradicting, correcting and disagreeing with Tim's statement in asserting that she has spoken to him about 117 aftercare. This challenging of knowledge threatens Tim's face in contrast with the chair's talk; perhaps, Tim is not telling the truth, has a poor memory or is not interested enough in his own services. At the same time, the care coordinator saves her own face by displaying herself as a proper professional who has informed Tim about the service to which he is entitled.

Moreover, the care coordinator invokes an 'independent witness', Anna, to authorise her definition of the situation (Smith, 1978). Initially, Tim offers his agreement with only part of the assertion (turn 5). Thus, the care coordinator directly asks him if he can "remember us talking, you can't remember us talking about that?" (turn 6). By repeating the word "remember" and the two-part format of the question ("can you"; "you can't"), the care coordinator again presents the situation as having actually happened, positioning Tim as not recalling the conversation. Here, there is an implicit allusion made that the problem is Tim's poor memory, aligning with his mental health service user identity. As the professional, the care coordinator holds the power of definitional privilege (Smith, 1978). In his reply, Tim does not dispute that the discussion has taken place and uses the word "honestly", which depicts that it is a genuine loss of memory on his part (turn 7). Indeed, he explicitly states "I know you did" and adds "I'm not saying you didn't", showing his acquiescence with the care coordinator's version of events. The chair closes this sequence in a delicate way by not taking a stand on the disagreement and offering Tim further information on 117 aftercare, thereby evaluating it in a positive manner (turn 8).

In summary, this short conversation is an example of disagreeing and non-aligned talk between Tim and his care coordinator. In the beginning of the extract, the chair treats Tim as the person to be asked questions about his own services. However, the conversation between the chair and Tim on services, especially on 117 aftercare, is interrupted instantly, as the care coordinator challenges Tim's first response of not having heard of this particular service. The care coordinator displays herself as having better knowledge on this matter, which violates Tim's epistemic rights over his recent history. Although Tim claims or remembers otherwise, the professional presents 117 aftercare as having been discussed with him. Eventually, Tim admits that the care coordinator has better knowledge and he has a bad memory, but this happens only after the care coordinator's strong counterarguments towards Tim's own knowledge of the situation.

'Contradictory talk' about the service user's recent medication

The final extract is from Pete's CPA meeting. The extract is taken from the very start of the meeting where the chair asks an open question directed to Pete.

Extract 4

1. Chair: Okay, so today, did you have any particular questions to ask? Did you have anything in mind which you want specific help with?
2. Pete: ((sigh)) Is there anything you could give me so I could– I hate sleeping tablets, I don't like sleeping tablets. They're addictive and you can get very dependent on them. I hate tablets altogether. I only realised that a while ago. When I stopped taking drugs, I didn't go on anything. I just stopped taking everything all at once and that made me subconsciously hate taking drugs, any kind of drugs.
3. Care coordinator: Because ((Pete)) you're not prescribed anything at the minute, are you, and you haven't been for a while?
4. Pete: But I understand better than myself that I do need to be prescribed something because I can't go on like this most of the time.

5.   Care coordinator: Excuse me. The problem we had in the past is you weren't taking your medication.
6.   Pete: Yes, I know I wasn't, but I was taking my medication before I stopped. No, yeah, I was, when I was taking my medication, I was taking drugs as well. When I was taking drugs, I was on drugs; I was actually taking my medication regularly.
7.   Care coordinator: Okay, well you weren't on–
8.   Pete: I know it doesn't change that fact. I know to the point of view where I'll sit at home and things will go on, and somebody will do that for me or somebody will do that for me, and I'll sit down. I can't stand it. It's horrible.
9.   Care coordinator: Pete, can I just say, the time that you've had with the early intervention team and then you were handed over to me, there was lots of medi-packs full of medication, so you hadn't been taking it then.
10.   Pete: No, I know I hadn't been taking them and I stopped taking them.
11.   Care coordinator: Yeah, and then you haven't been taking them properly all the time I've worked with you and when ((housing support worker)) just (..)
12.   Pete: But I was taking them.
13.   Care coordinator: (..) tidied out your flat there was, she said, eight medi-packs hidden.
14.   Pete: Eight, there wasn't eight. There were two.
15.   Care coordinator: She has no reason to tell untruths.
16.   Pete: Eight medi-packs? Boxes, no, there was two boxes of medi-packs.
17.   Care coordinator: No, she said there were eight medi-packs full of medication hid behind the kickboards in the kitchen.
18.   Pete: No, there wasn't, there was two of them.
19.   Care coordinator: Well, she had no reason to (..)
20.   Pete: Oh, I know what she means, there's eight packs of, yeah, I understand what she means by that. Yeah, I would agree on that because it was getting on my nerves because of the fact that she kept saying, 'your tablets are here, your tablets are there'. I had tablets from months ago hidden under there.
21.   Care coordinator: It doesn't take away then the fact that you weren't taking them.
22.   Pete: No, I wasn't taking them, but I didn't understand why I didn't want to take them, even though I know they were making me well. I'm not making excuses; yeah, I did hide them under there, and I didn't want to take my tablets.

The chair opens the meeting by giving Pete the right to choose what issues he wants to talk about, especially regarding help (turn 1). This underlines the importance of Pete's own knowledge of his support needs. Although Pete does not complete his reply to the original question, it is apparent from the turn that follows that he is requesting medication to help him sleep (turn 2). Pete emphasises how much he does not like sleeping tablets or, indeed, any medication by repeating the words "hate" three times in his reply. Thus, paradoxically, Pete has asked for something that he then states he does not want. The care coordinator starts her statement with a connective, which demonstrates her alignment; that is, Pete does not like medication and is not prescribed medication (turn 3). However, Pete then gives a dispreferred response, signalled by "but"; even though he has unequivocally stated that he "hates" medication, he now says that he does need to be prescribed "something" (turn 5). Here, the phrase "I understand better than myself" is interesting. Pete appears to position himself as being aware that although he hates medication, he recognises that he needs to be prescribed something. Here, Pete is implicitly attributing blame to the professionals in the meeting through the statement: "I do need to be prescribed something". In other words, the non-prescribing by the team is the reason he is not taking any medication.

Picking up on this, the care coordinator interjects to disagree and, thus, *challenges* Pete's own interpretation of his medication (turn 5). The care coordinator attributes the blame to Pete as an individual ("you weren't taking your medication") and identifies that this had been a "problem" for the team as a whole, not just her, in the past, by "we had". Once again, she is *challenging* Pete's own personal knowledge. In another apparently paradoxical reply, Pete initially agrees and then disagrees, signalled with the word "but" (turn 6). Although the care coordinator does not speak, Pete responds as if she has disagreed with him by stating: "No, yeah I was." Hutchby and Wooffitt (1998, pp 212–13) write that 'it is not simply that people are trying to persuade their co-participants: they are also designing their talk in anticipation of a sceptical or unsympathetic response'. Pete contends that when he was using illegal drugs, he was also taking his prescribed medication – a point he emphasises through repetition. Again, the word "actually" anticipates the care coordinator's likely disagreement (Oh, 2000).

Once again, the care coordinator does not continue with overt disagreement and partially accepts what Pete has maintained before starting to make another point (turn 7); that this is another dispreferred response is marked by the word "well": "Okay, well you weren't on".

However, Pete interrupts her turn and accepts that she does have a valid argument, obliquely alluding to being a passive recipient of a service in his home (turn 8). This is an example of 'indexicality'. Indexicality points to the 'essential incompleteness' of language (Garfinkel, 1967, p 29), as the meaning is intrinsically linked to the context in which it is said. The 'transient circumstances of its use assure it a definiteness of sense ... to someone who knows how to hear it' (Garfinkel and Sacks, 1970, p 338). That the care coordinator knows how to hear it is demonstrated in her response, as she refers to the period of time when Pete was a client of the early intervention team (turn 9).

Rather than immediately disagreeing, the care coordinator gently prefaces her disagreement with the words "can I just say" (turn 9). Here, she evokes physical evidence – produces facts (Potter, 1996) – that Pete had not been taking his medication, that is, the presence of 'medi-packs' (pre-sorted containers for prescribed medication), which had not been taken. By doing so, she both *adds* knowledge on Pete's personal knowledge and *talks on his behalf* by producing new knowledge on Pete's recent personal history. Pete concedes that this was the case, although the word "stopped" implies that he had been taking the medication at one time (turn 10). After affirming his reply, the care coordinator then extends her argument from the period with the early intervention team to "all the time I've worked with you", extending this to very recently when the housing support worker "just" tidied out his flat (turns 11 and 13). Although Pete interrupts to disagree, the care coordinator continues without a pause, using the reported speech of the housing support worker to authorise her version (Smith, 1978; Juhila et al, 2014). Again, Pete implicitly accepts this, although disagrees about the amount of medi-packs that were hidden (turn 16).

Following this, the care coordinator strengthens her authorisation by again using the reported speech of the housing support worker and adding further details, which positions the worker as a direct observer: "hid behind the kickboards in the kitchen" (turn 17). Again, Pete implicitly accepts that the packs were hidden in this way, although continues to dispute the amount (turn 16). The professional's account is also positioned as 'uncontaminated by previous prompting or definitional work which might be interpreted as a form of bias' (Smith, 1978, p 37) through the statement "she has no reason to tell untruths" (turn 15). Although Pete continues to dispute the number of packs, the combination of the care coordinator again using reported speech and starting to repeat that the worker had no reason to tell untruths (turn 19) leads him to accept this version of events, albeit maintaining that this is open to interpretation: "I know what she means ... I understand what she means by that" (turn 20). Although accepting that the tablets were hidden, Pete puts the blame for this onto the worker, also using reported speech to invoke the worker as somewhat authoritarian: "she kept saying, your tablets are here, your tablets are there". The care coordinator does not enter into any disagreement about this matter but simply repeats that Pete was not taking the medication (turn 21), a point Pete reiterates, showing affiliation. He then overtly agrees: "yeah I did hide them under there, and I didn't want to take my tablets" (turn 22). While the care coordinator does not explicitly acknowledge this agreement, this is reflected in the closure of this matter with a topic shift to the category of "sleep problems".

Overall, this interaction can be described as contradictory, first in the sense that Pete asks for some medication to be prescribed for him, while at the same time displaying a negative attitude towards taking tablets. It is also contradictory in another sense. The care coordinator and the chair do not comment on Pete's wish to get some medication (even though a contradictory wish); instead, the care coordinator moves the discussion to focus on Pete's previous use of medication. She produces a lot of detailed knowledge about Pete's recent history related to medication, and in doing so, gives evidence of how Pete has not used the medication prescribed for him in the past. This is not totally non-aligned talk between Pete and the care coordinator, since Pete partly accepts the care coordinator's narrative on his earlier medication use. However, the strong role that the care coordinator takes in telling this narrative violates Pete's epistemic rights as the main narrator concerning his own recent history.

Discussion and conclusion

This chapter has examined who displays epistemic rights to the service users' recent personal histories in mental health CPA meetings. According to cultural understandings, people have primary access to and ownership of knowledge concerning their personal lives and experiences. Therefore, in principle, access to this knowledge is asymmetrical. The service users can be assumed to have primary and more extensive experience-based access to knowledge regarding their own personal lives than the professionals; in other words, they have epistemic rights to this knowledge. However, in the CPA meetings, the housing support workers and the care coordinators displayed experience-based knowledge of the service users' recent situations at some points. This may be explained by the fact that the support workers are closely involved with the service users' everyday lives at the supported housing unit, and the care coordinators have regular contact with the service users related to their care plans.

The only ones 'not so knowledgeable' in the CPA meetings were the psychiatrists acting as chairs, who had no continuous everyday contact with the service users. They were more reliant on second-hand knowledge (see first-position and second-position assessments in Heritage and Raymond, 2005). It was notable that the chairs treated the service users as primary owners of knowledge concerning their lives by clearly posing their questions first to the service users. Despite this 'recipient design', the housing support workers and the care coordinators often participated by answering the questions. As demonstrated in this chapter, this participation was accomplished by using six devices: confirming service users' personal knowledge, adding some knowledge to service users' personal knowledge, fishing for personal knowledge from service users, producing positive assessments of service users, producing knowledge on behalf of service users and challenging service users' personal knowledge. By using these devices, the housing support workers and the care coordinators presented themselves as knowledgeable about the service users' recent histories alongside the service users. Having access to this knowledge and displaying it in the CPA meetings can also be understood as pertaining to their professional duties; they are responsible for reporting in the meetings how the service users have recently been managing their lives.

In analysing the meetings, special attention was paid to whether the talk concerning the service users' recent histories was joint or non-aligned between the service users and the professionals. Joint talk was prevalent, meaning that the professionals often just confirmed what the service users had just said, or they added some related knowledge and positive assessments on it. However, there was also non-aligned talk in the data. This tended to happen when there was a challenge: when the professionals challenged the service users' knowledge or the service user challenged the professionals' knowledge. At points where the professionals produced a lot of knowledge on the service users' behalf or were fishing for particular knowledge from them, it was hard to interpret whether talk was joint, non-aligned or neither.

Whether talk about service users' recent histories is joint or non-aligned between the professionals and the service users, an important question of epistemic justice still needs to be addressed. According to Fricker (2007), epistemic, especially testimonial, injustice occurs if speakers are not regarded as credible storytellers, and their capacity to produce trustworthy knowledge is suspected (see also Lee et al, 2019, p 488). At worst, this kind of mistrust questions the human value and worth of a speaker (Fricker, 2007, p 130). It can be argued that epistemic testimonial injustice is strongly present if speakers' knowledge about their own personal histories is not taken as such, but instead, it is seen as something that needs to be confirmed or even challenged by someone else. Epistemic injustice is also obvious, if people are disallowed from speaking on their own matters, and someone else speaks on their behalf without permission to do so. This kind of epistemic injustice can prevent the realisation of relational agency that takes service users as full participants in creating knowledge in multi-agency meetings (Edwards, 2011; see also Chapter 1). It can also produce processes of shaming and turn the meetings into degradation ceremonies for service users (Garfinkel, 1956; see also Chapter 2).

One of the conclusions of this study is that, occasionally, such epistemic injustice was present within the CPA meetings, where service users were not treated as trustworthy or able to tell and reflect on their own personal histories. This happened especially when the professionals challenged the service users' own interpretations of recent events. On occasion, challenging can have a professional justification, for example if service users are defined as incapable of telling about their situation due to serious illness. This kind of challenging demands careful ethical consideration and, often, interactional skills that save service users' faces in a conflicting situation and prevent the meeting from turning into a degradation ceremony.

However, it is clear that the meetings also included examples of epistemic justice and signs of integration ceremonies, meaning equal collaboration between the professionals and the service users in knowledge production (see Chapters 1 and 2). It can be argued that the meetings' shared talk about the service users' recent histories and the professionals' and service users' joint access to them demonstrate a close relationship based on trust between these two parties. Co-telling a story to 'outsiders' in the meetings strengthened the service users' voices, although the professionals have the ultimate power to make assessments of their situations.

Close analysis of the interactions in the CPA meetings presented in this chapter displayed aspects of talk that both enable and hamper service users' participation in such multi-agency meetings. It allows professionals to be aware of and reflect on the forms of language that enable service users' full participation in the care planning process. Hence, it also helps to achieve the policy-level aims of CPA that emphasise promoting social inclusion and recovery, and the principle of putting service users at the centre of the process.

Notes

1. Data derive from the research projects Responsibilisation of Service Users and Professionals in Mental Health Practices, funded by The Academy of Finland in 2011–2016. Following the ethical guidelines for social research in Finland and the UK, all participants were informed about the study in advance At the beginning of the meetings, participants were briefly re-informed about the study and signed consent forms.
2. Under this section, people who have been detained under certain sections of the Mental Health Act are entitled to free aftercare for services that have both of the following purposes: (a) meeting a need arising from or related to the person's mental disorder; and b) reducing the risk of a deterioration of the person's mental health condition.

References

Care Quality Commission (2016) *National Community Mental Health Survey*, London: Care Quality Commission.

Carpenter, J., Schneider, J., McNiven, F., Brandon, T., Stevens, R. and Wooff, D. (2004) 'Integration and targeting of community care for people with severe and enduring mental health problems: Users' experiences of the Care Programme Approach and care management', *British Journal of Social Work*, 34(3): 313–33.

Department of Health (1990) *Joint Health and Social Services Circular: The Care Programme Approach for People with a Mental Illness Referred to Specialist Psychiatric Services* (11 HC (90) 23/LASSL (90) 11), London: Department of Health.

Department of Health (1999) *Effective Care Coordination in Mental Health Services: Modernising the Care Programme Approach*, London: Department of Health.

Department of Health (2006) *Reviewing the Care Programme Approach: A Consultation Document*, London: Care Services Improvement Partnership, Department of Health.

Department of Health (2008) *Refocusing the Care Programme Approach: Policy and Positive Practice Guidance*, London: Department of Health.

Edwards, A. (2011) 'Building common knowledge at the boundaries between professional practices: Relational agency and relational expertise in systems of distributed expertise', *International Journal of Educational Research*, 50(1): 33–9.

Ekberg, K. and LeCouter, A. (2015) 'Clients' resistance to therapists' proposals: Managing epistemic and deontic status', *Journal of Pragmatics*, 90: 12–25.

Fricker, M. (2007) *Epistemic Injustice: Power and the Ethics of Knowing*, Oxford: Oxford University Press.

Garfinkel, H. (1956) 'Conditions of successful degradation ceremonies', *American Journal of Sociology*, 61(5): 420–4.

Garfinkel, H. (1967) *Studies in Ethnomethodology*, Englewood Cliffs, NJ: Prentice-Hall.

Garfinkel, H. and Sacks, H. (1970) 'On formal structures of practical actions', in J.C. McKinney and E.A. Tiryakian (eds) *Theoretical Sociology: Perspectives and Developments*, New York, NY: Appleton-Century-Crofts, pp 338–66.

Goffman, E. (1967) 'On face-work: An analysis of ritual elements in social interaction', in E. Goffman, *Interaction Ritual*, Garden City, New York, NY: Doubleday, pp 5–45.

Gould, D. (2013) *Service Users' Experiences of Recovery Under the 2008 Care Programme Approach*, London: National Survivor User Network and the Mental Health Foundation.

Hayano, K. (2012) 'Question design in conversation', in J. Sidnell and T. Stivers (eds) *The Handbook of Conversation Analysis*, Chichester: Blackwell Publishing, pp 395–414.

Heritage, J. (1998) 'Oh-prefaced responses to inquiry', *Language in Society*, 27(3): 291–334.

Heritage, J. (2010) 'Questioning in medicine', in A.F. Freed and S. Ehrlich (eds) *Why Do You Ask? The Function of Questions in Institutional Discourse*, Oxford: Oxford University Press, pp 42–68.

Heritage, J. (2012) 'Epistemics in action: Action formation and territories of knowledge', *Research on Language and Social Interaction*, 45(1): 1–29.

Heritage, J. (2015) 'Well-prefaced turns in English conversation: A conversation analytic perspective', *Journal of Pragmatics*, 88: 88–104.

Heritage, J. and Raymond, G. (2005) 'The terms of agreement: Indexing epistemic authority and subordination in talk-in-interaction', *Social Psychology Quarterly*, 68(1): 15–38.

Hutchby, I. and Wooffitt, R. (1998) *Conversation Analysis: Principles, Practices and Applications*, Cambridge: Polity Press.

Jingree, T., Finlay, W.M.L. and Antaki, C. (2006) 'Empowering words, disempowering actions: An analysis of interactions between staff members and people with learning disabilities in residents' meetings', *Journal of Intellectual Disability Research*, 50(3): 212–26.

Juhila, K., Jokinen, A. and Saario S. (2014) 'Reported speech', in C. Hall, K. Juhila, M. Matarese and C. van Nijnatten (eds) *Analysing Social Work Communication: Discourse in Practice*, London: Routledge, pp 154–72.

Lee, E., Herschman, J. and Johnstone, M. (2019) 'How to convey social workers' understanding to clients in everyday interactions? Toward epistemic justice', *Social Work Education*, 38(4): 485–502.

Oh, S. (2000) 'Actually and in fact in American English: A data-based analysis', *English Language and Linguistics*, 4(2): 243–68.

Pomerantz, A. (1980) 'Telling my side: "Limiting access" as a "fishing device"', *Sociological Inquiry*, 50(3–4): 186–98.

Pomerantz, A. (1986) 'Extreme case formulations: A way of legitimizing claims', *Human Studies*, 9(2–3): 219–29.

Potter, J. (1996) *Representing Reality: Discourse, Rhetoric and Social Construction*, London: Sage Publications.

Rautajoki, H. (2010) 'Tietämisoikeudet televisiokeskustelun vuorovaikutuksessa: Asiantuntijareviirit poliittisella areenalla', *Sosiologia*, 47(1): 24–40.

Raymond, G. and Heritage, J. (2006) 'The epistemics of social relations: Owning grandchildren', *Language in Society*, 35(5): 677–705.

Sacks, H. (1984) 'On doing "being ordinary"', in J.M. Atkinson and J. Heritage (eds) *Structures of Social Action: Studies in Conversation Analysis*, London: Macmillan, pp 413–29.

Smith, D. (1978) 'K is mentally ill: The anatomy of a factual account', *Sociology*, 12(1): 23–53.

Stevanovic, M. and Peräkylä, A. (2014) 'Three orders in the organisation of human action: On the interface between knowledge, power, and emotion in interaction and social relations', *Language in Society*, 43(2): 185–207.

Tew, J., Ramon, S., Slade, M., Bird, V., Melton, J. and Le Boutillier, C. (2012) 'Social factors and recovery from mental health difficulties: A review of the evidence', *British Journal of Social Work*, 42(3): 443–60.

8

Relational agency and epistemic justice in initial child protection conferences

Juliet Koprowska

Introduction

Multi-agency meetings in child protection in England are attended by professionals from different disciplines and by family members, typically parents and other close relatives. Initial child protection conferences (ICPCs), the focus of this chapter, take place early in the child protection process, when serious concerns about the welfare of children have been identified. The meetings consider the gravity of the concerns and make decisions about what needs to be done. ICPCs are enshrined in policy guidance (DfE, 2018) and have an explicit institutional function, providing a record of accountable multi-agency practice. Potentially they provide a forum for the co-creation of knowledge about the children's circumstances, taking into account the perspectives of different professionals and family members to inform the decision making. This chapter is principally concerned with the role of the chair, and the relationship between chairs' interactional behaviour and service user participation.

Involving families in child protection processes is more than a policy principle. There is a consensus that removing children from their parents is a last resort, and the child protection system aims to work with families to improve the situation of children so that they can stay at home and thrive. It appears, then, that an implicit function, or possible outcome, of the ICPC is to build a working relationship between professionals and service users. Do chairs accomplish this, and if so, how? This chapter uses the concepts of 'relational agency' (Edwards, 2011) and 'epistemic justice' (Fricker, 2007) to make sense of how chairs include family testimony and co-create an understanding of family circumstances.

The chapter first considers the child protection system in England and the place of ICPCs in child protection policy and process. Next, the concepts of 'institutional talk', 'relational agency', 'epistemic rights' and 'epistemic (in)justice' are introduced as the basis for the analysis. The data, which come from audio-recorded ICPCs in two local authorities in England, are discussed, and this is followed by an analysis of extracts from the ICPCs. Policy guidance offers no prescription for involving families in the meeting, and the analysis here shows how the behaviour of chairs may facilitate or obstruct their involvement. The conclusion suggests that leaning on institutional talk is associated with reduced relational agency and disregard for service users' epistemic authority. It also proposes that the chairs' approach owes more to the norms of their institutions than to personal preferences about leadership style.

Child protection and ICPCs

Child protection is a highly sensitive domain, where private troubles become public issues. In England, the protection of children from their own kin has been a matter of public concern since the late 19th century (for an account, see Ferguson, 2011). Theoretical explanations for familial harm to children have taken many forms over succeeding decades, and recently financial and material inequality rather than parental inadequacy is being highlighted by some writers (such as Featherstone et al, 2014). Nonetheless, professional intervention tends to focus on interpersonal and behavioural change in parents.

The intrusion of child protection services into the private world of the family can lead to covert or overt conflict between families and services. Many child protection 'service users' are involuntary. Infants and small children neither seek nor consent to social work involvement, while parents and carers may be reluctant participants yet their choice about cooperating is limited (Rooney and Mirick, 2018). Statutory policy in England (DfE, 2018) expects both interprofessional collaboration and family involvement in child protection processes, and while the importance of working directly with children has been emphasised (Lefevre, 2010; Ferguson, 2016), children lack the power and means to make choices and changes, so social workers and other child protection professionals frequently work with parents and carers. The acknowledgement of family difficulties at the same time as trying to elicit their involvement for the good of their children is an interactional challenge. ICPCs are the first in a series of meetings attended by both professionals and family members, and in this study the service users present were parents and other carers.

ICPCs are preceded by a 'strategy discussion' between local authority children's social care and other relevant agencies, when they decide whether there are significant concerns about the welfare of a child. If an ICPC is called, it must be held within 15 working days (DfE, 2018). During this time, relevant professionals embark on assessing the children's circumstances and produce written reports, which are shared with the family in advance of or just prior to the ICPC. A senior social worker chairs the meeting and is independent of the 'case', having no direct managerial responsibility for the family's social worker, and usually meeting the family for the first time immediately before the meeting. Family members are key participants but, significantly, not decision makers, this power being reserved to specific professional representatives.

The primary task of the ICPC is to make a decision about whether a child protection plan (CPP) is needed, and if so, on what grounds. ICPCs are therefore powerful and pivotal meetings, where face-threatening (Goffman, 1955) information about families is aired in the presence of professionals, some of whom are strangers to the family. Chapter 2 introduced Garfinkel's (1956) concept of the 'degradation ceremony', by which a person is stripped of their social status and identity in public, with criminal trials being a prime exemplar where an ordinary person is transformed into an offender. ICPCs potentially constitute degradation rituals, since parental shortcomings are frequently the reason for child protection concerns. Parents risk being stripped of their social role as suitable carers for their own offspring.

While some studies have explored family participation through interviews with participants (for example, Muensch et al, 2017), few analyse interaction *within* the meetings themselves. Because ICPCs take place at short notice, often at a time of crisis, they have rarely been researched directly (Campbell, 1997, Appleton et al, 2015 and Koprowska, 2016, being exceptions). Meetings that take place at both earlier and later stages of child protection processes have more often been investigated. Examples include core groups (see Chapter 4), family group conferences (Holland and Rivett, 2008; Yanfeng et al, 2017), reviews (Hall and Slembrouck, 2001) and public law outline meetings (Broadhurst et al, 2011; Dickens et al, 2013). ICPCs therefore occupy a site for interprofessional work and service user participation that has largely been hidden from view, while their influence is far-reaching.

Government guidance (DfE, 2018) defines the *function* of the ICPC but not the *structure*. There is considerable discretion for local authorities to choose their approach to the conduct of ICPCs, exemplifying street-level bureaucracy in action; government policy only comes into being through its enactment (Lipsky, 1980; Brodkin, 2011) and takes shape according to local institutional and interpersonal practices.

Institutional talk, relational agency and epistemic rights and justice

Chapter 2 introduced doubts and critiques concerning the concept of 'service user participation', querying whether service users have the right to refuse to participate. Parents and carers are not formally obliged to attend ICPCs, but this study only includes ICPCs where service users are present. Nonetheless, mere attendance does not equal participation, and this is where the chair's influence makes its mark. Asmuß and Svennevig (2009, pp 11, 12) point out that chairs 'have a special role in meetings in that they are given institutional authority to moderate the talk' and that 'there is also room for variation depending on such aspects as the purpose of the meeting, the chair's institutional authority and leadership style'. The following concepts are used to explore the way in which chairs use both their institutional authority and leadership style.

Institutional talk (Drew and Heritage, 1992) refers to talk that takes place in work settings, which both resembles and departs from informal talk, and is different in different work contexts. Meetings themselves are institutional events, and Boden (1994) states that their length must feel appropriate to the participants, so ICPCs must be sufficiently long to reflect the seriousness of the endeavour, requiring considerable concentration (Koprowska, 2016). During their education and training, professionals learn institutional talk and put it to use in daily encounters with each other; service users are not part of the professional tribe and may find this talk unfamiliar and obscure. In the meetings examined here, formal, legalistic language and professional jargon oriented to the institution contrasts with straightforward, direct use of everyday language.

Relational agency (Edwards, 2011, p 34) 'involves a capacity for working with others to strengthen purposeful responses to complex problems'. Relational agency is enacted in different ways between professionals who share a common language, while 'some translation may be needed' when professionals interact with service users (Edwards, 2011, p 34). It is a collaborative process of knowledge building that comes from understanding and incorporating multiple perspectives regarding the issue at hand.

Epistemic authority reflects the rights of the knower to speak with authority about any given matter (Heritage and Raymond, 2005).

Speakers modify their speech, often in subtle ways, to acknowledge their conversation partner's superior right to knowledge or to convey their own.

Epistemic injustice, specifically **testimonial injustice** (Fricker, 2007), meanwhile, refers to the way in which a person's epistemic authority is disregarded or undermined on the basis of identity. Particular groups of people may be subjected to epistemic injustice because of prevailing cultural prejudices, such as people from black, Asian and minority ethnic groups. In this chapter, it is parents thought to be failing their children whose testimony may go unheard as a result of their social status as degraded parents.

These concepts permit the examination of questions about the distribution of power, the co-creation of knowledge and how the chair's interactional approach produces or inhibits service user participation.

Data and the process of analysis

The data for this chapter are drawn from a corpus of 23 audio-recordings of ICPCs, 12 collected from one local authority (LA1) in 2015 and 11 from another (LA2) in 2017. Ethical approval was granted by the University of York, and all parties consented to the use of the recordings for research. The author observed five of the conferences in LA1. To the author's knowledge, all participants are white British. The LA2 study included semi-structured interviews with chairs, family members and social workers, but these data are not discussed in this chapter.

LA1 was unusual in making an audio-recording of every ICPC, enabling the administrator to check details when writing up the minutes. The recordings were kept for 20 days in case of disputes or complaints and then deleted. Audio-recording was not the norm in LA2 and recordings were made solely for the research project. In each case, administrators made the recordings. The families who gave consent for their ICPC to be included in the research do not differ greatly between the two authorities. Families in both LAs faced challenges with drugs, alcohol and relationship problems. Several were affected by intimate partner violence and its impact on their children. Some in each had had previous children removed from their care.

As can be seen from Table 8.1, meetings in LA1 were attended by a greater number of family members and professionals than in LA2. Seven people attended the smallest meeting (ICPC A10 in LA2), and 21 the largest (ICPC 03 in LA1), indicating the complexity of the chair's task. Table 8.1 also shows the children who were the subject of

Table 8.1: Characteristics of the ICPCs in the two LAs

				LA1		
ICPC	Chair	Family[a] present	Profs[b] present	Children no. and age	Decision: CPP/CIN[c] and category	Duration +/- minutes
01	RW[d]	M, F, MGM	14	3 aged ≤ 9 years	CPP Neglect	81
02	BF	M, F, PGM, MA	6 + R	4 aged ≤ 12 years	CPP Neglect	80
03	AG	M, F, MGM	16	3 aged ≤ 7 years	CPP Neglect	101
04	RW	M, F	4	Unborn, 4 removed	CPP Neglect	58
05	BF	M, F, MGM, C	7	18 months	CPP Emotional abuse	63
06	RW	M, MGM, GGM, GGF	9	4 years	CPP Neglect	74
07	BF	MSA, F, MGM	8 + R	Unborn	CPP Neglect	49
08	RW	M, F, MGM, PGGM, PA	7 + R	4 weeks	CPP Emotional abuse	96
09	SA	M, MGM	6	Unborn	CPP Neglect	45
010	SA	M, B	9 + R	4 months	CPP Neglect	75
011	JB	M, F, PGM	7 + R	Unborn, 2 removed	CPP Neglect	48
012	BF	M, F	9	4 & 11 years	CPP Emotional abuse	89
				LA2		
ICPC	Chair	Family[a] present	Profs[b] present	Children no. and age	Decision: CPP/CIN[c] and category	Duration +/- minutes
A1	1	M, MGF	9	Unborn, 1 aged <2 years	CPP Emotional abuse	73
A2	1	M, F, StF	5	4 years	CIN	101
A3	2	M, F	4	Unborn, 2 removed	CPP Emotional abuse	79
A4	1	F, PGM	5	5 years	CPP Neglect	91
A5	1	M, F	7	Unborn, 3 removed	CPP Neglect	81
A6	1	M	6	Unborn, 5 aged ≤6 years already on CPP	CPP Emotional abuse	64
A7	3	M, F, MGM, PGF	5	3 aged ≤ 7 years?	CPP Neglect	91
A8	3	M	5	11 & 15 years	CPP Neglect	80

A9	1	MGM, Supporter & C	5	10 years	CPP Sexual abuse	80
A10	3	M	4	4 years	CPP Emotional abuse	90
A11	3	M, F	6	Unborn, 1 aged <3 years already on CPP	CPP Emotional abuse	91

^a M = mother, F = father, StFa = stepfather, MGM/F/PGM/F = maternal/paternal grandmother/father; GGM/GGF = great grandmother/father, MA/PA = maternal/paternal aunt, C = child, B = baby.

^b Number of professionals plus chair and note taker. R = researcher.

^c CPP = child protection plan, CIN = child in need.

^d Initials of pseudonyms.

? = exact details unknown.

Source: Adapted from Koprowska (2019)

the concern, the decision made and the duration, with meetings in LA2 being somewhat longer.

In LA1, four different self-selected chairs were recorded. In LA2, the three chairs were selected by their managers and chosen because of their experience and expertise. LA2 had adopted the Signs of Safety approach of Turnell and Edwards (1999), which seeks greater collaboration with family members in child protection work. The commissioning manager's belief was that LA2's adaptation of the Signs of Safety model had changed the way that ICPCs were conducted and that family participation had improved. It is important to note that the corpus ICPCs were not collected randomly and cannot be regarded as representative of the work in either LA. Nonetheless, differences between the two collections are greater than the differences within each collection.

In both LAs, meetings follow a format similar to that described by Hall and Slembrouck (2001, p 149) and cited in Chapter 2 of this book: 'introduction, information gathering and assessment, discussion and decision making and planning'. However, LA2 meetings also resemble Gunther et al's (2015) care planning meetings, described in Chapter 2, with an 'orientation towards planning the service user's care and starting the plan's recording' and 'making a care agreement'. The two LAs document the meeting in different ways. In LA1, an administrator types the minutes of the meeting into a laptop, and subsequently produces copies of minutes that are sent to all participants. In LA2, the administrator's laptop is connected to a screen, which is visible to all participants. Some sections of the document are already populated with family details, and the record, which includes the care plan, is co-created during the meeting. The making of this record was an explicit focus of LA2 ICPCs, as shown in some of the extracts.

For the research project, the audio-recordings were transcribed, and the analysis relied on listening to the recorded material alongside an examination of the transcripts. None of the accompanying documents relating to the ICPCs were made available, other than a standard information sheet provided at LA1 meetings. For this chapter, the focus is on two aspects. The first examines the chair's conduct and interaction during the early stages of the meeting. The second explores instances of family members making contributions, solicited or otherwise, and their reception by the chair or other participants, including the making of the record. The data are presented in relation to the analytic concepts.

Analysis: effect of chairs' interactional approach on service user participation[1]

Institutional talk at the start of meetings

As noted in Chapter 2, meetings are task-focused and institutionally oriented, but also have symbolic functions and aspects of ritual. Social welfare meetings display a blend of formality and more informal conversational talk and Chapter 2 suggests that some informality arises because the professionals meet often and therefore know each other. The ICPC recordings display this feature, as Boden (1994) notes, after the main business of the meeting is over. Participants turn their attention to dates for next meetings and professionals audibly relax into discussions of their availability on particular days and weeks owing to other work commitments, holidays and part-time working.

However, everyday talk of a less casual kind emerges as an interactional choice or strategy on the part of the chair, and personal acquaintance is not the reason since chairs seldom know families prior to ICPCs. The degree of formality varies, as shown in the following extracts, illustrating the different ways the chair sets the scene for the conference. Contrasting features emerge:

- formal versus informal language;
- scripted institutional introductions versus shorter and more interactive exchanges;
- use of the passive voice and the third person "they" versus the inclusive "we" and direct address using "you";
- clarity versus ambiguity about participation – who is being addressed?

The first extract shows how chairs move between scripted, formal language designed specifically for ICPCs and everyday talk, perhaps in recognition that the group of addressees includes service users.

Extract 1: LA1

> Chair: ((unclear)) Initial child protection conference has been convened in respect of [Child], [Child] and [Child]. Before we get started I'm aware there's a *lot* of people in this room. If we can go round the table and just explain who everybody is, what their role is. If I can ask you all to use your name and your job title and a very brief description of what your involvement with the family has been or what your involvement with the case conference is. So my name is RW and I'm tasked with chairing today's meeting on behalf of the Safeguarding Children Board. That's independent of any day-to-day management of the case. (ICPC 01)

RW opens with the formal term "convened in respect of", and the extract closes with her identifying her institutional duty as "tasked with chairing today's meeting on behalf of". Between these formal statements she draws on the resources of everyday language to start introductions, acknowledging the large number of people present who may not be known to each other.

In this ICPC and the others she chairs, RW routinely asks everyone to include their "job title" in introductions: "if I can ask you all to use your name and your job title". She suggests other ways for people to define themselves, by "role", or by "involvement" with the family or conference. Nonetheless, family members seem to understand that the apparently inclusive "you all" does not include them, as nearly all name their relationship to the children who are the subject of the meeting. One grandmother in ICPC 08, however, takes up the job title invitation and identifies herself by her work role, which passes without comment. Meanwhile the mother in ICPC 01 glosses her role identity like this: "I'm [first name, last name], I'm a pare- the children's mother and a drain on society." This mother's self-identification suggests that she has already been the subject of a degradation ceremony; she supplies a degraded status for herself as "a drain on society", appearing to recognise this 'job title' as relevant to the ICPC context.

The next extract from the same meeting takes place immediately after introductions.

Extract 2: LA1

> Chair: So if I can just explain to people then the purpose of today's meeting is for agencies and family to share information about the ((unclear)) causes for concerns affecting the children to make a decision about whether or not people feel that there is a risk of significant harm to the children's health or welfare in the future as a consequence of neglect or abuse and if so a requirement to safeguard the child protection plan. Okay? As part of today's meeting it is really important that everybody feels that they're able to fully contribute to the discussion and to the decision making. It's really important that everybody feels that they've got all the information that they feel they need to help them to make the decision that will be asked of them. (ICPC 01)

In this extract the chair uses formal institutional language to explain the purpose of the meeting, and then frames expectations of participants in everyday language: "it is really important that everybody feels that they're able to fully contribute to the discussion and to the decision making". As with the request about job titles, the statement uses the collective term, "everybody". However, while family members may be invited to "contribute to the discussion", they will not contribute "to the decision making", which is the exclusive province of professionals.

In Extract 3, we see the chair leaning on ritualised institutional language to a greater degree.

Extract 3: LA1

> Chair: ... in respect of Unborn [last name]. The conference is convened in accordance with the [local] safeguarding procedures. The purpose of the conference is to consider whether the child is likely to suffer or is suffering significant harm and therefore requires a child protection plan or child in need plan. The information presented at the conference is confidential and should only be shared outside the conference if it's necessary to do so to safeguard a child. It is important that all conference members share any relevant information they have and that they all contribute to the decision making. If any party feels unable to do so, they should advise the conference chair of the reasons why. Conference members are asked to take care to distinguish between fact, observation, allegation and opinion. Discriminatory comments, behaviour or prejudice, or unacceptable language, shall be challenged by the chair or other conference members. If – if unhappy with either the process

or the outcome of the conference, a complaint can be made under the Safeguarding Board complaints procedures. Information explaining how to do so will have been sent out with the invitation to conference letter and can also be obtained on the SCB website. (ICPC 07)

The chair in Extract 3 audibly reads from an institutional document made available to all participants at LA1 ICPCs. He thus uses the terms "in respect of" and "convened in accordance with", terms that appear in 10 out of 12 LA1 conferences. He uses the formal term "Unborn" and a last name in naming the child. The importance of confidentiality is formally expressed, using the passive voice: "The information presented at the conference is confidential and should only be shared outside the conference if it's necessary to do so to safeguard a child." People present are referred to formally as "conference members" or in semi-legal language as "any party".

LA1 chairs usually take some time at the beginning of the meeting to read this document aloud or *talk* it with more spontaneity, revealing some differences in their leadership style. In both cases they ensure that all the institutional points are made and this practice appears to enact an institutional obligation more than an effort to communicate interpersonally. As an educated listener, the author found it hard to sustain concentration and follow the meaning, both during live observation and when listening to recordings. This raises questions about how less educated families or even professionals make sense of it. The practice appears to be an instance of Munro's (2010) 'doing things right', that is, following the letter of the law, rather than 'doing the right thing', and enabling everyone to understand and participate.

Notably, the chair in Extract 3 reads a standard sentence from the institutional document: "It is important that all conference members share any relevant information they have and that they all contribute to the decision making." This institutional script underlies RW's more everyday version in Extract 2: "it is really important that everybody feels that they're able to fully contribute to the discussion and to the decision making". Although only professionals have decision-making rights and duties, it is not clear whether participants register the error; certainly no one remarks on it in any ICPC.

"You all" and "everybody" are a form of collective reference to 'you' and 'they'. Lerner and Kitzinger (2007) discuss 'collective *self*-reference' (emphasis added) in their analysis of the use of 'we'. They propose that 'we' can be 'organisational', referring to a workplace or work group, 'relational', in describing a couple or family, or 'circumstantial', referring to the people here in this context (Lerner and Kitzinger, 2007, pp 526–7). As discussed in Chapter 2, chairs of multi-agency meetings may use 'we' to make relevant either the institution or the present participants of the meeting. In Extract 1 the chair uses "we" once, saying: "If we can go round the table", clearly referring to the people in the room. In the following extract, the chair uses "we" much more frequently and with a different effect.

Extract 4: LA2

> Chair: So the purpose of this conference today is to share information about current family circumstances, erm, and what's been going on, the situation at the minute, and we'll be looking at the background and we'll be looking at how agencies are involved or have been involved. And we'll be discussing and thinking about the level and nature of any risk to [Child] today as well, erm, and about whether she's suffering or likely to suffer significant harm which is is the ((unclear)) level for child protection, and about whether we need a child protection plan at the end of the meeting. So this conference, we'll be writing everything up as we go along so people can see what's, what's going on and if you don't agree I want, I want people to be able to say, please. Erm, and just to say, anything that anybody reads or we talk about today, it is confidential and I'd ask that we keep it like that, erm, and people can ask me if they need to talk about it with anybody else. (ICPC A4)

While the chair uses some formal, legal language, such as "level and nature of risk to [Child] ... likely to suffer significant harm", this is not the dominant discourse. There is a preference for everyday language, such as "what's been going on" and "if you don't agree". Rather than using third-person passive constructions as in Extract 3, the chair uses "anybody", "we" and "I" when referring to confidentiality: "Erm, and just to say, anything that anybody reads or we talk about today, it is confidential and I'd ask that we keep it like that." She then uses third-person collective references, "people" and "they": "people can ask me if they need to talk about it". Here references to "I" and "me" point to her institutional authority as chair; "we" and "people" are used to speak to all participants as interactants, rather than as an audience. She invites involvement from everyone when referring to the record being made on the screen: "we'll be writing everything up as we go along so people can see what's, what's going on".

The chair in Extract 5 also uses "we", and from the outset starts a dialogue with the expectant mother.

Extract 5: LA2

1. Chair: So welcome, this is an initial child protection conference that will involve Baby [last name], whose expected delivery date is still [date] of [month], as far as you know?
2. Mother: Yes.
3. Chair: Sometimes it's changed ((laughs)). Well, who knows when she'll come. So the purpose of today's meeting is to consider unborn baby's safety and to decide whether she – it is she – whether she's at continued risk of serious harm and we need a child protection plan, and then if we think she does, we'll look at what that plan needs to have in it. So let's start with introductions. Excuse me. I'm Chair 3, I'm the chairperson, and I'm from [local] Safeguarding Children. (ICPC A11)

In Extract 5, the chair draws on informal conversational resources as well as making reference to the institutional context. She opens with "So welcome" and switches to a formal term, "this is a child protection conference". However, where most LA1 chairs would continue with "convened in respect of", she says "that will involve Baby [last name]", her use of "Baby" contrasting with the formal "Unborn" in Extract 3. In addition, the chair in Extract 5 knows the baby's gender and uses it, talking about her arrival: "Well, who knows when she'll come." These devices personalise the infant who is the subject of the conference, and the chair's laughter helps lighten the tone.

Her use of "we" extends to implied decision making, as in Extract 4: "whether we need a child protection plan". It could be argued that this avoids clear identification of the active decision makers, and is thus as ambiguous as the terms "everybody" and "all conference members" used in Extracts 2 and 3. It is possible that the chairs in Extracts 4 and 5 are shifting invisibly from a 'circumstantial we' to an 'organisational we'. However, the combined effect of the frequent use of "we", everyday language, and addressing and interacting with family members, is an invitation to participate in the conference process as a whole. It can be understood as an interactional strategy to involve family members early in the conference and initiate an integration rite (Islam and Zephyr, 2009), 'attempting to establish unity of purpose between participants' (see Chapter 2).

Relational agency

Relational agency (Edwards, 2011) necessarily involves an appreciation of the value of different perspectives and knowledge. Edwards' work starts from the way in which professionals from different knowledge bases employ relational agency to work together to solve complex problems, and the concept is relevant also to how professionals work with service users.

In LA1, the chair routinely asks the social worker to provide what has been referred to as the 'warrant' for the meeting, often with instructions to be brief, pointing out that people have read the reports, seemingly wanting to reduce the volume of shaming information aired (Koprowska, 2016). While this shows a degree of sensitivity to family feeling, it does not amount to relational agency, since patterns of interaction give primacy to professional knowledge, and are frequently characterised by problem-saturated discourse about family difficulties. Some social workers use delicacy to avoid direct naming of difficulties, while others are more explicit in their use of denigrating terms. The process of the chair asking the social worker to account for the calling of the conference means that the social worker must identify problems; indeed, the family *is* the problem. Extract 6 is a particularly stark account from the social worker.

Extract 6: LA1

1. Chair: I'll turn to [SW] if you don't mind and if you could just outline really for us what were the prime decisions really that led to the decision to convene a conference this afternoon? Thank you.
2. SW: The original referral came in on [date] from the police. The police had received anonymous sources to say that the address of [XX] where [Baby] and [Mother] live was being used as a doss house and there was concerns about the number of people coming there and a certain person who had a number of high warning risk markers, that's why we first contacted [Mother]. ... there's been a number of other referrals ... stating of the concerns about drug use in the house and about the number of people that are coming whilst [Baby] is present. And then on [date] when I completed a home visit, [Mother] had an injury to her face, quite a large black eye and a number of bruises on her body. [Mother] told me [details of her account], yet when I checked that information out that was not true and that's what has led us to a strategy meeting on [date] to get together to share the concerns and to see where we are. So

whilst I've been doing my enquiries and assessment, things seem to be getting progressively worse regarding the number of referrals and I'm not quite sure that [Mother] agrees with me about that – about the risk that I feel that [Baby] is in at present. (ICPC 10)

In Extract 6, the social worker follows the interactional norms of LA1, orienting to institutional procedures such as the strategy discussion, and making clear that she has undertaken a thorough assessment, for example checking the veracity of the mother's account of her injuries. She talks to the chair about the family in the third person, while the mother becomes the audience. She describes the concerns frankly and unambiguously, mixing the colloquial and pejorative term "doss house" with the more institutional "high warning risk markers". She also suggests that she and the mother have different views of the risks. This account has the character of a degradation ceremony; the mother's reported disagreement with the social worker about the levels of risk to the baby is a mark of her unfitness, not a source of different knowledge.

In the following extract, differences between chairs' practices in the two LAs become more evident. The chair does not ask the social worker for a warrant for the meeting, but provides it herself, and addresses the family directly.

Extract 7: LA2

> Chair: We need to start by looking at, at why we've convened a conference today ((unclear)). So we start with, with past harm obviously unborn baby, that's quite limited but just to set the scene for why we're here. [Mother], you attended doctor's on [date] and they did a pregnancy test and that's, that was positive. You were believed at that point to be about 36 weeks pregnant. You've had no antenatal care and baby's health had not been monitored. You said at that time you were smoking 30 cigarettes a day and that, that from ((unclear)) there been a strong smell of cannabis, so they're all things that can impact on, on baby developing. So they're the reason why they're up on past harm. (ICPC A5)

Extract 7 shows that frankness also characterises talk in LA2, but with a marked difference about who addresses whom. The chair reads from and summarises the social worker's assessment report, talking directly to the family about its contents. She names the issues quickly and simply in a few lines: the lateness of the pregnancy test and lack of antenatal care, the mother's smoking and parental cannabis use. Her orientation to the institution is not framed in terms of procedures but takes the form of pointing the family members to the shared screen and what is written under the heading 'Past Harms' to facilitate their involvement in the conference. She displays relational agency in talking to them by explaining simply what the identified issues are and showing them how the record is being made.

This leads to an analysis of epistemic rights, where relational agency also plays a part.

Epistemic authority and epistemic injustice

In this final section, the epistemic authority of family members is analysed. Questions arise in ICPCs about the veracity of family testimony, as in Extract 6 above. Are family members reliable informants? How are their contributions received? In LA1, family circumstances are frequently discussed between the professionals; there are also instances where families are asked direct questions, and occasions where they volunteer information or proffer accounts and explanations. In LA2, the chair and other professionals frequently speak directly to family members. Is this difference related to reception of family testimony? Three kinds of reception have been selected for analysis, which will be discussed in turn:

- ignoring the contribution;
- qualified acceptance;
- explicit acceptance.

The chair in Extract 8 has been quizzing the child in need worker about what the mother knows and what she has been told, and the mother seems to believe that these questions could have been put to her directly, as she has already tried to make her knowledge relevant through a number of uninvited contributions. The conference has heard about the children climbing and hurting themselves.

Extract 8: LA1

1. Chair (addressing the child in need worker): Okay so including the concerns from 2004 right up until the current time?

2. Mother: [Talks for one minute, finishing with] When I'm cooking, I'm there all the time, so they can't climb and I always get them down when they try climbing.
3. Chair: Now what we're going to do, we're going to go back to the social worker. (ICPC 02)

In Extract 8, the mother interjects, speaking at length, and explains how she is managing the children's behaviour better. Prior to the extract the chair has already responded to the mother as an 'unratified participant' (Goffman, 1981; see also the discussion in Chapter 2) by not acknowledging her contributions, and in the extract again makes no reference to her account. He uses "we" and uses his institutional authority to select the next speaker, identifying the social worker as a ratified participant.

In the next extract, the chair is talking with the social worker to confirm a story of redemptive change in the mother.

Extract 9: LA1

1. Chair: In your report, [SW], you said that actually a lot of what [Mother] has just said is – is being evidenced in her contact currently with the four older children, so she is being – you said she's being very consistent with contact.
2. SW: Yeah.
3. Chair: And that taking responsibility, she's taking advice and support now from the social workers with regards her older children, so we are seeing some of what you're saying being put into – to practice with the older children.
4. Mother: Yeah, I used to think it was everyone else's fault, why did they take *my* kids when I didn't do nothing wrong?
5. Chair: ((inbreath))
6. Mother: And now I realise it *was* my fault.
7. Chair: ((inbreath)) Just sticking for a minute with the concerns that have been identified in the report, [SW], about risk of drugs and the and the impact of drugs and alcohol. (ICPC 04)

The mother in this extract, like the mother in Extract 8, tries to contribute to the narrative with evidence from her own reflections. She interjects with an account of how she has changed. The chair indicates with two inbreaths that the mother has talked out of turn. She resumes her dialogue with the social worker, ignoring the mother's claim of redemptive change, to initiate a problem-saturated focus on drug and alcohol use.

This 'disciplining' of unsolicited contributions is reserved for family testimony. Although there is one instance of a chair cutting short a social worker's (long and rambling) warrant in ICPC 09, professionals are not ignored in this way, indicating that parents are experiencing epistemic injustice based on their identity as parents. Chairs in LA2 do not ignore family contributions, although they do sometimes respond to spontaneous, out-of-turn contributions by asking the service user to wait until a professional has finished speaking.

The following extract shows the chair inviting comment from the parents, seeming to position them as ratified participants.

Extract 10: LA1

1. SW: ... and we've also got concerns for a number of missed health appointments for the children erm and they being deregistered at the GP as well erm.
2. Chair: Okay, thank you. So is there anything there [Mother] or [Father] you'd just want to comment on?
3. Mother: I've never had an appointment missed for [Child] or [Child]. I've never missed no health appointments; I don't understand that (.) and 'deregistered', what what's that mean?

Subsequent talk with the health visitor tries to establish whether the children are registered with a GP; the health visitor resolves to "double-check" (ICPC 01).

The mother challenges the information presented – "I've never missed no health appointments" – and questions the meaning of "deregistered". While the chair's invitation seems to suggest that the parents' testimony will be relevant, the challenge is not accepted as it stands. Some discussion takes place but the matter is not resolved by accepting the mother's account. The health visitor, who lacks the relevant information, takes responsibility for checking, thus assuming epistemic authority. Evidently her future testimony will be more reliable than the mother's current claim. It is interesting that shortly afterwards, when the parents are asked if the children are registered with a dentist, their negative response is immediately believed. It is upgraded through a statement that becomes a question from the chair, who says: "Right. So th-have they *never* been registered with a dentist the children?" In this instance, the parents' epistemic authority to admit a deficit is accepted.

The next extract shows qualified acceptance of the parents' claim to have most of the necessary items for their forthcoming baby.

Extract 11: LA2

1. Chair: There's a worry about you've not made any preparation for baby's needs, such as cot and a pram, erm any food, oops, sorry, and what a baby needs to be fed, to be clean, and to be warm and dry. Sorry, I've misread that. And that's the worry, because baby's due next week. I don't know, I – where are you up to with that?
2. Father: We've got everything apart from a pushchair.
3. Mother: Her pushchair, now we've got everything.
4. Chair: Right, right, so since this was written…
5. Father: Yeah.
6. Chair: So can we just add that in please, [note taker]? 'Now got everything except for' – okay.
7. Note taker: Yep.
8. Father: Which ((unclear words))
9. Mother: Yep, this afternoon hopefully. Yeah.
10. Chair: Okay, and have you seen the stuff then [social worker]?
11. SW: No, but…
12. Chair: Or is that what you're going to go and have a look at and see what's what?
13. SW: Yeah, yeah. (ICPC A5)

In Extract 11, the parents have had several children removed in the past and have only recently revealed that another baby is about to be born. The chair outlines concerns and asks the parents directly about their preparations. The parents state that they have "everything apart from a pushchair", and the chair acknowledges this by asking the note taker to include it in the record. However, it is qualified acceptance, since she also establishes that the social worker is going to verify the parents' claims. The family's testimony is given some credence in the interaction and by inclusion in the record but the social worker is required to confirm its veracity.

In the following extract, concern has been expressed about the father's rent debts. He is not present and the mother is asked about them. The individual speaking with the mother is not the chair but an unidentified female professional (Prof).

Extract 12: LA2

1. Mother: It wasn't actually anything to do with him-
2. Prof: Oh.
3. Mother: It was Housing Benefit – they lost the paperwork-
4. Prof: Oh right.
5. Mother: -and they wouldn't backdate it. They'd only backdate a month and then they wanted, like, £800 off him which obviously...
6. Prof: So it wasn't through any bad management...
7. Mother: No, no, no, nothing.
8. Prof: Okay. (ICPC A6)

In this extract, the professional spontaneously accords the mother epistemic authority about the matter, as her "Oh" indicates that this is news to her (Heritage, 1984). According to Heritage (2018, p 159), 'oh is ... frequently associated with the prompt registration of information transfer'. The professional takes in this information from the mother and changes her epistemic stance, confirmed in "Oh, right", while her use of "Okay" indicates acceptance and closure (Schegloff and Sacks, 1974[1973]).

In the next extract, evidence of 'information transfer' is even more explicit.

Extract 13: LA2

1. Father: I think the main thing what we need is the same rules. See, when they're at Mum's house they've got one rule, when they come to my house they've got different rules. We need to...
2. Chair: Oh, okay. So that's, that's a complicating factor, isn't it, that you, you have different rules. (ICPC A7)

In Extract 13, the chair also uses "Oh, okay", indicating she accepts the father's information. She then enacts epistemic justice through the implied inclusion of the father's testimony in the record, under 'complicating factors'. This is more than an orientation to institutional requirements; it is inclusion in the plan of work for family and services.

In the final two extracts, the chairs engage with the families, using relational agency and according them epistemic authority to provide an account of their lives that will lead to a more complex understanding of the problems.

Extract 14: LA1

1. Chair: Well, I mean, is this a common feature between, with [Father]? I mean, we know that it's…
2. Father: I'm not, overall, I'm not an angry person at all – well, I'm not violent, am I? You'd say – the times that I – this incident, it all sprung off because ((unclear)), I'll try and sort this out now. I was rattling, basically ((voice drops away))
3. Chair: Sorry you're saying it's one-offs?
4. Father: Yeah, yeah.
5. Chair: When you're trying to resolve an issue?
6. Father: I was trying to resolve it and I was trying to sort it out myself.
7. Chair: Okay.
8. Father: Like I always have done.
9. Chair: Yeah.
10. Mother: I think, at the time though I was under a lot of pressure cause like I say, I had not long lost ((unclear)) my mother. She'd just died about a month before, the day before [an important occasion] so you know, I was struggling myself and he was struggling with cold turkey. I needed his support at that point and obviously he wasn't able to give me it and that was pretty much why we were arguing.
11. Chair: So you you were were at the end of things there, you were were struggling emotionally?
12. Mother: Yeah me on my own, you know, I've gone through a great loss.
13. Chair: Yes. How many times have you tried to go cold turkey [Father]?
    The chair then talks with the father about his efforts to stop using drugs, and concludes:
14. Chair: So, we've highlighted a two-year period where things have gone down for you as a family, correct? (ICPC 12)

The LA1 chair in Extract 14 is engaged in discussion with another professional, as in Extracts 8 and 9, but once the father starts to speak, the chair explores both his account and the mother's. The chair recognises their authority to know about their experience and their emotions. He responds sensitively and empathically first to the mother and when closing the topic: "So, we've highlighted a two-year period where things have gone down for you as a family, correct?", and only after this does he turn back to the social worker to ask about one of the children.

The last extract illustrates a feature characteristic of LA2 chairs' interactional behaviour. They refer early on to the screen on which the record of the meeting is co-created in full view, and they speak directly to all present, often showing that they are specifically including family members, as in this case. Families are treated as valued contributors with important knowledge about themselves and their aspirations.

Extract 15: LA2

1. Chair: And to be cared for by a safe, appropriate and so-sober adult, and for [Father] to access support in relation to his alcohol, and, and I think we can take alleged out, cause you are using drugs [Father], aren't you? You know, you've said that, so we'll take that 'alleged' bit out there. So about you rec-, getting support, about, about those things. What about for, for you, [Father] and [Paternal Grandmother], what would you want to achieve for, for [Child]? It's all right everybody around the table having their goals, isn't it, what about you?
2. Father: For [Child] to be like [Name of older child].
3. PGM: To be a normal little five-year-old.
4. Chair: Right. [3–4 minutes of grandmother and the less talkative father expressing their hopes]
5. Chair: … Going to – [Father] the – what your mum's saying, are those things that you would agree with or is there anything else you would want to add? You know, your mum's saying: 'I just want her to grow up to be a normal five-year-old with stability and security.'
6. Father: Yeah, of course.
7. Chair: … And know that we'll always be there for her and for her to get her confidence back and be not so frightened. (ICPC A4)

In Extract 15 the chair is switching between dictating to the note taker and speaking frankly to the father about his drug use. This could become a degradation ceremony, with his considerable difficulties becoming the focus. Instead, it becomes an integration ceremony in which the support services for the father are written in, and family hopes and wishes for the child are sought. The chair uses relational agency to ask the father and grandmother about their goals, so that the plan includes their perspective and their knowledge. They take turns to speak for some time, especially the grandmother, with the chair responding energetically with "Right", "Yeah!". She then begins to quote key phrases from their talk as she dictates to the note taker and encourages the father to express his views. Writing their words into the shared plan for the child confirms the value of their testimony and accords them epistemic justice.

Discussion and conclusion

ICPCs are sites authorised by government policy for discussion and decision making about the welfare of children and family life. They are potentially fraught occasions, where discrediting information about families is discussed, to the point where they can resemble degradation ceremonies. Inevitably there is sometimes distrust and suspicion on both sides; families do not always tell the truth, downgrading or disguising their difficulties, while professionals possess legal powers that families fear. The meetings can become a battleground for competing accounts where service users and professionals cannot reach agreement. Yet professionals must try to work with parents and carers, and service users, however reluctantly, need to work with child protection services.

Analysis of data from ICPCs in two LAs in England two years apart shows more differences than similarities in interactional practices. In LA1, a lengthy organisational script written in institutional language sets the scene for the meeting, even when it is spoken rather than read. It seems oriented to making all relevant points, ticking all organisational boxes, rather than being 'translated', with relational agency, to engage and involve service users. In addition, the script is inaccurate; it makes the participation of families ambiguous, with inclusive "you all" statements that do not or cannot include them. The next interactional event consists in the chair asking the social worker to provide an account of the reasons for calling the conference. This entails listing deficits and problems about the family in the third person, creating the potential for a degradation ceremony, although some social workers soften their accounts and present redeeming features (Koprowska, 2016).

As a result, family participation in the early stages of an LA1 ICPC often takes the form of passive listening to professional accounts. The main ratified role for family members is as audience. This does not appear to be sufficient for service users, some of whom make unsolicited contributions in their own defence at this stage and later in the meeting. On occasion, service users' interjections are explored with empathy and their epistemic authority is acknowledged, but more often they are met with testimonial injustice where their contributions are ignored. Verbal and non-verbal communication from chairs indicates that families have talked out of turn. Their transgressive behaviour in the meetings may contribute to the professional view that they are not competent parents. The family and the professionals seem to be on opposing sides, with parental failings made central to support the case against them and in favour of their children's needs. Questions must arise about how such processes further the welfare of children. A final point is that in LA1, the meeting is a talking affair; the families have no way of knowing how their knowledge or views are being included until the minutes are issued later.

In LA2, families are ratified addressees from the outset of the conference, with chairs providing brief explanations of the process, mostly using accessible everyday language. Families are directed to the screen where the record of the ICPC is co-created during the meeting, and actively encouraged to correct errors and bring in new information. The chair talks through the concerns that have arisen, referring to the social worker's report but addressing the family, rather than asking the social worker to provide a third-person account. Chairs give these accounts in frank unambiguous language, naming problems factually, and incorporating new information from family members about their knowledge, hopes, plans and opinions. Service users are interactants, not the audience. While family accounts are not always taken at face value, with professional verification planned, they are not ignored. Family members must regard themselves as ratified participants, given that they speak at some length in LA2 ICPCs, and they know what is being written about them on the screen, on a similar footing to other participants. Professionals and parents usually seem to be on the same side, trying together to do their best for the children, giving these ICPCs the character of a rite of integration (Islam and Zyphur, 2009).

These interactional factors are consequential for service user participation and, by implication, for the building of collaborative working relationships between professionals and families for the safety and welfare of children. This chapter has examined different interactional approaches seen in ICPCs. One of the questions it raises is whether these differences reside in the personal leadership style of the chair, or whether their interactional conduct is the product of local norms regarding institutional authority. To put it another way, is this personal discretion at an individual level, or organisational discretion at a policy level? Given the differences between the two authorities, it seems more likely that the LA2 chairs' use of less institutional language, more direct talk and more interaction with service users is a function of institutional discretion about how they use institutional authority rather than personal discretion about their leadership style.

This study also raises issues of justice and morality. In ICPCs, it seems likely that according people their epistemic rights will have better outcomes for children and their families – but that is beyond the scope of this chapter to say for certain.

Note
1   Extracts are used for longer passages of talk. The analysis also draws on shorter quotes from other ICPCs within the study.

References

Appleton, J.V., Terlektsi, E. and Coombes, L. (2015) 'Implementing the strengthening families approach to child protection conferences', *British Journal of Social Work*, 45(5): 1395–414.

Asmuß, B. and Svennevig, J. (2009) 'Meeting talk', *Journal of Business Communication*, 46(1): 3–22.

Boden, D. (1994) *The Business of Talk: Organizations in Action*, Cambridge: Polity Press.

Broadhurst, K., Holt, K. and Doherty, P. (2011) 'Accomplishing parental engagement in child protection practice? A qualitative analysis of parent-professional interaction in pre-proceedings work under the Public Law Outline', *Qualitative Social Work*, 11(5): 517–34.

Brodkin, E. (2011) 'Policy work: Street-level organizations under new managerialism', *Journal of Public Administration Research and Theory*, 21(2): i253–i277.

Campbell, L. (1997) 'Family involvement in decision making in child protection and care: Four types of case conference', *Child & Family Social Work*, 2(1): 1–11.

DfE (Department for Education) (2018) *Working Together to Safeguard Children: A Guide to Inter-Agency Working to Safeguard and Promote the Welfare of Children*, London: HMSO.

Dickens, J., Masson, J., Young, J. and Bader, K. (2013) 'The paradox of parental participation and legal representation in "edge of care" meetings', *Child & Family Social Work*, 20(3): 267–76.

Drew, P. and Heritage, J. (eds) (1992) *Talk at Work: Interaction in Institutional Settings*, Cambridge: Cambridge University Press.

Edwards, A. (2011) 'Building common knowledge at the boundaries between professional practices: Relational agency and relational expertise in systems of distributed expertise', *International Journal of Educational Research*, 50: 33–9.

Featherstone, B., White, S. and Morris, K. (2014) *Re-Imagining Child Protection: Towards Humane Social Work with Families*, Bristol: Policy Press.

Ferguson, H. (2011) *Child Protection Practice*, Basingstoke: Palgrave Macmillan.

Ferguson, H. (2016) 'What social workers do in performing child protection work: Evidence from research into face-to-face practice', *Child and Family Social Work*, 2(3): 283–94.

Fricker, M. (2007) *Epistemic Injustice: Power and the Ethics of Knowing*, Oxford: Oxford University Press.

Garfinkel, H. (1956) 'Conditions of successful degradation ceremonies', *American Journal of Sociology*, 61: 420–4.

Goffman, E. (1955) 'On face-work: An analysis of ritual elements in social interaction', *Psychiatry*, 18(3): 213–31.

Goffman, E. (1981) 'Footing', in *Forms of Talk*, Philadelphia, PA: University of Pennsylvania Press, pp 124–59.

Gunther, K., Raitakari, S. and Juhila, K. (2015) 'From plan meetings to care plans: Genre chains and the intertextual relations of text and talk', *Discourse and Communication*, 9(1): 65–79.

Hall, C. and Slembrouck, S. (2001) 'Parent participation in social work meetings – the case of child protection conferences', *European Journal of Social Work*, 4(2): 143–60.

Heritage, J. (1984) A change-of-state token and aspects of its sequential placement, in M. Atkinson and J. Heritage (eds) *Structures of Social Action: Studies in Conversation Analysis*, Cambridge: Cambridge University Press, pp 299–345.

Heritage, J. (2018) 'Turn-initial particles in English: The cases of oh and well', *Language and Interaction*, 31: 155–90.

Heritage, J. and Raymond, G.T. (2005) 'The terms of agreement: indexing epistemic authority and subordination in talk-in-interaction', *Social Psychology Quarterly*, 68(1): 15–38.

Holland, S. and Rivett, M. (2008) '"Everyone started shouting": Making connections between the process of family group conferences and family therapy practice', *British Journal of Social Work*, 38(1): 21–38.

Islam, G. and Zyphur, M. (2009) 'Rituals in organisations: a review and expansion of current theory', *Group and Organisation Management*, 34(1): 114–39.

Koprowska, J (2016) 'The problem of participation in child protection conferences: An interactional analysis', *International Journal of Child and Family Welfare*, 17(1/2): 105–22.

Koprowska, J. (2019) *The Impact of a Signs of Safety Approach on Participants' Discourse and Experience during Child Protection Conferences*, York: University of York.

Lefevre, M. (2010) *Communicating with Children and Young People: Making a Difference*, Bristol: Policy Press.

Lerner, G. and Kitzinger, C. (2007) 'Extraction and aggregation in the repair of individual and collective self-reference', *Discourse Studies*, 9(4): 526–57.

Lipsky, M. (1980) *Street-Level Bureaucracy: Dilemmas of the Individual in Public Services*, New York, NY: Russell Sage Foundation.

Muensch, K., Diaz, C. and Wright, R. (2017) 'Children and parent participation in child protection conferences: A study in one English local authority', *Child Care in Practice*, 23(1): 49–63.

Munro, E. (2010) *The Munro Review of Child Protection. Part One: A Systems Analysis*, London: Department for Education.

Rooney, R.H. and Mirick, R.G. (eds) (2018) *Strategies for Work with Involuntary Clients* (3rd edn), New York, NY: Columbia University Press.

Schegloff, E. and Sacks, H. (1974 [1973]) 'Opening up closings', in R. Turner (ed) *Ethnomethodology*, Harmondsworth: Penguin Education, pp 233–64.

Turnell, A. and Edwards, S. (1999) *Signs of Safety: A Solution and Safety Oriented Approach to Child Protection Casework*, New York: Norton.

Yanfeng, Y., Haksoon, A. and Bright, C.L. (2017) 'Family involvement meetings: Engagement, facilitation, and child and family goals', *Children and Youth Services Review*, 79: 37–43.

Conclusion

Kirsi Juhila, Tanja Dall, Christopher Hall and Juliet Koprowska

Analysing collaboration and participation in multi-agency meeting interactions

This book has examined how policy trends that promote interprofessional collaboration and service user participation are implemented (or not) through frontline practices in multi-agency meetings. The challenges faced by service users are seen as complex and interconnected, demanding many kinds of expertise for them to be understood, assessed and resolved. As a result, collaboration and participation together have become the prevailing approach in health and social care policy in Western welfare states. Bringing together diverse viewpoints of professionals and service users is also thought to create boundary spaces that, at their best, produce joined-up thinking and constructive debate, resulting in novel ideas. Chapter 1 has provided a more thorough introduction to the trend and its 'selling points'. In the literature, concepts such as 'relational turn', 'relational agency' and 'responsive process' have emerged in an effort to understand collaborative and integrated welfare and its potential for generating new common knowledge (Edwards, 2011). In this literature too, collaboration and participation are perceived as positive and desirable ideals. However, a number of concerns about the policy approach have also arisen and been presented in the literature. As outlined in Chapter 1, instead of equal collaboration, the policy may lead to:

- loss of specialised expertise by professionals and service users;
- a blurring of professional responsibilities;
- increased responsibility being placed on service users to participate;
- asymmetrical power relations between participants;
- comprehensive surveillance of service users' lives.

An overarching theme for the contributions in this volume has been whether and how collaborative and integrated welfare is present in frontline practices. There is a scarcity of research into the frontline practices of social welfare organisations, where professionals and service users encounter each other to tackle complex problems and implicitly do not always share the same goals. Hence, this book has focused on studying these interactions in multi-agency meetings in different settings, through audio- and video-recordings. Multi-agency meetings are boundary spaces in which professionals from different welfare agencies, service users and their lay representatives are brought together. As such, they are key practices in the realisation of policy aims and serve as a vantage point from which to study how policies are actually achieved in practice and what shape they take in everyday talk and interaction.

Chapter 2 drew on existing literature to introduce ways of understanding meetings as organisational rituals and ceremonies that can take on aspects of degradation (Garfinkel, 1956) and integration. This conceptualisation has proved to be significant in the empirical analysis of meetings in terms of the impact on service users. Are service users subjected to shaming processes (degradation) or are they included as active participants in discussions about their personal problems and lives (integration)? The analysis of the meetings described in this book has demonstrated that the answer to this question is not one or the other; elements of both kinds of processes have been found in all them. Chapter 2 also illustrated the detailed and multifaceted interactional work that meetings entail. It is through situated interaction that meetings are brought into being. The nature of collaboration and participation are interwoven with interaction, something that becomes clear through the examination offered by the empirical chapters of this book. In this concluding chapter, the core conclusions of these analyses (Chapters 3–8) are summarised and synthesised through four themes:

- the role of the chair and turn-taking;
- information-giving and decision-making roles;
- alignments, affiliation and different uses of the term 'we';
- owning, prioritising and producing knowledge.

Role of the chair and turn-taking

Multi-agency meetings, like others, usually have a clear structure with an agenda, aims and expectations about how participants will contribute (see Chapter 2 for a thorough overview). In many workplace and business settings, meetings are attended on a regular basis by experienced participants who know how the meeting is structured and what to expect. Multi-agency meetings in social welfare are different, especially when considering the position of service users. As Hall and Dall argue in Chapter 2, what is relevant, rational and typical in a meeting is closely tied to the organisational context, with Boden (1994, p 35) noting that 'meaning is constituted in the interplay of people and objects under the concrete conditions of a particular setting'. Professionals often know each other and have attended similar meetings, so the ceremonial activity about to take place is familiar to them. Conversely, for service users these kinds of meetings are rare, sometimes a 'once in a lifetime' experience. Even for service users who participate in several meetings, these all concern their own 'cases', whereas for professionals they are part of their work routine. For this reason alone, service users cannot be as knowledgeable about institutional meeting procedures as professionals, putting them at a disadvantage. This becomes visible in the turn-taking in interaction where professionals mostly take the lead by asking questions and introducing topics for the service user (or other professionals) to respond to. This is the predominant structure described in all of the empirical chapters, even though they take place in different countries and welfare sectors.

The asymmetrical starting point of multi-agency meetings in social welfare makes the role of the chair crucial, visible in the way the chair sets the scene. How the chair describes the agenda, asks participants to introduce themselves, allocates turns of talk and raises topics affects the collaborative nature of the meeting. The analyses provided in this book show that the chair can play a key role in creating participatory boundary spaces both for service users and for professionals from different disciplines. Sometimes the chair creates a collaborative space for more equal conversations between parties. The analysis in Chapters 3, 4 and 8 demonstrates how chairing may vary with the formality of the meeting, the individual style of a given chair or institutional norms. Furthermore, in Chapter 5, Raitakari, Ranta and Saario illustrate how the chairing role may shift between individuals as topics develop and the professional with the most expertise about a particular topic takes the leading role. Nowhere in the meetings examined in this book are there examples of service users leading the conversation, emphasising the institutional authority connected to being the chair (see Asmuß and Svennevig, 2009).

Opening the meeting is part of the chair's role. The way they explain its purpose and invite participants to introduce themselves determines the kind of contribution that is expected from each participant. For example, Koprowska illustrates in Chapter 8 that some chairs orient to institutional requirements, speaking at length in formal scripted language, while others use everyday language and speak directly to service users, eliciting participative responses from the outset. Dall and Caswell demonstrate in Chapter 3 how participation roles may also be more subtly introduced through the ways in which different kinds of participation are addressed by the chair.

The chair is responsible for inviting participants to make a contribution and to some extent controls turn-taking in meetings (Asmuβ and Svennevig, 2009). A critical moment for displaying this responsibility is at the start, in terms of who is addressed as the first speaker, and who is given the authority to introduce the key topics of the meeting. Chairs often take this role themselves, since they usually represent the agency that is hosting the meeting and thus have prime responsibility for processing the case (as seen in Chapter 4). They may also address a professional, a service user or both as 'owners' of and therefore the most knowledgeable about the case. Chapter 5 shows chairs engaging immediately with service users to talk about their current concerns, yet service users being addressed first does not always mean that they are treated as competent people or equal partners in meetings. Whether this happens depends on how they are addressed, what kinds of issues they are enabled to raise and how these are treated, not only at the beginning of the meeting but also during the whole meeting, as discussed in the next section. The same is true for other participants when the chair addresses them as representatives of particular kinds of professional knowledge. This can be seen as the chair's boundary work in the meetings (Chapter 4). Whether this boundary work leaves room for creating boundary spaces and for enabling the emergence of new knowledge is a critical question from the point of view of collaborative and integrated welfare. Hall and Slembrouck's analysis in Chapter 4 makes visible how this may come down to the style of the individual chair, while Dall and Caswell in Chapter 3 show examples of how the chair may use the institutional context as a resource for legitimising drawing certain boundaries, for instance by referencing the legal framework.

Information-giving and decision-making roles

Social welfare meetings are often structured in terms of certain phases, starting from orientation and introductions, proceeding with information gathering about the service user's situation and problems, including professional assessments, and ending with decisions about next steps in the service user's care pathways (Chapter 2). Given that joined-up thinking and constructive debate are understood as the hallmarks of collaboration in multi-agency settings, it is essential to see how information, assessments and decisions are produced in the meetings. Who are the authorised speakers and how are different participants' turns of talk responded to? How are they taken into account in making assessments and decisions?

According to the analyses in this book, service users have an important role in the information-gathering phase (see, for instance, Chapters 3 and 8). This role is made important via interactional activities. The chair often asks service users direct questions with a 'you format', especially at the start of the meeting, but also later on when new topics emerge, as seen in Chapters 5, 7 and 8. Service users are thus authorised to speak about their own circumstances and perspectives, and how they see their own situation, needs and possible problems. Furthermore, some professionals may also be invited to give information about the 'case' as knowledgeable experts, for example if they are service users' key workers, care managers or responsible for particular interventions. Information given by different parties may be compatible, but can also be conflicting and signal an absence of collaboration. Juhila, Morriss and Raitakari (Chapter 7) illustrate one such instance, where a service user's telling of his own recent behaviour is challenged by a home support worker who claims to know otherwise. If service users' information is treated in conflict situations as less valuable or even questionable, the meeting can skew towards a degradation ceremony, as the service users' capacity to produce trustworthy accounts is negated (Fricker 2007; see also the discussion in Chapters 7 and 8).

As service users describe their situation, emotional talk may emerge. This may seem contradictory to the formality of meetings, but as Bülow and Wilińska illustrate in Chapter 6, both institutional and emotional elements of the context of multi-agency welfare meetings are entertained and hardly distinguishable from each other. Moral reasoning about social problems and the ensuing emotions enter the meeting room. Chapter 6 reflects on this feature by considering the processes of claiming and giving sympathy during institutional encounters. Service users make sympathy claims, to which other participants respond verbally or non-verbally. Not responding to or directly rejecting claims for sympathy in these situations will threaten service users' face, and thus provide yet another possibility for degradation. On the other hand, accepting and offering sympathy creates moments of sharing that may build towards integration even if not directly impacting on the outcome of meetings in terms of decision making.

Taking a central role in the information-gathering phase does not equate to having a powerful position in the meeting overall, especially if participation in the assessment and decision-making phases is withheld. Service users are then treated as sources of information for other participants to arrive at conclusions about their 'case', and this can be true for more peripheral professionals too. Participants who are positioned as having core expertise or a legal mandate have decisive power in the meetings, and this may extend beyond the meeting itself in the form of plans about how to proceed. This power is traditionally vested in some professionals and not others, which may create interactional asymmetry as seen in Chapter 3. However, as the analyses in the book demonstrate, assessments and decisions can also be made on a shared and equal basis between professionals and service users during meetings. Chapter 5 provides one such example from a setting where the meetings are rather informal without a strict agenda defined in advance, and decision making about several 'minor' concerns takes place throughout the meeting. Boden's (1994) distinction between decisions as outcomes and decision making as a process of negotiation is relevant here. The chapters in this book have illustrated how questions of collaboration and participation are not just a matter of seeing one's fingerprint on the final decision. Rather, they are ongoing achievements that make relevant a preoccupation with the detailed process of decision making. As Huisman (2001, p 72) suggests, we should 'locate the emergence of decisions at the turn-by-turn level of the interaction in which participants exchange information and opinions'. It is in the incremental process of actions and responses that participation emerges, not in single utterances or final decisions.

Alignments, affiliation and different uses of the term 'we'

Since multi-agency meetings have several participants, talk and interaction are rarely a straightforward exchange of perspectives, nor do they consist only in individual opinions and voices. Instead, there may be a variety of nuanced positions, often with alliances of various kinds created during the course of the meeting interaction. The detailed examination in this book has brought out the richness of these alliances, and the ways in which they may disrupt or support the idea of shared agency and collaboration. As stated above, the role of the chair, turn-taking, information giving and decision making in the multi-agency meetings relate to and create a basis for various alliances.

Participants in the meetings use personal pronouns in different ways. In terms of collaboration, the use of the collective self-reference 'we' is extremely important. As demonstrated in this book, it can be used in either exclusive or inclusive ways. The 'inclusive we' can cover all members of the meeting including service users, and the role of the chair in initiating this kind of collaborative talk is often crucial. Chapter 3 demonstrates how the use of the 'exclusive we' is also prevalent. Frequently it seems to exclude service users so that 'we' covers only professional participants. Service users are then either addressed with the pronoun 'you' ('talked to') or bypassed ('talked about'), as seen in Chapter 8. Using the inclusive and exclusive 'we' becomes powerful boundary work, as it defines which participants are regarded as experts competent to tackle the complex problems in question. Excluding service users from 'we' makes them passive listeners, who are only occasionally allowed to contribute to discussions. This can make meetings humiliating and degrading, whereas belonging to an inclusive 'we' can have an integrative effect.

However, as demonstrated in the book, both the 'inclusive we' and the 'exclusive we' can come into play during the course of a single meeting as alliances between the participants form and break up. The concept of 'alignment' – meaning mutual cooperation and shared stances on ongoing activities – and the concept of 'affiliation' as emotionally displayed alignment, are useful in locating these variations as seen in Chapters 5 and 6. Alignment often takes place dyadically within the context of the group, with 'partners' changing as in a dance.

Alignment with service users – and between all participants – is typical at the beginning of the meetings, when people introduce themselves. It also occurs when the agenda is set (see Chapter 5) and when the service users participate in producing information about their situation (see Chapter 3). Correspondingly, the shift towards professionals' mutual alignment tends to occur when the meeting proceeds to the assessment and decision-making phases. Nevertheless, it would be an oversimplification to claim that this is always the case. Sometimes one (or several) professionals align with the service user, making other professionals 'overhearers', and form an alliance ('we') 'against' other participants in the meeting. Chapters 4 and 7 contain examples of such instances, which typically happen if the service user and the professional know each other beforehand, and their previous professional–service user relationship is based on mutual trust. In these cases, the professional may position themselves as the service user's advocate in the meeting. However, Juhila, Morriss and Raitakari (Chapter 7) touch on the fine line between the professional and the service user 'talking as one' in an alliance, and the professional talking on behalf of the client in a way that may become patronising and disempowering.

The alignment between service user and professional in the meeting may be momentary. This occurs especially when emotions are at stake. For example, in Chapter 6, Bülow and Wilińska show that when a service user makes verbal or non-verbal sympathy claims concerning the difficulty of their situation, one of the participating professionals responds with a sympathising turn, creating a moment of affiliation. However, this kind of affiliation may not last until the end of the meeting or influence the assessment and decision making. The professional may disaffiliate if the service user intensifies their claims, and other participants may regard these 'emotional moments' as appearing outside the frame of a 'proper meeting'. Nonetheless, accomplishing empathy and sympathy towards the service user, their everyday life, sorrows and difficulties may prevent the meeting turning into a degradation ceremony. Sometimes professionals initiate affiliation turns with the purpose of supporting and encouraging the service user's voice to be heard in the challenging multi-agency meeting context, as seen in Chapters 4, 5 and 8. Furthermore, the professionals may avoid overt alignment with other professionals, if they estimate that it will threaten the position of the service user (see Chapter 4).

Professionals, too, are occasionally excluded from the professional 'we'. Sometimes professionals accompanying the service user in meetings are treated as informants rather than belonging to an assessment or decision-making group (although the opposite can also be justified). Chapter 3 contains one such example. Occasionally a professional may fall under other professionals' scrutiny, and thus be excluded from the alliance of other professionals, for example when their earlier actions and interventions are assessed. As demonstrated in Chapter 4, it is also not uncommon for some professionals to struggle to establish their roles and specialised expertise in the meetings.

Owning, prioritising and producing knowledge

When several participants with special professional and experiential expertise come together, different types of knowledge and perspectives on a 'case' are present. In this book, such differences in knowledge and expertise have been approached as phenomena that are produced and attended to by participants in the interaction. Orientation to different types of knowledge becomes visible especially when certain participants are invited – usually by the chair – to talk on certain topics at a certain phase of the meeting. As demonstrated in

Chapters 4 and 7, how participants come to be recognised as owner of a certain knowledge type is a matter of interactional achievement. For example, services users are often asked to talk about their personal situation, feelings, needs and wishes at the beginning of the meeting, thus providing experience-based knowledge for other participants to consider and assess. Furthermore, professionals are addressed according to their specialised areas of knowledge to complement understanding about a 'case'. Allocating and taking turns based on different areas of expertise demonstrate participants' respect for the boundaries at play; the meetings in this book include artful boundary work about who is regarded as having epistemic rights to what (see for instance Chapters 4 and 7).

Different types of knowledge are not always treated equally in meetings. Knowledge can be produced as conflicting and hierarchical in the sense that certain types are treated as more trustworthy and reliable than others, while others are downgraded or ignored, as seen in Chapters 4, 7 and 8. In terms of service user participation, the way their experience-based knowledge is encouraged and responded to is pivotal. The analyses in this book have demonstrated instances of encouragement and respect for service user knowledge, as well as patronising and challenging reactions (see Chapters 5 to 8). Depending on the reaction, service user knowledge can be treated as of equal value to professional knowledge in building common knowledge, or merely as information that supplies 'raw material' for professional assessments and knowledge construction about a 'case'. The second approach can be seen as violating service users' epistemic rights concerning their own lives, as discussed in Chapters 7 and 8. This violation becomes stronger when service users' experiential knowledge is questioned and challenged, and alternative interpretations or evidence are produced.

Service users as meeting participants do not just talk about their own lives and experiences. They can also take a strongly participatory role and add to, challenge and resist professionals' knowledge. Although this happened rarely in the meetings analysed in this book (see Chapters 5, 7 and 8), such resistance can be responded to – or indeed resisted – in different ways. It can be treated as an important contribution that modifies common knowledge created in the meetings, or dismissed as unreliable. It can also contribute to the shift in alignments and relate to the emotional dimensions of the meeting. In such a context, service users' resistance can therefore produce new understandings of the situation and personal troubles (see Chapter 6). Moreover, professionals also challenge or ignore one another's knowledge and prioritise some areas of expertise over others.

Remarkable are various (dis)alignments in knowledge construction between service users and professionals. These occur especially when one of the professionals and the service user have a close working relationship so that they know each other well beforehand (see Chapters 6 and 7). They then produce a 'shared' history and the associated knowledge in the meetings. Sometimes this happens unanimously, creating a strong influential joint voice, or conversely with disagreements, creating competing types of knowledge and violations of service users' epistemic rights. On other occasions, this may happen via recognition and acknowledgement of multiple roles that both professionals and service users occupy, resulting in various understandings of the problem (see Chapter 6). Epistemic rights may also be violated (Fricker, 2007) when professionals talk on behalf of service users by using their prior professional knowledge. An important finding is a 'here-and-now' affiliation between some professionals and service users in the meetings. The professionals position themselves as sympathising with the service user's situation, and thus also display themselves as knowledgeable about it (see Chapters 4 and 6). Sometimes this affiliation remains momentary, and does not contribute to the ultimate building of knowledge (see Chapter 6). Sometimes it can be crucial; affiliation between a service user and professional can constitute a source of authority (see Chapter 4).

Concluding remarks

All the themes discussed in this concluding chapter – the role of chair and turn-taking, information giving and decision making, alignments and displaying knowledge – are played out in organisational and institutional contexts where multi-agency meetings are located. While the meetings analysed in this book differ in terms of aims, participants, formality and so on, participants talk these different contexts into being as they orient to each other and the activity at hand.

Differences in formality especially stand out. Generally speaking, formal meetings have a strict structure and rather tight responsibilities for each participant. They are often occasioned by legislation and established procedures, according to which the chair manages topic progression and the allocation of turns of talk. Formal meetings are also framed by the expectation of reaching a certain (shared) decision about the 'case' discussed. The empirical chapters in this book show that service user participation in the meetings is often involuntary or reluctant, yet being absent can have serious consequences such as financial sanctions or the termination of services. Nonetheless, it is possible even for meetings with formal legal functions to create informal spaces characterised by everyday inclusive talk, enabling service users to participate more freely.

Meetings that are less formal in their entirety tend to have a more flexible agenda. Participants gather together to discuss and negotiate different options concerning service users' complex situations. From the point of view of service users, informal meetings may constitute boundary spaces that allow for and even facilitate their participation to a stronger degree. If there is no strict agenda or specific (legally bound) decisions to be made, meetings serve more as arenas for joint talking about how to define and address key problems, and how to proceed with a 'case'. In these meetings, service users have more room to raise the topics they regard important in their own lives and can also join in decision making regarding the next steps in their care pathways. However, if decisions are not made on a formal basis, the service user lacks the opportunity to make a complaint if the informally promised services are not being provided. Creating inclusive boundary spaces is dependent on all participants' non-exclusionary actions in the meetings. In formal meetings service users' roles often reduce to merely being information givers and service user knowledge is treated as the raw material on which professionals base their assessments and decisions.

From the professionals' point of view, too, the degree of formality/informality matters. Tightly controlled meetings offer less space for dialogue between professionals and thus less relational agency. If the chair allocates turns to professionals solely according to their specific area of expertise and knowledge, and they are expected to present only their agency's perspective on a 'case', the professionals may be constrained from contributing to discussion and negotiation of a shared understanding. As with the role of service users in less formal meetings, professionals too may find that a looser meeting structure creates more spaces for cross-professional talk. This is not to say that interprofessional collaboration is only achieved with informal meetings, and cannot happen in formal settings. Rather it brings attention to the constitutive character of meeting talk in relation to policy implementation.

The analyses of multi-agency meetings in this book have demonstrated that what happens in meeting interaction is critical for the successful implementation of collaborative and integrated practice. At the beginning of this book, a number of concerns regarding interprofessional collaboration and service user participation were raised. The empirical chapters provide some insight into the realities of service user participation. First, the chapters make it clear that bringing service users into meetings does not automatically ensure that they are involved with decision making and care planning. While service users might be encouraged, even expected, to state their point of view, their participation in agenda setting, assessment and decision making is more questionable. At worst, their personal lives are under comprehensive top-down surveillance by the 'army' of various professionals. The asymmetrical relationship between professionals and service users is clear in all meetings, but the book also contains examples of how service users' position may be strengthened. For instance, less formal meeting structures, an orientation towards service users as more than sources for information and recognition of their experiential knowledge may be more conducive to active participation. This may be realised through an awareness of interactional devices such as inclusive/exclusive pronouns, affiliation and alignment, sympathy displays and the use of direct address and everyday informal language.

How the policy aim of interprofessional collaboration is realised is similarly complex. Several of the empirical chapters report concerns that increased interprofessional work may blur responsibility for the 'case' as a whole as well as single tasks. To the extent that a united front of agreement is presented to service users (such as through a unified 'we'), any specific responsibilities in decision making or subsequent service provision may become blurred, and sometimes a clear decision and next steps remain unclear. The risk of blurring responsibilities becomes even more salient when certain professionals on the one hand take decisive roles in meetings, occasioned by chairing roles, particular organisational affiliations or areas of expertise, and on the other, do not explicitly take responsibility for future tasks. As interprofessional meetings may become vague about who is to carry out a particular task, they may also disguise professional asymmetries in decision making. The chapters of this book point to the formality of meetings, recognition of a variety of knowledge types and perhaps a shared chairing role as ways to mitigate such asymmetries. Once again, interactional devices such as inclusive/exclusive pronouns, affiliation, alignment and direct talk about plans may facilitate these efforts.

For both service users and professionals, multi-agency meetings have the potential for being integration ceremonies that make possible the creation of common knowledge and the establishment of shared goals. At the same time, however, there is the risk that meetings become degradation ceremonies that devalue the knowledge and status of both service users and professionals. The chapters in this book illustrate the contingent nature of meeting interaction. On the one hand, they make visible the discretionary room that affords participants some agency in how they enact meetings. At the same time, the structuring of meetings is also visible, as legal frameworks, epistemic hierarchies and participant roles such as chair, facilitate certain (inter)actions more than others. As these – largely tacit – dimensions of professional practice are made visible, an opportunity for reflection is created that may inform and inspire both practitioners and policy makers, producing reflective 'discursive mindfulness' (Juhila and Pösö, 1999; Hall and White, 2005; Kirkwood et al, 2016; Matarese, 2020).

In terms of research, this volume has provided insights into how interprofessional collaboration and service user participation are interactionally achieved. It has demonstrated the value of examining the minute turn-by-turn interactions in meetings, offering unique insight into collaborative processes as they occur. Important questions remain about how asymmetries of knowledge and power play out in practice and how they may be managed to facilitate relational agency and the creation of common knowledge among participants. This relates not only to the various degrees of formality and informality of the institutional meetings, but also how institutional and affective tasks are approached. All in all, it points to the notion that emotions are neither redundant in nor contradictory to the institutional agenda. In terms of developing practices, the detailed scrutiny of the multi-agency meetings in different social welfare settings provides grounds for the following conclusions.

First, creating collaborative thinking and novel common knowledge among participants with different professional backgrounds, institutional responsibilities and personal experiences is a challenging task. It makes demands on professionals in particular. It requires a willingness to listen to various viewpoints carefully, treating them as equal contributions to the discussion, and a readiness to abandon previously held views in favour of new insights created jointly in the meeting. Second, interprofessional collaboration is easier to achieve than collaboration that also includes service users. Third, and related to the second, is that the asymmetry in power between professionals and service users can be mitigated but not eradicated through interactional practices. This asymmetry is especially difficult to manage in formal meetings, where final decisions about services are made by the professionals. Fourth, alignments and emotionally sensitive affiliations between service users and professionals are an effective tool to advance service user participation. Finally, if service user participation is to be achieved, the chair's skill is pivotal in creating an interactional environment that enables service users to bring in their voice and be heard as competent members with epistemic rights and authority.

More generally, we might want to question if too much is expected of multi-agency meetings as the main site for the implementation of collaborative and integrated working in social welfare. Given the concerns raised in this book about the degradation and exclusion of service users and professionals, of power struggles and asymmetries, and the discretion available to powerful participants, perhaps current practices should be more explicitly scrutinised. Questions could be asked about the structuring of meetings, especially where formal and highly consequential decisions are made. Should service users more often be legally represented, as is the case in other settings (for example, employment, special education and social security)? Should chairs more often be independent of the professionals directly involved in the case? Should meetings be subjected to outside scrutiny, for example in the form of inspection systems? Should there be options for appeals? For more informal meetings, perhaps the informality could be acknowledged and encouraged with, for example, service users and their supporters enabled to chair meetings, while the use of more relaxed settings may also mitigate the intimidating aspects of formal meetings. Exploring these questions would require different and more wide-ranging research and policy initiatives. It is hoped that this book has made the case for such questions to be asked.

References

Asmusβ, B. and Svennevig, J. (2009) 'Meeting talk', *Journal of Business Communication*, 46(1): 3–22.

Boden, D. (1994) *The Business of Talk: Organizations in Action*, Cambridge: Polity Press.

Edwards, A. (2011) 'Building common knowledge at the boundaries between professional practices: Relational agency and relational expertise in systems of distributed expertise', *International Journal of Educational Research*, 50(1): 33–9.

Fricker, M. (2007) *Epistemic Injustice: Power and the Ethics of Knowing*, Oxford: Oxford University Press.

Garfinkel, H. (1956) 'Conditions of successful degradation ceremonies', *American Journal of Sociology*, 61: 420–4.

Hall, C. and White, S. (2005) 'Looking inside professional practice: Discourse, narrative and ethnographic approaches to social work and counselling', Editorial, *Qualitative Social Work*, 4(4): 379–90.

Huisman, M. (2001) 'Decision-making in meetings as talk and interaction', *International Studies of Management and Organisations*, 31(3): 69–90.

Juhila, K. and Pösö, T. (1999) 'Local cultures in social work: ethnographic understanding and discourse analysis of probation work', in S. Karvinen, T. Pösö and M. Satka (eds) *Reconstructing Social Work Research: Finnish Methodological Adaptations*, Jyväskylä, Finland: SoPhi, pp 165–207.

Kirkwood, S., Jennings, B., Laurier, E., Cree, V. and Whyte, B. (2016) 'Towards an interactional approach to reflective practice in social work', *European Journal of Social Work*, 19(3–4): 484–99.

Matarese, M. (2020) 'Discursive mindfulness among practitioners analyzing social work communication', in L. Grujicic-Alatriste (ed) *Language Research in Multilingual Settings: Communicating in Professions and Organizations*, Cham, Switzerland: Palgrave, pp 95–123.

Postscript

At the time of completing this book (June 2020), most of the world is gripped by the coronavirus pandemic, with various regimes of lockdown, quarantine, social distancing, isolation and closure. The multi-agency meetings we have studied in this book are likely to have taken on new forms as the world – and health and social care – come to terms with this new reality. We quoted Hughes et al (2011, p 136) in Chapter 2, that the practice of meetings that are 'face-to-face ... in close proximity' would not comply with current social distancing requirements. Yet most of these meetings are essential for the everyday work of social welfare professionals and are consequential for the lives of service users.

We do not know what multi-agency meetings look like at the moment. There seems to be a variety of responses between different countries and settings. It is likely that most of the meetings we observed have been postponed, scaled back or are taking place virtually, although there are some reports of plans to organise meetings with social distancing restrictions (Turner, 2020b). For example, we understand that the rehabilitation meetings described in Chapter 3 were postponed but are restarting with social distancing. Child welfare meetings (examined in Chapters 4 and 8) are taking place using virtual meeting or teleconference applications, according to official local authority websites in the UK. These websites provide little detail of how virtual meetings currently are being organised. Guidance from the Royal College of Psychiatry in the UK recommends that CPA meetings (examined in Chapter 7) should look at 'alternative ways of sharing information, such as written feedback or teleconferencing' (Courtney, 2020, p 3).

We suggest that the themes identified in this book will be relevant in examining these new arrangements. For example, we noted the importance of the ways in which the chair encourages and gives credence to professionals' and service users' contributions. However, one local authority in England described (in April 2020) a system of organising multi-agency meetings in which the chair gathers information and opinions from professionals and service users and then makes a decision on future action, with seemingly no discussion between other professionals or service users (posted on 2 April 2020) By

September 2020 the system was described as 'semi-virtual': the chair, social worker and parents would meet in the same room, social distanced, but other professionals would join by video link. In the absence of a face-to-face discussion, the chair would continue to make the decision on the case and outline the child protection plan. No doubt other arrangements for multi-agency meetings will be developed in response to the changes in coronavirus pandemic.

We also noted the importance of how service users are included in the meetings. An internal survey of telephone conferences in child welfare carried out by another local authority in the UK found high levels of non-attendance by service users at the beginning of lockdown restrictions, partly because of a lack of appropriate devices or software. However, it also found that service users who did 'attend' telephone conferences preferred not being in the meeting room with the professionals, seemingly mitigating some of the features of degradation ceremonies. A survey carried out by the professional journal *Community Care* (Turner, 2020a, 2020b) similarly found that young people were more confident about participating in virtual meetings. The survey also reported that families who were provided with appropriate equipment increased their attendance. However, there were concerns that telephone conferencing in particular hindered participation in the meeting, with families unsure who was 'in the room'. The survey quoted the chief executive of a non-governmental organisation saying that this is 'far from partnership work as envisaged by the Children Act' and 'must not become the new normal'. Concerns have also been raised by professionals about the confidentiality and safety of service users if others are in the home overhearing the meeting. One of the *Community Care* articles reported that contributors to meetings needed to be more 'succinct' and that they were 'denied visual cues', further restricting participation. Even so, it concluded: 'A significant proportion of social workers expressed a preference for virtual meetings to continue in at least some circumstances, both in terms of time saving and convenience, and in order to offer greater choice and flexibility for the people they support' (Turner, 2020a).

These reports are only the beginning of discussions about multi-agency meetings and are not research evidence. If some form of digitally mediated meeting is to become a regular feature, there is a large literature in business and medicine that compares face-to-face and virtual meetings (we are not aware of any research in social welfare). For example, Jabotinsky and Sarel (2020, p 5) summarise:[1] 'Generally speaking, face-to-face interactions are usually considered to be a worthy instrument that yields many benefits, such as smoother communication, higher levels of trust, strong(er) motivation to succeed, higher satisfaction, and more positive perceptions of others.'

Virtual meetings offer new and extra challenges for collaboration and participation practices. Saatçi et al (2019) note that it is not only a lack of appropriate information technology (IT) skills and equipment that places constraints on being heard and acknowledged, but also how the camera, microphone and screen are set up in the meeting rooms. While technologies are becoming ubiquitous and smarter, Saatçi et al (2019, p 58) emphasise the unpredictability and uncertainties of remote communication: 'while video-mediated communication itself transforms the look, gestures and manners of bodily conduct, it also broadens the already given asymmetries stemming from the diversity of the social and cultural background of participants'.

Sivunen (2016, pp 204–8) sums up the winners and losers in virtual meetings in terms of *presence* and *absence*. With appropriate technology, skills and attitudes, a virtual participant can 'feel engaged', 'transported to another place' and have a 'sense of being together'. Conversely, a lack of access leads to disengagement, 'being inattentive and emotionally disconnected' and distracted by 'technological invasion'. Many professionals and service users are equally likely to find such technologies challenging and alienating.

From a wider perspective regarding the legitimacy of virtual meetings, we can ask whether absence from the complex interactions of the meeting room undermines the authenticity of the meeting to achieve its ambition. Jabotinsky and Sarel (2020) note:

> For instance, consider a financial regulator who must decide whether to allow board members in public companies to conduct their meetings online. As board meetings require the participants to exchange information about the state of the company, an obvious question is to which degree information flows effectively in Video Conference meetings compared to Face to Face meetings. If the quality of the information flow is similar in both communication forms, the regulator can safely authorize board members to communicate virtually. Conversely, if the flow of information is hindered when interactions take place via Video Conference, regulators may need to impose various monitoring measures to compensate for the loss of information. (Jabotinsky and Sarel, 2020, p 4)

Similarly, the leader of the UK House of Commons recently required Members of Parliament to attend debates in person: 'This House plays an invaluable role in holding the Government to account and debating legislation, which can only properly be fulfilled when Members are here in person' (Mogg, 2020).

Perhaps as lockdown systems ease, there will be a return to the meeting room, or perhaps experiments with virtual systems will continue. Either way, issues of how the meeting is managed, the relative importance given to the information and knowledge of service users and professionals, and the influence of affiliations and alliances, as examined in this book, remain crucial. The current disruption provides an opportunity to reconsider the extent to which the multi-agency meeting promotes interagency collaboration and service user participation.

Note

[1] See article for details of the appropriate research papers.

References

Courtney, K. (2020) 'COVID-19 and people with intellectual disability', https://www.rcpsych.ac.uk/docs/default-source/members/faculties/intellectual-disability/covid-19-facultypsychid.pdf?sfvrsn=86f6a7da_2.

Hughes, J., Randall, D., Rouncefield, M. and Tolmie, P. (2011) 'Meetings and the accomplishment of order', in M. Rouncefield and P. Tolmie (eds) *Ethnomethodology at Work*, Basingstoke: Ashgate, pp 131–50.

Jabotinsky, H. and Sarel, R. (2020) 'Shall we meet? An experimental comparison of video conferences and face-to-face meetings', *SSRN*, 30 April, https://ssrn.com/abstract=3589431.

Mogg, R. (2020) *Hansard*, 2 June, Column 727.

Saatçi, B., Rädle, R., Rintel, S., O'Hara, K. and Klokmose, C. (2019) 'Hybrid meetings in the modern workplace: stories of success and failure', in H. Nakanishi, H. Egi, I. Chounta, H. Takada, S. Ichimura and U. Hoppe (eds) *Collaboration Technologies and Social Computing*, 25th International Conference, Kyoto, Japan, 4–6 September, proceedings, pp 45–6.

Sivunen, A. (2016) 'Presence and absence in global virtual team meetings: physical, virtual and social dimensions', in J. Webster and K. Randle (eds) *Virtual Workers and the Global Labour Market*, London: Palgrave Macmillan, pp 199–217.

Turner, A. (2020a) 'Most social workers say COVID-19 has negatively hit their work and the lives of those they support', *Community Care*, 28 May, https://www.communitycare.co.uk/2020/05/28/social-workers-say-coronavirus-negatively-affected-services-people-they-support/.

Turner, A. (2020b) 'From "harsh" virtual hearings to digital treasure hunts: Remote social work under COVID-19', *Community Care*, 12 June, https://www.communitycare.co.uk/2020/06/12/childrens-services-coronavirus-technology-virtual-hearings-digital-treasure-hunts/.

Index

A

abstinence 117
acceptance 74, 118, 182, 212, 215
accessible services 117
accountability 49
accusation 160, 162
act, ability to 84, 120
action, plan of, in child protection 84
action-oriented pathways 17
active participants 9, 74
active social citizenship 21
actors, powerful 117
addiction 21, 73, 76, 131
adding 177, 179, 182, 189, 191
adult risk 3
advice giving 102, 130
affiliations 118, 145, 226, 230–2
affirmation 55
agendas 44, 50, 93, 121, 133
agreement 42, 54, 67, 75, 108, 128
alcohol 76, 127, 130, 132, 179, 201, 213, 218
alignment 42, 95–6, 145, 177, 180, 183, 230–2
 of professionals 102–3, 106, 109
 service user participation 116–18, 121, 123, 128, 130, 134, 135
alliances 66, 141, 144, 145, 165
altercasting 88, 99, 102, 103, 105
Appleton, J 84
Arminen, I 45, 56
Aronsson, K 158
artefacts 45
Asmuβ, B 3, 37, 43, 44, 46, 200
assessment 44, 63, 85, 108, 175–7, 184, 211
assessment process 22, 199
ATLAS.ti 120
attendance at meetings 3
audience 155, 219
audio recordings 2, 68, 119, 176, 201
authority 18, 66, 68, 91, 103, 110, 212–14
autonomy 117

B

babies 102, 103, 104, 207, 209, 215
backstage 68, 78, 90

Barnes, R 50
barriers 116, 117
Bedford, R 88
behaviour 39, 107, 198, 229
Bergner, R 37
Beyer, J 36, 40
bills 178, 179, 182, 183
Bittner, E 35
Boden, D 40, 41–2, 43, 48, 53, 99, 200, 204, 227, 230
bodily movements 149, 150, 166
bonding 158
boundaries 4, 10, 14–18, 21, 123, 133, 226
 blurring 25, 225, 236
 in child protection 83, 87–9, 98, 107–8
 dissolving 102, 109
 managing 52, 64, 91
Bucher, S 88, 98, 102, 106, 110
bureaucratic procedures 37, 130, 172, 184

C

Calder, M 84, 86
Cameron, A 11
care, coordinated 11, 23, 173, 176
care agreement 44
care culture 16
care plan 22, 23, 45, 54, 172, 173, 203
Care Programme Approach (CPA) 5, 171–7, 190–2
Care Quality Commission 173
Carpenter, J 172
case conferences 23, 38, 84, 90, 142
ceremonies and rituals 34
chair, the 34, 56, 64, 77–80, 93, 109, 183–5
 and meeting structure 98
 role of 44–7, 66–8, 197–205, 206–12, 226–8
challenging 177, 182, 185, 191, 214
Chesters, J 12, 13
child deaths 83, 84
child protection 83–9, 98, 101, 107–9, 133, 197–9, 228
child protection meetings 37, 38, 45, 47, 49, 50, 52, 90, 197

247

child protection plan (CPP) 85, 91, 198–9
children, removing 197, 201
choices 19, 25, 53, 115, 128, 130, 134, 135
citizenship, duty of 9, 22
clarity 204
Clark, C 141, 144, 145, 146
Clifton, J 53, 54
Climbié, Victoria 84
coding 69, 120
coherence and coordination 9
collaboration, what is 3, 10, 12
collaborative and integrated welfare 11, 75, 80, 84, 101, 173, 225, 238
collaborative participation 116, 118, 120, 121, 124, 130, 133–5, 220
collective self-reference 66–8
common knowledge 15, 17, 20, 24, 135, 174, 225
common language 15, 87
communication 13, 23, 24, 43, 87, 115, 136, 157
communicative events 4, 10, 89
competence 84, 115, 121, 136
competition 5, 17, 87
complaints 39, 120, 235
complex lives 87, 119
complex problems 10, 18, 63, 65, 173, 200, 210, 219
compliance 35
compliments 51
conceptualising 4, 20, 79
confirmation 177, 179, 180, 191
conflicts 5, 15, 23, 36, 69, 86, 88, 100
consensus 53, 84
constructionist theories 15
contradictory talk 186–90
conventions and constraints 3, 6, 33
core group meetings (CGMs) 83, 85–9, 90–1, 98, 109–10
coronavirus pandemic 241–2
Cromdal, J 158
cross-professional dialogue 109
crying 149
cultural-historical activity theory 14
cultural prejudice 201

D

Dall, T 63, 227, 228
Danish welfare/employment services 5, 63, 64, 68
  alignment and participation 116, 117, 119–21
  epistemic rights 176–7, 192, 201–4
  frames and boundaries 83, 87, 90–7, 102

sympathy and micropolitics 141, 147–50, 164
  on the use of 'we' 64, 68–75
debts 178, 215
decision making 2, 64–8, 128, 134, 136, 226
  and the chair 197, 206–7
  in meetings 36, 44, 52–5, 74–5, 219
  and power 18, 79, 130
  roles 228–30
  and the service user 118, 120–1
degradation ceremonies 36–9, 142, 174, 192, 199, 211, 218
delicacy 33, 52, 56, 210
Denmark 5, 63
denouncer 37, 38
dentist 214
Department of Health 172
depression 147
detoxification 132
devices 177, 191
diet 96
disability 22, 143
disability pension 56, 68, 69, 70, 73, 77
disagreements 184–6, 188, 189, 211
disappointment 150
discourse identities 48
discrimination 117
discursive theories 15, 88, 121, 132
disempowering 38, 232
distrust 219
doctors 48, 147, 150, 151, 158, 211, 214
domestic abuse 94
drugs 178, 180, 186, 201, 211, 213, 217, 218
drug tests 37, 98
drug using 5, 115, 116, 119, 127, 130
dysfunctional 22

E

early intervention 84
education 2, 47
Edwards, Anne 14, 16, 20, 79, 203, 210
Edwards, S. 203
effectiveness 43
Ekberg, K 50, 175
embarrassing topics 52, 55
emotional support 123, 124, 130, 133, 141
emotions 5, 87, 142–4, 147–9, 150, 166, 229
empathy 102, 118, 123, 132, 145
employers 141, 151, 158
employment services 2, 5, 63, 64, 73
empowerment 39

Engeström, Y 14, 15
England 5, 6, 83, 84, 90, 171, 172, 176, 198
epistemic authority 200, 212–13, 216
epistemic justice/injustice 191–2, 197, 212, 219
epistemic rights 5, 171, 174–6
Epstein, W 38, 39–40
ethics code 19, 68
ethnomethodological perspective 41, 90
everyday language 119, 200, 204, 208, 209, 226
everyday life 117, 130, 136, 176, 183, 190, 232
evidence 13, 52
'exiting' 120
experiental 11
experts and expertise 4, 16, 17, 25, 49, 65, 174

F

face-to face encounters 15, 33, 87
failings 84
fake addresses 37
families 3, 11, 38, 52, 86, 87, 90, 197
and difficulties 198, 210, 212
family participation 219
family support 83
feminist scholars 117
field positions 88
financial matters 11, 65, 68, 119, 146, 174
Finland 5, 11, 115, 116, 176
fishing 177, 179, 183, 191
Flinkfeldt, M 143
food 96
footing 149, 158, 165, 166, 220
Ford, C 46, 48
formality 33, 39, 44, 109, 150, 155, 176, 204, 234
Fox, A 115
fragmented services 9, 11
framing 5, 83, 87–90, 91, 109
Freiss, E 51
Fricker, M 191
friends 38
frontline practices 6, 10, 12, 14, 24, 174, 225
functional integrity 35

G

Garfinkel, H 36, 38, 199
gateway services 117
gaze 149, 155, 163
Gephart, R 35
gesturing 5, 161–4

Glenny, G 12, 13, 17, 18, 22
global issue 10
goals 3, 12, 15, 19, 24, 35, 40, 44, 84, 226
Goffman, E 49, 88, 89, 149, 155, 166
Gould, D 173
graduation ceremonies 36
Gunther, K 44, 47, 203
Gustafson, K 37

H

Hall, C 3, 44, 45, 47, 88, 118, 203, 227, 228
Halvorsen, K 44, 53
Hammick, M 12
'hard to reach' groups 117
Harlow, E 86
Harris, J 34, 38
headteacher 100, 106
health boards 38
health issues 63
health survey 173–4
health visitors 86, 102, 103
Henneman, E.A 3, 12
Heritage, J 177, 216
Hesel, P 38
hierarchies 4, 17, 25, 47, 110, 144
histories 171, 174–6, 190
Hitzler, S 3, 53, 54, 55, 56, 63
holistic 11, 13, 22
Holmes, J 45, 51
home conditions 98
homelessness 119, 121, 123, 125, 128
home visits 33, 39, 55, 105, 119
Hopwood, N 20, 79
Horwath, J 86
housing 86, 95, 98, 119, 124, 128, 132, 177
benefit 216
support workers 171, 176, 179
Housley, W 49
Hughes, J 35, 41
Huisman, M 54, 230
human resources 147, 151, 160, 162
human rights 19, 115
humour 51

I

identities 21, 48, 87, 91, 143, 179, 199, 201, 213
illness 143, 162, 166, 192
imprisonment 38
inappropriate conduct 67
inclusion 41–3
independent living 124
indexicality 189
individuals 3, 11

influence 19, 118
informality 45, 86, 90, 91, 99, 110, 119, 235
information gathering and sharing 74, 84–7, 216, 228–30
initial child protection conference (ICPC) 84, 85, 198–9
injuries 210, 211
injustice 5
institutional context 44, 234
institutional roles and sympathy 164–5
institutional talk 200, 204
integrated welfare 1, 3, 10, 11
integration ceremonies 6, 135, 192, 218, 236
interactional practices 34–5, 39–42, 43–50, 87–90, 116, 204–10
interdisciplinary approach 86
interpretations 14, 20, 35, 53, 89, 134
interprofessional collaboration 12–19, 43, 54, 66, 78, 93, 115, 236–7
interventions 63, 84, 87, 91
intolerant attitudes 16
Islam, G 36, 40

J

joined-up thinking 11, 15, 18, 225
judgements 1, 143, 166, 171
Juhila, K 118, 135, 229, 231
justifying solutions 88
juvenile justice 38

K

Kangasharju, H 66, 145
key worker 172
Kitzinger, C 66, 67, 207
knowledge 5, 15, 35, 64, 171, 197, 210, 226, 232–4
Koprowska, J 49, 52, 227
Koschmann, M 36, 40, 41
Kvarnström, S 19, 21

L

labour market 63, 143
language 35, 69, 87, 118, 149, 189, 192, 204
  and service user participation 78–9
lay people 33, 123, 226
leadership style 220
learning disabilities 105
LeCouteur, A 50, 175
Lees, A 87
legal basis 9, 33, 65, 79, 116, 172, 234
legitimacy 12
Leontyev, L.S 14
Lerner, G 66, 67, 207

life experiences 117
linguistic devices 35
Linköping, Sweden 147
living arrangements 120
local authorities 6, 199, 201
long-term sick leave 142
long-term unemployed 21
low-skilled jobs 147
low-threshold meetings 5, 115
Lowton, K 23

M

marginal status 117
Markaki, V 46, 48, 56
Måseide, P 34, 56
Matarese, M 118
McDonald, J 36, 40, 41
media 84, 142
medical meetings 34, 38
medical staff 161
medical status 18, 150
medication 123, 159, 176, 182, 187, 188, 190
meetings, organisation of 44–7
meetings as interactional occasions 34–5, 43
meetings as rituals and ceremonies 36–43
meeting structures 4, 34, 226–8
meeting talk, literature on 4
mental health 22, 44, 71, 119, 171–6, 190
Mental Health Act 184, 185
Messmer, H 3, 53, 54, 55, 56, 63
Meyer, J 34
micropolitics 5, 141, 144–7
military demotion ceremony 37
Miller, G 38, 39, 56
minority ethnic groups 201
Mittler, H 86
Mondada, L 46, 48, 56
monopolies of practices 17
moral considerations 39, 41, 84, 118, 143, 160, 229
Morrison, M 12, 13, 17, 18, 22
Munro, E 85
Murray, H 37

N

National Community Mental Health Survey 173–4
negativity 22
neglect 92, 206
negotiation 3, 45, 54, 86, 133, 171
neoliberalism 9, 85
next of kin 33
non-aligned talk 186, 191

Index

norms 34, 40, 41, 143
nursery 95

O

objects 14, 21
obligations 46, 90, 91
observations 90
organisational ceremonies 36–43, 42, 55, 226
organisational framework 79
organisational goals 40
orientation 3, 13
outcomes 14
outpatient clinic 119, 121, 131, 132

P

pain 72, 147
palliative care team 52
parents/carers 19, 86, 93, 99, 110, 197, 198
participation 1, 11, 19, 44, 67, 89, 119, 149, 197, 201, 204, 219–20
Parton, N 84
passivity 134, 189, 204, 219
pathways 11, 17, 116, 127, 128, 176
patterns 25, 40, 50, 141, 210
Peck, E 35, 38
Peräkylä, A 119, 174
Perälä, R 45, 56
personal difficulties 124, 166
personal lives/histories 4, 25, 177, 190, 236
perspectives 36, 63, 166, 197, 210, 229
physical health 174
placement visits 55
planning 11, 19, 22, 83
  care planning 3, 54, 192, 203, 236
  and meetings 23, 44, 47, 99
police 2, 85
policy and policy trends 11, 22, 24, 80, 83, 88, 142, 225
politeness 33, 51, 52, 109, 150
Pomerantz, A 179
positioning 5, 25, 118
positive assessments 177, 179, 184, 191
posture 5
poverty, living in 37
power relations 16, 21, 68, 79, 117, 126, 144, 165, 201, 225
predetermined attributes 21
prediction of cruelty 85
problematic behaviour 108
problems 11, 35, 63, 101, 119, 127, 173, 228
procedures 2, 11, 20, 23, 52, 78, 84
pronoun 'we' *see* 'we'
psychiatrists 171, 176, 191

psychosocial support 119
public discourse 37, 142, 198
public enquiries 83

Q

qualitative mixed method 90

R

Raitakari, S 227
Ranta, J 227
ratified participant 213, 220
Raymond, G 177
reality 41–2, 89
recovery 173, 180
redemptive change 214
Reeves, S 115
rehabilitation 63–6, 70–8, 141, 143, 147, 151
relational agency 14–16, 64, 173, 192, 200, 210–12, 237
relational practice 20, 135, 143
relationships 86, 87
repetition 36
reports 44
research 3, 4, 14, 174, 204, 226
respect 115, 128, 130, 132, 135
responses 14, 98, 225, 228
  minimal 118, 126, 129, 133, 154, 184
responsibilities 3, 9, 11, 18, 21, 24, 64, 66, 71, 86
restorative justice 38
return to work 5, 68, 141–6, 147–9
reviewing 3, 172
revolving door 22
rights 9, 19, 21, 24, 46, 67, 91, 115, 143 *see also* epistemic rights
risk 63, 85, 124, 173, 176, 210
rites of passage 36
rituals and ceremonies 34, 36–43
roles 24, 64, 71, 78, 87, 226
  in child protection 83
Rowan, B 34
Ruusuvuori, J 119, 145

S

Sacks, H 46, 66
sacredness 36, 41
safeguarding 84, 206, 209
safety 179
safety, child 99–100
Sarangi, S 44
saving face 185, 192
school attendance 106–8
school nurse 86, 100, 106, 107
scripted language 204
self-casting 88, 98, 102, 103, 105

self-determination 21, 115, 136
self-harm 173, 181
self-identification 205
self-sufficency 142
self-trust 117, 135
service transition 127
service users 2–3, 19, 22, 25, 53, 65, 116–19, 225
 and decision making 79
 histories 174–6
 and interactional approach 204–8
 and knowledge 233
 and meeting talk 33, 74, 180–4
 presence 23–4, 200
Shadwell, S 86
shaming 37, 38, 192, 210, 226
shared experiences 145
shared framework 71
shared goals 2, 12, 22
shared responsibility 9, 11, 16, 17, 77, 89, 165, 235
sharing information 206
sick leave 142
Signs of Safety 203
silent listener 143
skilled professional 147
Slembrouck, S 3, 44, 45, 47, 88, 203, 228
smoking 211, 212
Snow, D 88
social anxiety 73, 76
social care packages 11
social engineering 21, 22
social inclusion 173
social insurance 5, 119, 142
social workers 17, 86, 91, 98, 110, 124, 147, 199
 and child protection 49, 52, 86, 198, 219, 242
solutions 14, 35
speaking time 64, 65, 90
specialisation 9
specialist nurse 104–7
spiral informality 45, 120
state, role of the 9
Statement of Values and Principles 173
status 1, 67, 110, 144, 199
Stevanovic, M 174
stigmatisation 21, 22, 25
storytellers 191
strategy discussion 199
stress/burnout 142, 151
Strong, P 38
structural problems 11
Stubbe, M 45, 51
stylistic unity 35
subordinate communication 157

substance abuse 21, 45, 116
suicide 173
summaries 46
supported housing unit 180
support measures 19, 38, 65, 83, 174, 182, 183
surveillance 225
Svennevig, J 3, 37, 43, 44, 45, 46, 50, 51, 200
Swartzman, H 34
Sweden 5, 141, 142
symbols 37, 41
sympathy 141, 144–7, 229
 claiming 150–4
 and institutional roles 164–5
 non-verbal 155–63

T

talk 33, 64, 145, 150, 177, 180, 192, 226
 institutional talk 200–4
 meeting talk and interaction 43–50, 71–5
tasks 15, 132
teachers 48, 86, 100, 106
teamwork 23
technical solutions 86
testimony 214, 219
Thomas, J 115
Thompson, K 87
'tick-box' 172
timeout 71
tissues 155
topics 87, 91, 98, 120, 134, 176, 227
 changing 100, 123, 160
 control 3, 44, 46, 50–2, 65
training periods 159
transportation 72
traumatic childhood experiences 123
treatment plan 23
Trice, H 36, 40
trust 22, 191, 192
Turnell, 203
turn-taking 34, 47–50, 90, 98, 123, 134, 143, 149

U

unemployment 22, 72
United Kingdom 11, 83
unratified participant 213
unskilled worker 72
user-centred approach 11

V

values 12, 34, 36, 40, 41, 219
victims 85, 179

video recordings 2, 147
violence 201
Virkkula, T 49
voices 15, 21, 126, 128
vulnerable people 17, 24, 56, 116, 117, 128, 135
Vygotsky, L.S. 14

W

washing (practical tasks) 181, 182, 183
'we' 63, 66–8, 69–78, 132, 204, 208, 226, 230–2
welfare dependency 22
welfare of children 197, 199, 219
welfare policy 9
wellbeing 13, 19

witnesses 37, 38
work 39, 68, 72, 77, 141, 143, 150, 159, 166, 174
work-incentive programme (WIN) 38–9
working relationships 220
Working Together 84
work rehabilitation 146, 163
World Health Organisation 10
written care programme 172

X

Xyrichis, A 23

Y

young people 242

www.ingramcontent.com/pod-product-compliance
Lightning Source LLC
Chambersburg PA
CBHW070917030426
42336CB00014BA/2444